本书为作者承担的 2021 年陕西省社会科学基金项目“框架语义学视域下国际期刊论文中 Knowledge Emotions 研究”成果（立项号 2021K021）
本书出版得到西北工业大学精品学术著作培育项目专项资金支持

Knowledge Emotions in Academic Discourse

A Cognitive Semantic Perspective

学术语篇中的“知识情绪”

认知语义视角

王 倩 著

中国海洋大学出版社
· 青岛 ·

图书在版编目(CIP)数据

学术语篇中的“知识情绪”：认知语义视角：英文 / 王倩著 . -- 青岛：中国海洋大学出版社，2023. 11

ISBN 978-7-5670-3679-6

Ⅰ. ①学… Ⅱ. ①王… Ⅲ. ①英语－语言学－研究－英文 Ⅳ. ①H31

中国国家版本馆 CIP 数据核字(2023)第 203863 号

出版发行	中国海洋大学出版社		
社　　址	青岛市香港东路 23 号	邮政编码	266071
出 版 人	刘文菁		
网　　址	http://pub.ouc.edu.cn		
订购电话	0532－82032573(传真)		
责任编辑	邵成军	电　　话	0532－85902533
印　　制	青岛国彩印刷股份有限公司		
版　　次	2023 年 11 月第 1 版		
印　　次	2023 年 11 月第 1 次印刷		
成品尺寸	170 mm ×240 mm		
印　　张	15. 25		
字　　数	266 千		
印　　数	1—1 000		
定　　价	58. 00 元		

· Table of Contents ·

Chapter One
Introduction

1.1 Research background

Academic writing generates and disseminates disciplinary knowledge in a specific field of study. Scholarly publications are not only deemed the endpoint of scientific research being conceived, conducted, written up, peer-reviewed, and finally accepted by peers but are also seen as an invaluable means for researchers to gain national and international recognition as disciplinary experts. Hence, a substantial body of studies has examined research articles (RAs)—a prestigious academic genre and rhetorically sophisticated artifacts for generating new knowledge and communicating scientific inquiries (Hu & Cao, 2015) shaped by a multitude of complex social interactions within academic discourse communities (e.g. Berkenkotter & Huckin, 2016).

Academic writing was traditionally expected to be objective, faceless, impersonal and seen as an embodiment of detached reasoning and rationality. However, it has now been regarded as a "privileged form of argument" (Hyland, 2011, p.193) deployed by academic writers to encode concepts, express authorial attitudes, and interact with or engage the intended audiences to persuade them. As such, attitude markers are essential linguistic resources deployed in academic writing to achieve writer-reader interaction (Hyland, 2005a, 2005b). These markers explicitly signal authorial stances and are realized by attitude verbs (e.g. *prefer, agree*), adverbs (e.g. *hopefully, unfortunately*), and adjectives (e.g. *remarkable, inappropriate*). Hyland (2005a) maintains that "attitude markers indicate the writer's affective, rather than epistemic, attitude to propositions, conveying surprise, agreement, importance, frustration, and so on" (p.180). While extant research conducted on attitude markers in RAs abounds (e.g. Abdi, 2002; Del Olmo, 2014; Gillaerts & Van de Velde, 2010; Hyland & Jiang, 2018b; McGrath & Kuteeva, 2012), less attention has been given to subtypes of attitude markers, for example, surprise or interest markers. Some research, however, has shown that surprise markers such as *unexpectedly, to our surprise,* and *surprisingly* are not uncommon in RAs (Tutin, 2015). Hu and Chen (2019) investigated the use of surprise markers in RAs from two disciplines (i.e. Applied Linguistics and Counseling Psychology) and proposed a Surprise frame with five frame elements. The Surprise frame has augmented our understanding of how the emotion of surprise, together with its linguistic expressions, partakes in knowledge construction across disciplines.

Labeled as one of "epistemic emotions" or "academic emotions" in some studies (e.g. Chevrier et al., 2019; Muis et al., 2015; Vogl et al., 2021), Silvia (2009) included surprise in a family of knowledge emotions. Knowledge emotions that arise from people's beliefs about their prior thoughts and knowledge are essentially "associated with thinking and comprehension" (Silvia, 2009, p.48). In other words, knowledge emotions are crucial to fostering, generating, and constructing scientific knowledge (Silvia, 2010, 2019). For example, surprise markers in scientific writing that "involve the reader as a witness" are contributive to "interlocutive dialogism" manifested in the writer's anticipated response and understanding from the readers (Tutin, 2015, p.415). The other two knowledge emotions listed by Silvia, viz. confusion and interest, are also intrinsically cognitive in nature. They promote learning, exploring, and reflecting because they occur when something violates what people expect or believe and, consequently, invoke efforts to address the resultant incongruity. In other words, they motivate us to engage in cognitive reappraisal and resolve the discrepancy between what is expected and what is experienced (Silvia, 2019; Tsang, 2013). When a conflict or misalignment is detected between our prior knowledge and incoming information, the knowledge emotions can be induced, thereby initiating a cognitive reappraisal of the stimulus. According to Scherer (2001), surprise calls for expectedness checking. We become surprised when something goes against the background of our expectation or experience (Teigen & Keren, 2003). Then driven by our psychological need to resolve the discrepancy, we are motivated to find an explanation for this unexpectedness (Tsang, 2013). This might explain why feeling surprised is, in essence, associated with acquiring new knowledge.

With regard to interest, while it serves as a "counterweight to anxiety by making unfamiliar things appealing" (Silvia, 2013, p.34), feeling interested could also be viewed as a form of intrinsic motivation that promotes subsequent exploration of knowledge because the activation of interest may assist in closing a gap in our understanding or expanding our skills and competence (Silvia, 2013, 2019). Similarly, confusion or feeling mentally challenged stems from the appraisal of an event characterized by unfamiliarity, novelty, complexity, and lack of comprehension (Silvia, 2013, 2019). Responding actively and thinking through something difficult to understand enable us to engage in deep learning, thereby fostering the growth of knowledge (Silvia, 2013, 2019). In this sense, the knowledge emotions, to a large extent, gear up our mind in terms of intellectual pursuits for a better and more thorough understanding of the world we live in.

Attitude markers that index academic writers' affective attitude toward propositional content are a means of achieving writer-reader interaction (Hyland, 2005b). As remarked by Kukla (2000), our attitudes are constructed by human minds and are subject to multiple sociocultural factors. Moreover, the socially constructed knowledge and truth are accepted by a community of people with shared experiences and understanding, and are ever changing (Cottone, 2007). To date, some research has indicated that the evolving scientific context (e.g. Chen & Hu, 2020a; Hyland & Jiang, 2016b, 2018b), disciplinary background (e.g. Abdi, 2002; Hyland, 2005a), research paradigms (Chen & Hu, 2020b; Hu & Cao, 2015), and cross-cultural differences (e.g. Mu et al., 2015) could influence the use of attitude markers. However, what remains unclear is how the deployment of specific types of attitude markers, i.e. surprise, interest, and confusion markers, might be mediated by a range of factors such as disciplinarity, gender, geographically defined communities, and the changing social context.

The disciplinary discourse community is apparently the most relevant professional community to academic writing. Gender is chosen as another contextual factor because gender differences, as one fundamental social stratification, "saturate our language and cultural outputs, immersing us in chains of signification so familiar and incessant that they comprise the very fabric of our lives, desires, comfort and phantasy" (Francis, 2012, p.6). Academic authors' geo-academic location is examined because knowledge transmission cannot be detached from the geographical or physical space where knowledge is produced (Agnew, 2007). Notably, in an increasingly globalized academia, the internationalization of knowledge is connected to power relations and writings are "constitutive of power-knowledge systems" (Gregson et al., 2003, p.6). In addition, the diachronic perspective, along with a synchronic perspective, has a greater potential to produce a comprehensive and dynamic description of the use of knowledge emotion markers in academic writing since knowledge-making practices and scientific communication occur in an ever-changing world.

To begin with, academic writing reflects discipline-specific ways of claiming an individual researcher's identity, status, authority, and knowledge in a field. Thus, academic discourse bears close connections with writers' cognitive styles and their epistemological beliefs grounded in the particular disciplinary communities with "shared patterns of interaction" (Hyland, 2009, p.22). Hence, a disciplinary nexus, which involves disciplinary epistemology, established discursive practices in presenting arguments, and mechanisms for gaining social acceptance, among other things, can influence how authors interact with other academics in the field. Given the importance of discipline-specific knowledge-making practices in academic communication, the past decades have witnessed a growing number of studies examining cross-disciplinary variation in academic literacy practices from a metadiscoursal perspective (e.g. Hyland, 2005a, 2005b) and a cross-cultural perspective (e.g. Mu et al., 2015; Mur-Dueñas, 2010). These scholarly inquiries have illuminated cross-disciplinary differences in the strategic manipulation of rhetorical and interactive features that contribute to a successful writer-reader relationship within disciplinary cultures. Nevertheless, a missing element from the extant literature is attention to the expression of knowledge emotions that may also help convey authorial stances, achieve interactions with the intended readers, and partake in the construction of scientific knowledge in academic writing. Therefore, the cursory understanding of the knowledge-making nature of knowledge emotions in RAs across disciplines calls for more empirical research.

Apart from differences in the construction of authorial attitudes caused by disciplinary variation, another variable—gender—may also play a role in shaping the conventions of academic prose. Numerous scholars have addressed the topic of gender and language choice, but the findings obtained for gender-related academic discourse have been somewhat divergent. Some found gender-related interactional styles (Tse & Hyland, 2008) or gendered writing characteristics (Shirzad & Jamali, 2013), whereas others did not find a significant difference in the written argument patterns of males and females (e.g. Lynch & Strauss-Noll, 1987; Rubin & Greene, 1992). These findings, although inconclusive, point to the role of gender as a potential variable in research on academic writing. However, possible gender differences in deploying knowledge emotion markers in academic writing remain under-researched. It can be expected that the investigation of gender-related norms and values manifested in the use of knowledge emotion markers could further our knowledge of how gendered characteristics may influence the writer's knowledge-making practice to gain authority and acceptance in a specific academic community.

Third, scientific research and academic writing, although involving a huge number of scholars, publishers, and research/higher education institutions across the globe, are locally situated practices and context-bound (Hyland, 2015). The concept of geo-epistemology assumes that knowledge production and circulation cannot be detached from the immediate physical space involved (Agnew & Livingstone, 2011; Mignolo, 2012). Geography matters in knowledge production because "important facets of knowledge are embedded in the place-based routines of individuals and organizations" (Polanyi, 2012, p.48). Geo-epistemology captures how knowledge production, diffusion, and interpretation are related to geographical locations exhibiting different historical, academic, and cultural trajectories (Agnew, 2007). Due to the uneven distribution of academic resources across geographical regions (Hyland, 2015), global research and development (R&D) activities in North America and Europe dominate the production and dissemination of academic knowledge (Kieńć, 2017; Larson, 2018), and academics in these areas are privileged in scholarly publishing and have easier access to and dominate the knowledge production world. It has been noted by Collyer (2018) that there exist staggering inequalities in global academic knowledge production, especially when English has become the default language for academic dissemination and communication (Hyland, 2015; Lillis & Curry, 2013; Mauranen et al., 2020). In fact, linguistic imperialism or hegemony has been well documented in a body of literature (Canagarajah, 2002; Phillipson, 2013; Pennycook, 2017), indicating that knowledge of science, in its modern meaning, is equivalent to colonial science. As a primary mode of communicating scientific knowledge, academic discourse is socially constructed and infused with power relations in the international context (Bennett, 2014). Therefore, there is good reason to expect that researchers' geographical locations or affiliations with institutions in the Center or Periphery (Canagarajah, 2002) might influence their academic writing and knowledge-making practices. However, to date, there is only limited research on the potential influences of geo-academic locations on academics' discursive practices, particularly on such impacts brought about by authorial attitudes and writer-reader interaction. Exploring the link between geographic areas and knowledge-making practices valued by scholars could contribute to understanding the possibly distinct ways of conceiving, constructing, and transmitting knowledge in Central or Peripheral academic communities in the global context.

Finally, the dynamically evolving nature of genres is another factor that could influence writer-reader interaction in academic writing. As conditions of social activity are in flux, writing conventions evolve following social changes. To date, many studies have sought to examine diachronic changes in the interpersonal aspects of academic writing, for example, the use of hedges, boosters, and attitude markers in the abstracts of RAs (Gillaerts & Van de Velde, 2010) and the use of engagement markers and other interactive features in RAs across disciplines (Chen & Hu, 2020a; Hyland & Jiang, 2016a; Hyland & Jiang, 2016b; Hyland & Jiang, 2018a). These studies on how disciplinary writing changes and develops with time have enlightened our understanding of the evolution of scientific thinking and philosophy. However, it should be noted that inquiries focusing on knowledge emotion markers in academic discourse are still very limited. Examining possible changes in the employment of knowledge emotion markers in academic discourse may extend our understanding of how writer-reader interaction evolves in a specific domain. This line of research should warrant more scholarly explorations.

1.2 Research questions

Given the connection of knowledge emotions to knowledge-making practices and the lack of research on the role of knowledge emotions in constructing scientific knowledge, this study sets out to examine to what extent the expression of knowledge emotions is mediated by factors including an academic author's disciplinary background, gender, geo-academic affiliation, and temporal location. The following research questions(RQs) are proposed to guide the study.

1) What semantic frames of knowledge emotion markers can be identified in research articles?

2) Do academic writers from different disciplines differ in using knowledge emotion markers in their RAs?

3) Do male and female academic writers differ in using knowledge emotion markers in their RAs?

4) Do academic writers affiliated with geographically defined research communities differ in using knowledge emotion markers in their RAs?

5) Has the use of knowledge emotion markers in RAs changed over a time span of 30 years?

1.3 Significance of the present study

By addressing the RQs presented earlier, this study is expected to make theoretical and practical contributions to the current literature.

Conceptually, the study represents a novel attempt to extend the application of frame semantics to linguistic analysis at the intra-sentential level to that at the inter-sentential or even discoursal level by developing an analytical framework that explicates the frames of knowledge emotion markers in RAs. As some frame elements associated with knowledge emotion markers may take extra-sentential positions, this exploratory attempt will create new possibilities of applying frame semantics to discourse analysis and thus have the potential to open up a new direction for studies on academic discourse. Furthermore, the proposed knowledge emotion frame could capture the linguistic and cognitive properties of knowledge emotion markers deployed in RAs based on a more coherent and unifying frame-based analysis of these cognitive emotions. In addition, this study can contribute to understanding how disciplinary differences may mediate the use of knowledge emotion markers to reveal the knowledge-making conventions of a particular field. Moreover, the study provides a new empirical perspective for gender-specific discourse in science communities. Additionally, it is positioned to offer insights into how authors' geo-academic locations might influence the use of knowledge emotion markers. Finally, the diachronic description of changes in the use of knowledge emotion markers may add to our understanding of how scientific philosophies evolve. Taken together, this study, aiming to conduct a fine-grained analysis of the employment of knowledge emotion markers, has the potential of augmenting our understanding of how academic discourse is strategically deployed to construct, disseminate and communicate scientific knowledge.

Practically, the findings of this study can provide important insights for English for Academic Purposes (EAP) instruction and novice researchers seeking entry into their discipline-specific discourse community through academic writing. Specifically, an in-depth portrayal of knowledge-construction practices involving knowledge emotion markers could alert both L1 and L2 writers to new ways of deploying linguistic resources for more effective academic communication. Furthermore, the findings of the study may assist L1 and L2 novice researchers in acquiring a more disciplinary-sensitive repertoire of knowledge emotion markers to convey an appropriate authorial identity in their transformation from an apprentice to an expert. In addition, the findings of this study are also expected to enhance the academic literacy of students on postgraduate programs, L2 research writers in particular, by informing them of potential discursive strategies that can be employed to construct scientific knowledge in academic writing, thus "facilitating their participation in the academy" (Martínez, 2005, p.176).

Chapter Two
Literature Review

2.1 Knowledge emotions in psychology research

Emotions signaling our affective states have long been heatedly discussed in psychology studies. Emotions are "short-lived, feeling arousal-purposive-expressive phenomena that help us adapt to the opportunities and challenges we face during important life events" (Reeve, 2005, p.294). Concerning the relationship of emotions and cognition, some researchers were skeptical about the possible role of people's emotional responses in developing reliable beliefs (e.g. Hookway, 2003). However, emotions, now deemed an essential component of human rationality, were found to contribute to a variety of cognitive performances, particularly in complex learning (Pekrun & Linnenbrink-Garcia, 2014), the exploration of specific kinds of knowledge (Candiotto, 2019; Pekrun et al., 2017) and enhanced cognitive processing of new information (Vogl et al., 2019). Given the connection of emotions to knowledge-generating qualities (Chevrier et al., 2019; Silvia, 2019; Vogl et al., 2021), Silvia (2009) listed a family of knowledge emotions including surprise, interest, and confusion to specify how these emotions motivated us to learn, explore and reflect. According to Silvia (2009), there were at least two reasons for labeling some emotions as knowledge emotions. First, events that triggered knowledge emotions essentially reflected the state of our knowledge. Simply put, these emotions emanated from our appraisals of "what we know, what we expect to happen, and we can learn and understand" (p.49). Second, knowledge emotions were fundamental to learning and expanding our world knowledge.

A prototypical situation for eliciting knowledge emotions was the appraisal of cognitive incongruity brought about by incoming discrepant information (Kang et al., 2009; Silvia, 2019; Tsang, 2013). In other words, when the information we received contradicted our prior expectations and beliefs, the discrepancy interrupted our ongoing cognitive process and, consequently, initiated a cognitive reappraisal of the unusual, unexpected, and new information. For example, surprise, seen as an interruption mechanism (Meyer et al.,1997), was evoked by schema-discrepant events (Noordewier et al., 2016; Reisenzein et al., 2019). When our attention was oriented to the unexpected stimulus, we were driven by the psychological need to explain the experience-expectation inconsistency (Tsang, 2013). To date, surprise has been researched widely in emotion psychology and was argued to facilitate the recall of contents matching surprised facial expressions (Parzuchowski & Szymkow-Sudziarska, 2008). In addition, the emotion of surprise could increase one's attention to the discrepant stimulus (Topolinski & Strack, 2015), elicit an individual's interest that enhanced meaningful engagement (Renninger & Hidi, 2016), and possibly prompt a person's curiosity (Loewenstein, 1994) as well as interest (Silvia, 2005a).

While we felt surprised when an event deviated from what we expected to perceive or experience, feelings of interest would be induced from the perception of a knowledge or understanding gap that urged us to investigate and explore (Silvia, 2008). This emotion has been extensively researched in mainstream emotion psychology (e.g. Silvia, 2008; Litman, 2008), empirical aesthetics (e.g. Silvia, 2005b, 2013), and educational contexts for its association with positive learning outcomes (e.g. Reeve, 2013; Renninger et al., 2014; Schraw et al., 2001).

While there has been much research on the emotions of surprise and interest, confusion has received less attention in psychology studies (Vogl et al., 2020). Confusion occurred when we experienced cognitive incongruity or conflict with prior knowledge and were unable to process and resolve the discrepant situation immediately (Nerantzaki et al., 2021; Pekrun & Stephens, 2012) or understand the encountered new and complex events (Silvia, 2013, 2019). To date, among a handful of studies on confusion, some examined facial expressions of confusion (Rozin &

Cohen, 2003) and the role of confusion in aesthetic experience (Silvia, 2010); other studies probed into the positive role of confusion in task engagement (D'Mello & Graesser, 2012) and promoting desirable learning outcomes if incongruity could be ultimately resolved (D'Mello et al., 2014; Lehman et al., 2012).

Although emotions were induced due to our cognitive appraisals of events, they involved different appraisals (Silvia, 2019). Silvia (2019) summarized the appraisal space for interest, confusion, and surprise (see Figure 2.1). In this figure, things characterized by unexpectedness, unfamiliarity, novelty, and complexity could elicit surprise, interest, and confusion. However, interest and confusion involved one additional appraisal—coping potential. Coping potential referred to our evaluations of our ability to handle and manage what we experienced (Lazarus, 1991). We would find something interesting when involved with a high coping-potential appraisal (Silvia, 2013, 2019). In other words, interest could be evoked when we were able to understand the new and unfamiliar event. Confusion, however, involved a low coping-potential appraisal (Silvia, 2013, 2019). This suggested that we would feel confused when we appraised the event as incomprehensible (Silvia, 2013, 2019). The hypothesis about the appraisal space for interest and confusion was tested by Silvia and Berg (2011), who reported that when presented with short film clips, film experts found these clips more interesting and less confusing than novices who showed the opposite feelings toward these film clips. By the same token, Silvia (2013) demonstrated that experts in the arts expressed much more interest and less confusion in appreciating visual art than novices did.

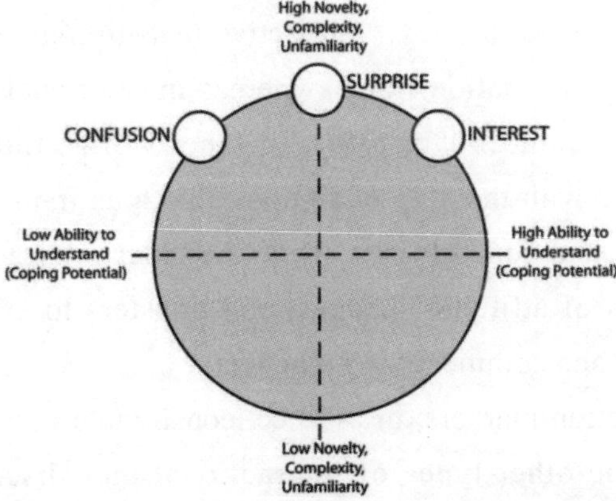

Figure 2.1 The appraisal space of surprise, interest, and confusion (Silvia, 2019)

In summary, the extant literature on knowledge emotions in psychology has evidenced their contributory role in people's knowledge-seeking and explorative behaviors.

2.2 Knowledge emotions as evaluative resources in writing

Fundamentally different from physiological changes brought about by emotions, linguistic expressions of emotions were defined as "the intentional, strategic signaling of affective information in speech and writing in order to influence partners' information and reach different goals" (Caffi & Janney, 1994, p.328). Thus, the expression of emotions served a communicative function as a socially situated act. Knowledge emotions in RAs were part of emotive communication, purporting to interact, engage or persuade readers strategically. To date, most studies revolving around knowledge emotions have been conducted primarily from a metadiscoursal perspective (Hyland, 2005b) or within the appraisal framework (Martin & White, 2005).

Metadiscourse, according to Hyland (2005b), was "the cover term for the self-reflective expressions used to negotiate interactional meanings in a text, assisting the writer (or speaker) to express a viewpoint and engage with readers as members of a particular community" (p.37). The model proposed by Hyland (2005b) distinguished between "interactive" (textual) and "interactional" (interpersonal) functions of metadiscourse in a text. Interactive metadiscourse primarily involved the "management of information flow," whereas interactional metadiscourse was "more personal" (Hyland, 2005b, p.44). In other words, the former concerned with orienting readers with the help of signposts such as frame markers, transition markers, sequencers, and code glosses, while the latter referred to the interaction-oriented expressions of attitudes, hedges, and boosters to engage readers more overtly by evaluating and commenting on the text.

Knowledge emotion markers, in essence, constitute a part of attitude markers and connect with the other types of interactional metadiscourse (i.e. hedges, boosters, and self-mentions) discussed by Hyland (2005a). As noted by Hyland

(2005b), "attitude markers indicate the writer's affective, rather than epistemic, attitude to propositions, conveying surprise, agreement, importance, frustration, and so on" (p.180). Thus, linguistic evaluative resources manifested in expressions such as *surprisingly, interestingly*, and *confusingly* could communicate authorial stances and attitudes in discourse. In addition, the intensity of knowledge emotions could be mitigated by hedges such as *somewhat surprisingly, perhaps interestingly*, and *slightly confusing* or enhanced by boosters such as *very surprisingly, the most interesting,* and *highly confusing*. Moreover, self-mentions explicitly identify experiencers of those emotions, as revealed by such examples as *to our surprise, my interest in...* and *the authors were confused by what has been reported.*

Apart from being addressed from the metadiscoursal perspective, knowledge emotion markers were also examined within the appraisal framework (Martin & White, 2005). The appraisal framework, emanated as an extension of Systemic Functional Linguistics, encompasses linguistic evaluative resources for interpersonal stance negotiations as well as ideological positions in discourse. The appraisal framework consists of three evaluative systems: attitude, engagement, and graduation, with each system being comprised of its own subcategories (Martin & White, 2005). Attitude system describes linguistic expressions involved with feelings such as emotional disposition, ethical judgement and aesthetic evaluations. The engagement system deals with dialogistic positioning against "the backdrop of alternative opinions, points of view and value judgments against which all texts operate" (Martin & White, 2005, p.94). The graduation system pertains to the modulation of intensity or degree of evaluation. In the appraisal framework, affect, judgment and appreciation resources constitute the attitude system. Affect resources refer to the appraiser's emotional reactions with positive and negative valence, showing reactions to behaviors, texts/processes, or phenomena (Martin & White, 2005). Judgment resources pertain to evaluations of human behaviors in line with a series of normative standards. Appreciation resources, consisting of our "reactions" to things (does this appeal to me?), their "composition" (balanced or complex), and their "social value" (is this worthwhile?), deal with evaluations of manufactured or natural objects and abstract structure (Martin & White, 2005, p.56). Graduation, realized through force and focus resources, involves strengthening or downgrading utterances in context. Force encompasses assessments in terms of the degree of intensity and amount while Focus concerns with grading by prototypicality by which different classes are sorted. If a phenomenon is evaluated as prototypical, sharpening resources are used, as instantiated by boosters and intensifiers (Martin & White, 2005). In contrast, softening resources such as hedges are used if a phenomenon is evaluated as lying on the outer margins of a semantic category (Martin & White, 2005). For example, adverbs like *extremely* or *very* indicate graduation with upscale/sharpening features.

From the perspective of appraisal theory, expressions of knowledge emotions such as surprise or confusion fall into the attitude system. Specifically, they are affective responses, as illustrated by *We were* ***surprised*** *to find far lower rates of depression in the population with greater racial diversity and lower socioeconomic status, contrary to what had been reported in the scientific literature* or *Given such conflicting professional advice, many ESL teachers are understandably* ***confused*** *and frustrated.* Furthermore, knowledge emotion markers can also indicate a judgment about people or behavior. For instance, *He is a very interesting person* conveys a judgment of the person's character, and *Surprisingly, she did not respond to my question* communicates a judgment about a behavior. Moreover, knowledge emotion markers are also indicators of appreciation, for example, signaling our "reactions" as illustrated by *The results reported are very interesting* or the "composition" of something as instantiated in *The situation is complicated.* Finally, knowledge emotion markers are also associated with the graduation system since these emotions can either be sharpened/upscaled or softened/downscaled, suggesting varying intensity levels. For example, "force" resources can be employed to enhance or mitigate the degree of evaluation, as illustrated by expressions like *much to our surprise, particularly interesting, highly confusing*, and *slightly confusing*. Similarly, knowledge emotion markers can also be used to indicate the prototypicality or centrality of a phenomenon or an attitude, as illustrated by the examples of *I am kind of surprised, We are genuinely interested in...* and *This is really confusing.*

As made clear by the discussion above, attitude markers such as surprise or interest served primarily textual and interpersonal metafunctions of language (Halliday & Matthiessen, 2013) in the metadiscoursal and appraisal frameworks. Examining such explicitly used linguistic devices as functional markers within the metadiscoursal framework indeed captured the interactive feature of writer-reader communication. Knowledge emotion markers that signaled the writer's affective evaluations toward the expressed propositions represented the writer's overt attempt to make them "coherent, intelligible and persuasive to a particular audience" (Hyland, 2005b, p.39). In this sense, metadiscourse analysis is functionally oriented. Similarly, as an interpersonal semantics approach, the appraisal framework offers explanations for evaluative meaning-making via linguistic resources in the writer-reader communication. As noted by Martin and White (2005), the appropriately chosen evaluative positioning projected "a professionally acceptable persona and appropriate attitude" (pp.13-14), thereby enhancing one's disciplinary credentials. Thus, the appraisal framework that focuses on interpersonal functions realized by evaluative linguistic resources used is also functionally oriented. Undoubtedly, these two frameworks have enlightened our understanding of the discoursal features of academic writing. However, it should be noted that these two analytical frameworks treat all attitude markers as one broad category and do not pay attention to any specific type of attitude markers (i.e. knowledge emotion markers expressing surprise, interest, and confusion). Thus, it remains unclear whether the observed diachronic differences in the use of attitude markers over the last 50 years (Hyland & Jiang, 2018a) apply to all the attitude markers or just some of them. Furthermore, these approaches tend to overlook the possible interaction of attitude markers with other types of metadiscoursal resources such as hedges, boosters, and self-mentions. As a result, the tendency to boost or hedge one particular type of attitude in different disciplines or across times is still largely unknown. Moreover, these frameworks do not distinguish the semantic meaning of attitude markers between its subcategories. For evaluative resources such as knowledge emotion markers falling into the same semantic field, these frameworks could not account for their key semantic features and cognitive properties in academic writing.

As noted earlier, knowledge emotion markers, as a subtype of attitude markers, are an essential cognitive resource for fostering the creation and growth of knowledge (Silva, 2019). Knowledge, consisting of ideas, beliefs, concepts, and facts (e.g. Tulving, 1985), is, by nature, semantic. Therefore, to better understand how knowledge emotion markers relate to knowledge construction, a fine-grained and semantically-oriented conceptual framework is needed to capture their cognitive semantic features and reveal their possible interaction with the other metadiscoursal resources. To this end, frame semantics provides the needed apparatus for accomplishing the task.

2.3 Frame semantics and academic writing

Due to the semantic nature of knowledge, frame semantics proposed by Charles Fillmore could provide a powerful conceptual tool for developing semantic frames for an understanding of the use of knowledge emotion markers. Frame semantics (Fillmore, 1985; Fillmore & Baker, 2010), deemed a cognitive linguistic framework of language understanding, assumes that a word's meaning is construed in relation to our background knowledge acquired from different types of previous experience. According to Fillmore (1985), a semantic frame is a script-like coherent structure of concepts, which constitutes a schematic representation of an event, a particular situation, or a relation. Fillmore provided the Commercial_transaction frame depicting participation in a scenario of commercial transactions with different roles to exemplify what a frame is. This frame includes roles such as *buyer* (someone who has money and wants to exchange it with goods), *seller* (someone who has goods and wants to exchange it for money), *goods* (the item that is exchanged for money), and *money* (any circulating medium of exchange, including coins or paper money). The buyer yields money and takes the goods, and the seller yields the goods and takes the money. The roles (i.e. *buyer*, *seller*, *goods*, and *money*) are participants, props, and conceptual elements that constitute the frame elements (FE) of the Commercial_transaction frame.

According to Ruppenhofer et al. (2016), frame elements can be classified into core and peripheral elements "in terms of how central they are to a particular frame" (p.23). "A core frame element instantiates a conceptually necessary component of a frame while making the frame unique and different from other frames" (Ruppenhofer et al., 2016, p.19). In other words, core frame elements could uniquely define a frame and capture the essential aspects of an evoked frame. For example, in the Commercial_transaction frame, *buyer, seller, goods*, and *money* are all core elements of the frame because they are crucial to understanding the frame. The Commercial_transaction frame cannot exist without a buyer or a seller. In contrast, peripheral frame elements relate to those that characterize the scene more generally, such as the medium, time, degree, or place when an event occurs (Ruppenhofer et al., 2016). For instance, frame elements such as time, place, and degree in the Commercial_transaction frame are peripheral because they do not uniquely distinguish the frame but merely provide additional information.

A semantic frame can be evoked or activated by lexical units, in other words, linguistic expressions. In the Commercial_transaction frame, lexical units are verbs such as *buy, spend*, or *charge*, nouns such as *price, goods*, or *money*, and adjectives such as *cheap* and *expensive*. Although these lexical units essentially belong to the same semantic frame, the choice of a lexical unit reveals a particular perspective from which the frame is viewed. For example, the verb *buy* foregrounds the buyer role and backgrounds the seller role, while the verb *sell* does the opposite (Fillmore, 1985). Frame semantics relates linguistic semantics to our encyclopedic knowledge, assuming that our entire knowledge of lexical items' frames is required before we can understand the meanings of these lexical items.

Informed by frame semantics, the Berkeley FrameNet research project (Baker et al., 2003; Ruppenhofer et al., 2016) is a unique online database documenting a wide variety of frame semantics descriptions and syntactic information for the core English lexicon. This project, drawing on hand-tagged semantic annotations of example sentences, aims to provide reliable information concerning each item's valences or combinatorial possibilities. The FrameNet project documents semantic frames, their frame elements, and relations between semantic frames evoked by lexical units. For example, the relationship of Inheritance refers to a semantic relationship where "each semantic fact about the parent must correspond to an equally specific or more specific fact about the child" (Ruppenhofer et al., 2016, p.80). In other words, Inheritance relation describes a connection between a child and a parent frame in which a child frame has all the semantic characteristics and properties of a parent frame as exemplified by the relationship between Commerce_buy (frame for *buy*) and Getting (frame for *get*). The frame Commerce_buy inherits from Getting because when we buy something, we get it. The Perspective_on relation indicates "the presence of at least two perspectives or different points of view on the Neutral frame (non-lexical and non-perspectivized)" (Ruppenhofer et al., 2016, p.82), as shown in the frames of Buying and Commerce_goods-transfer.

The Commercial_transaction frame that evokes a schema involving an exchange of various items (e.g. money and goods) between the *buyer* and *seller* includes two subframes, i.e. Commerce_goods-transfer and Commerce_money-transfer. The Buying frame provides a perspective_on the Commerce_goods-transfer subframe because Commerce_goods-transfer and Commerce_money-transfer are perspectives of Buying. The Using relation involves "a particular frame making reference in a very general kind of way to the structure of a more abstract, schematic frame" (Ruppenhofer et al., 2016, p.83). For example, the Product_delivery frame uses the Commerce_goods-transfer frame because the former describes the transferring activities of goods.

The central idea of frame semantics is to identify and describe "schematic representations of the conceptual structures and patterns of beliefs, practices, institutions, images, etc. that provide a foundation for meaningful interaction in a given speech community" (Fillmore et al., 2003, p.235). This suggests that frame semantics lays an emphasis on contextualized meaning in a text because related studies also set out to explain the reasons for the creation of a linguistic item in a speech community. However, the application of frame semantics in academic discourse research has been relatively limited, possibly due to the greater emphasis of FrameNet on intrasentential constituents of frame elements in an evoked semantic frame. Notably, Paltridge (1997) constituted an attempt to examine the macrostructure of RAs through the lens of frame semantics. This study, centering on notions of prototype, inheritance and intertextuality, aimed to uncover how language users could "recognize a communicative event as an instance of a particular genre" (p.2). In addition, it addressed the properties of a genre prototype and demonstrated how other texts of a similar genre could influence a text. However, as the author acknowledged, this study described linguistic features of collected texts within a systemic functional approach. Although this function-oriented approach examined how language functions socially and was produced and comprehended in research settings, it did not investigate the salient semantic frames of linguistic markers used for knowledge building in scholarly communication.

Among a very small number of studies that explored scientific knowledge construction drawing on frame semantics, Faber and her collaborators demonstrated how specialized knowledge was represented in frame-based terminologies (Faber,

2012; Faber et al., 2007; Faber et al., 2009). For example, Faber et al. (2007) examined the connections of linguistic and graphical descriptions of specialized concepts via frame analysis. Similarly, frame relations and their representation in the EcoLexicon terminological knowledge base in the field of Environmental Engineering were examined by Faber et al. (2009). It was suggested in this study that a map of semantic frames and their relations could facilitate access to the semantic framework of graphic resources in a concept. Another study conducted by L'Homme and Robichaud (2014) showed how frame semantics could characterize properties, processes, and events of terms used in Environmental Studies. This research primarily reported the authors' use of methodologies informed by the FrameNet project to unveil semantic relations. L'Homme and Robichaud (2014) maintained that frame relations of field-specific conceptual scenarios could be built by comparing the argument structures of terms and their shared relations in a terminological database. These studies have illuminated the application of frame semantics in scientific knowledge representation. However, they tended to be more conceptually oriented and thus have done little to reveal the potential of frame semantics for unmasking the cognitive properties of semantic frames evoked by a scientific term.

The review of the extant literature above pointed to a paucity of research on a semantically-oriented analysis of frame representations in academic discourse because previous studies mainly focused on studying knowledge-making practices or the rhetorical structure of academic discourse at a macro level. Two highly relevant studies to the present investigation of knowledge emotion markers in academic discourse were Hu and Chen (2019) and Chen and Hu (2020b). The former study, informed by frame semantics, proposed a Surprise frame with five distinct frame elements for examining the use of surprise markers in RAs from two disciplines (applied linguistics and counseling psychology). It undoubtedly has augmented our understanding of the role of surprise markers in knowledge building and construction. The latter study, drawing on the proposed Surprise frame as an analytical framework, examined how disciplinary background (applied linguistics vs counseling psychology) and research paradigm (qualitative vs quantitative) might affect the use of surprise markers. Moreover, drawing on a longitudinal corpus, Chen and Hu (2020a) examined diachronic changes concerning the use of surprise markers in applied linguistic RAs. They found some time-related discrepancies in the use of surprise markers in publications from two different periods separated by 30 years.

Motivated by these studies, the present study constitutes an attempt to further explore the use of knowledge emotion markers, particularly interest and confusion markers, in academic discourse. As noted earlier in this section, frame semantics can provide the powerful apparatus needed for analyzing the characteristics of frame elements, the distribution of these frame elements, and the relations between different semantic frames. In this light, it is well positioned to help unveil the semantic and cognitive features of linguistically expressed knowledge emotions so that we can understand how these emotions partake in knowledge construction and dissemination in academic discourse.

2.4 Disciplinary variations and academic writing

The concept of discipline captures how academics engage in knowledge construction as academic community members and helps "demarcate philosophies, epistemologies and academic identities" (Lau & Gardner, 2019, p.257). Examining the ways academics write in particular communities can reveal the discursive characteristics of disciplinary inquiry and knowledge-making practices such as persuasive appeals typically employed, means of critiquing ideas and framing arguments, and tactics for engaging with readers.

Disciplinary variation, well documented in Becher's (1989) concept of "academic tribes," arises from the epistemological orientations, norms, and cultures underpinning different academic communities (Hyland & Bondi, 2006). In recent decades, a line of research that gathered momentum has probed into disciplinary differences in the prestigious academic genre of RAs from a metadiscoursal perspective (e.g. Abdi, 2002; Dahl, 2004; Hyland, 2005a, 2005b; Hyland & Jiang, 2018a). Findings from this strand of research supported the belief that authors across disciplines sought different ways to claim knowledge in academic discourse (e.g. Hyland, 2008; Peacock, 2006; Samraj, 2004). For example, Abdi (2002) explored the interactional metadiscoursal features of RAs in social and natural sciences and found significant disciplinary differences in the use of hedges and attitude markers.

Natural science writers displayed more certainty toward their propositions, using fewer attitude markers than social science writers. Another corpus-based study done by Vold (2006) examined the use of epistemic modality markers in RAs in Linguistics and Medicine. It was demonstrated that while no significant difference was observed in the relative frequencies of epistemic markers between the two disciplines, there did exist substantial differences in the choice of types of modality markers. In a similar vein, Peacock's (2006) study undertook a cross-disciplinary comparison of the use of boosters in RAs sampled from leading journals in six disciplines (i.e. Linguistics, Business, Law, Public and Social Administration, Physics, and Environmental Science). The findings showed that the linguistics and law RAs used boosters most frequently, whereas the physics RAs deployed them least frequently. Furthermore, the RAs in the hard disciplines (i.e. Physics and Environmental Science) used a narrower range of boosters denoting evidence-based and implicit claims than those in the soft disciplines. In a series of studies, Hyland (2001, 2005a, 2008) analyzed stance and engagement markers in 240 RAs from eight disciplines: Sociology, Applied Linguistics, Philosophy, Marketing, Microbiology, Mechanical Engineering, Physics, and Electrical Engineering. Hyland (2001), for example, examined self-mentions, including self-citations and first-person pronouns and possessive adjectives (i.e. *I, me, my, we, us,* and *our*), in the aforementioned corpus. The results showed that first-person pronouns only appeared in the soft disciplines. Stance markers analyzed in Hyland (2005a) covered a broad spectrum of lexico-grammatical resources such as hedges, boosters, and attitude markers. In this study, hedges were found to be frequently deployed in all disciplines, although they occurred more frequently in the soft disciplines. In addition, the soft disciplines (i.e. Sociology, Applied Linguistics, Philosophy, and Marketing) employed more boosters than the hard disciplines (i.e. Microbiology, Mechanical Engineering, Physics, and Electrical Engineering). Interestingly, a similar pattern was observed in the use of hedges across the disciplines. Taken together, these findings suggested that the disciplinary nature of knowledge production could influence the rhetorical practices adopted across disciplines.

More recently, Zou and Hyland (2020) explored cross-disciplinary differences in the use of writer-reader engagement resources in academic blogs. The study found that bloggers from the soft disciplines employed a significantly higher number of reader mentions, questions, and directives, whereas bloggers from the hard disciplines preferred to choose discursive resources that helped enhance author authority. Yoon and Römer (2020) reported that writers from the soft disciplines tended to deploy epistemic and attitudinal features more extensively than those from the hard sciences. A more recent study done by Jiang and Hyland (2021) examined disciplinary effects on the use of metadiscursive nouns by academic writers. It was suggested that scientists from the hard disciplines increasingly relied on quality nouns to highlight the significance of their study, while their counterparts in the soft disciplines exhibited preferences for evidential nouns for knowledge-claiming.

A plethora of genre studies have examined different sections/aspects of RAs from a cross-disciplinary comparative perspective, for example, abstract (Jiang & Hyland, 2017; Khedri et al., 2013), introduction (Samraj, 2002), citation (Hu & Wang, 2014; Hyland & Jiang, 2019), and post-method sections encompassing Results/Findings, Discussion, and Conclusion (Cao & Hu, 2014). For example, Khedri et al. (2013) compared 60 abstracts of RAs in Economics and Applied Linguistics and reported both similarities and differences in interactive metadiscourse between the two disciplines. Drawing on an analysis of dialogic contraction and expansion informed by Bakhtinian dialogism, Hu and Wang (2014) demonstrated both cross-disciplinary (Applied Linguistics and General Medicine) and cross-linguistic (Chinese and English) differences in citation-based dialogic engagement.

These scholarly inquiries have illuminated cross-disciplinary differences in the strategic manipulation of rhetorical and interactive features that contribute to a successful writer-reader relationship within disciplinary cultures. Nevertheless, the studies examining the use of attitude markers in RAs tended to treat them as a broad category and thus overlooked subtypes of attitude markers in scholarly communication, for example, knowledge emotion markers. As noted earlier, knowledge emotion markers can help convey authorial positions, achieve interactions with the readership, and partake in the construction of scientific knowledge in academic writing. Therefore, there is good reason to expect that academics' expression of knowledge emotions to achieve writer-reader dialogue may vary across disciplines. Apparently, further investigation into knowledge emotion markers is needed to add to our understanding of the deep-seated disciplinary knowledge-making practices.

2.5 Gender-related effects and academic writing

The interaction of gender and academic discourse has been investigated in a plethora of studies (e.g. Cameron, 2010; Talbot, 2010; Tannen, 1994), but evidence generated from the extant studies on gender-preferential discoursal features is mixed and inconclusive. For example, Read et al. (2004) reported that female academics gave more attention to the presentational aspects of their writing, while male academics tended to be more argumentative. Likewise, Peterson (2002) maintained that males' writing was more powerful and aggressive, whereas females' writing was more empathic. To further reveal gender-related linguistic differences in texts, Newman et al. (2008) analyzed a large number of text samples, revealing that women were more inclined than men to make stronger commitments to the propositions presented. Furthermore, in a study of the academic writing quality of MA students' theses, Shirzad and Jamali (2013) found significant differences between male and female students in terms of syntactic complexity. Specifically, the male students were found to prefer the use of *I* to denote their involvement as agents in their writing.

Apart from the studies mentioned above, some researchers have argued that gender differences might influence the choice of metadiscoursal resources in academic writing (Ädel, 2006; Crismore et al., 1993; Francis et al., 2001; Tse & Hyland, 2008). For example, Crismore et al. (1993) investigated gender-based differences in the academic discourse produced by Finnish and American male and female writers and found that Finnish females used hedges most often, whereas American males used them least frequently. Furthermore, Ädel (2006) reported associations between gender and the propensity to employ different types of metadiscourse.

Further contributing to this line of work, Tse and Hyland (2008) discussed the role of gender in academic interactions based on a corpus of academic book reviews and interviews with researchers from two disciplines (Philosophy and Biology). This study identified some gendered rhetorical practices in constructing an appropriate disciplinary identity and revealed a strong interplay between gender and disciplinary identities. In this study, it was found that no simple, clear-cut relationship between gender and language use could be located. Male and female writers' disciplinary writing showed more similarities than differences. However, one quite interesting observation about gender difference was in the use of boosters to reinforce arguments. Females were inclined to employ boosters to intensify their positive comments, in contrast with men who tended to deploy them to heighten their confidence in a judgment. In a more recent study, Liu (2019) further examined the effects of gender and disciplinary affiliations on the use of intensifiers in academic lectures and found significant differences between the two genders and across academic disciplines. The males employed a significantly higher number of intensifiers than the females did, and intensifiers were used far less in the hard sciences than the soft ones. The author observed that the language choice of male lecturers was influenced far more by the genre of the lecture than by discipline. In contrast, the language use of female lecturers was substantially affected by both discipline and gender. This study pointed to gender as an important mediator in academic communication.

It should be noted that while the aforementioned studies indexed gender-based characteristics in writing, other studies observed few such characteristics in male and female writing. For example, neither Lynch and Strauss-Noll (1987) nor Rubin and Greene (1992) found gender-related differences in the use of assertions in the written arguments produced by male and female students. As reported in Lynch and Stauss-Noll (1987), discernable gender differences were detected only in informal writing rather than in formal writing. Francis et al. (2001) also found more similarities than differences in academic writing styles employed by male and female students. The male students' writing did not use phrases indicating tentativeness less frequently than the female students' writing, although the former showed a bold writing style more frequently. Generally, university assessors could not identify an author's gender while marking, indicating that few gender characteristics were visible in the written texts produced (Francis et al., 2003). Similarly, Robson et al. (2002) showed that both male and female university students employed a substantial number of bold statements to express certainty in their essays.

In summary, previous research findings, although inconclusive, have reveal gender as a potential variable in academic writing practices. Despite the light the current literature has shed on the role of gender in shaping academic discourse, to my best knowledge, gender differences in deploying knowledge emotion markers in academic writing remain under-researched. Moreover, the inconsistent findings concerning the possible mediating effect of gender on writing call for more scholarly attention. Thus, the present study seeks to approach gender-related characteristics in academic writing from a different empirical perspective. It is expected to provide new insights into gender-preferential discourse in academia.

2.6 Geo-epistemological contexts and academic writing

Research activities and academic writing are contextualized social practices (Hyland, 2015). Consequently, academic writing is possibly influenced by, for example, the sociocultural environment where scientific communication occurs or even academics' research institutions that are geographically defined. Researchers in China, for example, share certain experiences of academic training and international publications with researchers elsewhere. However, their attitudes, epistemological beliefs, and academic practices might also be shaped by the norms valued in the local community where they conduct their research. Thus, there is reason to expect that values adopted globally by the disciplinary community and upheld locally by individual academics' research contexts could shape scientific discourse (Mauranen et al., 2020).

The concept of geo-epistemology hypothesizes that knowledge per se and knowledge generation processes are inseparable from the physical space in which knowledge is produced and are contingent upon respective geographical locations, histories, and identities (Agnew & Livingstone, 2011). Our conceptual perspectives developed from the immediate environment cannot be detached from the local domain where we work or live. Of course, given the mobility of academics worldwide, the location where an author works may not necessarily match his/her nationality. For example, some academics affiliated with institutions situated in North America are nationals of Asian countries and vice versa. However, academic values, attitudes, and conventions are socially constituted and thus are possibly shaped by the local community in which academics conduct their research activities. In addition, universities and research institutes, as prestigious knowledge production sites, are supposed to contribute to endogenous societal development (Mansell, 2014). As such, authors' institutional affiliations are suggestive of the local academic community to which they belong. The term geo-epistemology well captures how geographical locations tend to influence the process of production and interpretation of knowledge because of historical, academic, and cultural trajectories. Hence, regional intellectual and epistemological assumptions acquired in geographically-defined research sites could be manifested in the presentation and organization of knowledge with community-preferred patterns of alignment.

In an earlier study examining how geo-epistemological culture may influence the way scientific discourse is produced, Tight (2007) found that North American and British higher education scholars tended to write without referring to anything (e.g. publications, policies, and experience) coming from outside their systems. In contrast, their counterparts from Australia, the Netherlands, and Chinese Hong Kong tended to reference the research literature, experience, or evidence outside their system. In addition, Tight also noted that North American researchers' writings exhibited a higher degree of explicitness in theoretical and methodological approaches than those produced by their counterparts from other countries. This may be attributable to the scholars' different perceptions of what would constitute more appropriate, rigorous scientific research. Hence, geo-epistemological culture could possibly impinge on discourse, playing a role in shaping writing conventions for scholarly communication.

In the contemporary world where scientific communication operates on a global scale, English has become the *lingua franca*, i.e. the premier vehicle of international scholarship and the principal medium of disseminating and exchanging scientific knowledge (Lillis & Curry, 2013). This linguistic dominance has made scholars from the Inner Circle (Kachru, 1985) in general and those based in the United States, in particular, have easier access to and dominate knowledge production markets compared to those scholars in the Periphery[①] (Canagarajah, 2002). In one study that compared French, Spanish, and English medical research discourse, Salager-Meyer et al. (2003) reported that researchers from French and Spanish were

① The Periphery was initially used to group counties that were geographically and economically disadvantaged in contrast to the prosperous Center and thus lacked the resources or, sometimes, the will to engage in the most prestigious scholarly endeavors or knowledge-making practices (Canagarajah, 2002).

more "passionate" in academic criticism than the relatively indirect, "veiled and 'politically correct' tone of English" (pp.223-235). The authors noted that in the global context, French and Spanish discourse styles were gradually subject to the international Anglo-influenced standard.

Since having access to knowledge is a prerequisite for new knowledge creation (Graham et al., 2011), it is not surprising that researchers from the Center, namely the Anglophone and other European countries, have enjoyed a disproportionately large percentage of academic publications due to this kind of "academic imperialism" (Fewer, 1997, p.764). Consequently, the non-Center participants of the international academic community are greatly disadvantaged in gaining more visibility, better recognition, and more professional credit through publishing in high-profile Center-affiliated journals. Gregson et al. (2003) pointed out that the internationalization of knowledge was "inevitably caught up in a complex web of power relations that connect power and knowledge...; writings themselves are constitutive of, and not just reflective of, power-knowledge systems" (p.6). The Center-Periphery divide is thus by no means a relation of difference but an indicator of power relations. Notably, Canagarajah's (2002) study on the geopolitics of academic writing critically evaluated the Western textual conventions, publishing communities, and social norms governing academic writing, through which the forms of intellectual hegemony stemming from the linguistic dominance of English were unveiled. As Canagarajah (2002) pointed out, the production of scientific knowledge is ideological, value-ridden, and contextual. When science involves a Center-Periphery relation, it is almost impossible to separate knowledge from the location where it is produced. Due to the uneven distribution of academic resources between the Anglo-American countries and the developing world, staggering inequalities exist in knowledge production skewing toward the global North (Collyer, 2018; Graham et al., 2011). Thus, academic discourse possibly interacts with geographically defined intellectual styles and writing traditions in a disciplinary community.

Notably, some research (Acharya, 2014; Alejandro, 2018; Wemheuer-Vogelaar & Peters, 2016) probed into the Western-dominated scholarly work in the discipline of International Relations (IR). Acharya (2014) noted that despite the increased interaction between scholars from the Western and the non-Western academic spheres, it is "the universities, scholars, and publishing outlets in the former sphere that dominate and set the agenda" (p.648). It was maintained in this study that scholars from the West seemed more involved in theory production, and those from the non-West supplied raw data for testing theory. Alejandro (2018), however, argued that it is the economic and political drivers in the Periphery such as India that have made IR researchers focus more on policy work, just because "national policy-oriented non-theoretical works have answered the needs of their national context of production (p.72). Wemheuer-Vogelaar et al. (2016) further revealed how the regional context shaped academic practices of IR scholars, although they more often than not identified themselves with issue-based research communities crossing geographic boundaries. It was reported that Western scholars (e.g. United States, Canada, and Western Europe) were more likely to eschew traditional paradigmatic analysis in their publications, whereas non-Western researchers (e.g. Latin America or East Asia) were almost twice as likely to choose Marxism as a theoretical framework. Moreover, the Western scholars' strong preference for qualitative or quantitative methods in doing research was observed, in contrast to the non-Western scholars' propensity to conduct policy analysis. In addition, scholars from the West most likely identified themselves with the global community, while their non-Western counterparts predominantly opted for national or subnational communities in research practices.

To conclude, extant research suggests that academic conventions in different research communities academics geographically belong to might mediate their scholarly practices. Therefore, it could be surmised that scholars' affiliation with the Center or Periphery may influence their use of attitude markers in general and their expression of knowledge emotions in particular. However, studies investigating the use of knowledge emotion markers as important linguistic devices to communicate scientific knowledge by researchers from different research regions are rather scant. Therefore, the present study constitutes an attempt to reveal possible connections of different geographically located research communities and their shared/specific ways of valuing, constructing, and transmitting knowledge.

2.7 Diachronic changes and academic writing

The dynamic and fluid nature of genre accommodates changing circumstances. When disciplinary norms and practices within a particular academic community change, the form, content, and rhetorical features of academic writing also respond to these changes. The diachronic evolution of referential behavior in medical RAs from 1810 to 1995 was addressed by Salager-Meyer (1999). It was found that author-centered features were noticeably on the wane, with a concomitant movement toward a more gentle, neutral, and less critical style of writing in modern medical written discourse. Furthermore, articles published in different periods were characterized by different referential patterns. For example, general and specific references and verbatim quotes were typical of nineteenth-century articles, while the use of footnotes typified the early twentieth-century articles. End-lists were characteristic of the articles published in the late twentieth century. Also focusing on RAs in the discipline of Economics, Shaw and Vassileva (2009) examined language-community as another variable in a diachronic study. They analyzed a corpus of 91 articles from Economics journals between 1900 and 2000 and probed into changes with academic practices from a cross-linguistic perspective. It was found that most earlier RAs were more like accounts instead of following a problem-oriented format. Not until 1973, articles started to follow the format, and accounts died out earlier in the British and Danish articles than in German and Bulgarian ones. Co-authorship became a dominant practice around 1993, and sections of journal articles became obligatory by the same year. In addition, first-person pronouns were observed in the British sample, whereas other languages tended to make the author less visible. Interestingly, the introduction and conclusion of articles in other languages resembled the British sample, which was attributable to the widespread use of English as the default language for academic communication and publication. Globalization and increasing professionalization of the discipline might also account for these developments.

In a series of studies, Hyland and Jiang examined diachronic changes in the use of metadiscourse in RAs. They found significant changes over time in textual features and rhetorical practices of scientific prose, revealing the interplay of language choice and its contexts of use. For example, Hyland and Jiang (2016a), drawing on a 2-million-word corpus of RAs from different disciplines (e.g. electrical engineering, biology, applied linguistics, and sociology), sought to investigate diachronic changes in the use of engagement markers, an array of rhetorical features in academic writing. They found an overall decline in the deployment of explicit engagement over 50 years and cross-disciplinary differences. In another study based on the same corpus, Hyland and Jiang (2016b) delved into diachronic changes in authorial projection in academic writing and noticed the declining use of overt authorial stance expressions in the soft disciplines but a rise of explicit stance features in the hard disciplines. More recently, Hyland and Jiang (2017) analyzed perceptions of the informality of academic writing and found a small increase of "informal elements" due to the increasing use of first-person pronouns, unattended references, and sentences starting with conjunctions and conjunctive adverbs. Academic writing in the hard sciences became less formal, whereas the trend was the opposite for the soft disciplines. Furthermore, Hyland and Jiang (2018a) examined a subset of the articles in the aforementioned corpus from four disciplines for the use of the evaluative that structure. Although still widely employed today, the incidence of the structure has declined by approximately 20% across the four disciplines over the past 50 years. Drawing on the same corpus, Hyland and Jiang (2018b) focused on the interactive features of research articles and found a significant decline in the use of interactional metadiscourse markers in the soft disciplines, in contrast to a substantial increase in the hard disciplines.

More recently, Poole et al. (2019) investigated diachronic variation in the use of epistemic stance features from 1972 to 2017 based on a specially compiled corpus of texts concerning a biochemical process known as chemotaxis. They reported a decrease in the use of modal auxiliaries and non-modal hedges but an increase in the use of boosters in these articles over time. Moreover, there was an increase in the use of epistemic stance markers connoting a level of certainty and confidence in formulating propositions but a decline in the use of hedges. Contrary to the decreasing use of boosters in biology found in Hyland and Jiang (2016b), Poole et al.'s study revealed divergent trends in the use of epistemic stance markers when a corpus of specialized texts focusing on a particular topic was examined. Along the same line, Rezaei et al. (2021) reported an overall decline of stance features in research articles of applied linguistics except for self-mentions from 1996 to 2016.

These enlightening studies have evidenced how stance features in academic discourse have evolved. Based on the findings regarding historical changes in the use of attitude markers, it could be posited that the use of specific types of attitude markers might also show some diachronic changes. However, to date, only one study conducted by Chen and Hu (2020a) probed into diachronic changes in the use of surprise markers in RAs of Applied Linguistics from 1985 to 2015. Thus, the present study attempts to add a new empirical dimension to the current literature by investigating diachronic changes in the expression of knowledge emotions, interest and confusion in particular, in RAs. Such research promises to increase our understanding of current academic writing as a complex and multi-level task and help us gain new insights into the evolution of scientific thoughts and academic writing to communicate such thoughts.

Chapter Three
Research Methodology

3.1 Research design

This study adopted a mixed-methods analytical approach, combining a large corpus of sampled RAs and interviews with academic writers from different disciplines. In addition to corpus-based analyses, qualitative interviews that could "get inside the heads" of informants (Cohen et al., 2011, p.62) or "[extend] the researcher-analyst's gaze beyond the text" (Lillis, 2008, p.361) were conducted to investigate how specialists perceived the employment of knowledge emotions in RAs. Four recognized disciplinary experts from four disciplines (Biology, Mechanical Engineering, History, and Applied Linguistics) were invited to participate in a semi-structured interview. They were asked to explicate their motivations or intentions for deploying knowledge emotion markers and comment on their own or other academics' use of these markers. The semi-structured interviews were open-ended, allowing the informants to raise relevant issues concerning the topic under discussion, whereby their in-depth views could be elicited (Mackey & Gass, 2016). When used as additional and supplementary data, emic perspectives (Swales, 2019) would provide "insider accounts" and be central to our understanding of what is relevant to researchers themselves concerning the deployment of knowledge emotion markers.

The mixed-methods approach, which balanced the external lenses taken by the corpus analyst with the internal perspectives from the disciplinary experts, helped triangulate findings (Greene, 2007). It was hoped that the combination of quantitative and qualitative inquiries could provide more nuanced and situated understandings of how these knowledge emotion markers contribute to the construction of scientific knowledge in academic discourse.

3.2 Corpus data collection

3.2.1 Corpus building

Becher (1989) put forward a typology of academic disciplines with four broad knowledge domains (Table 3.1). To ensure that the corpus covers all the domains, this taxonomy which divides academic disciplines into two dimensions (hard/soft, pure/applied) was consulted when sampling the disciplines for inclusion in this study.

Table 3.1 Becher's four knowledge domains (Becher, 1989)

Disciplinary Group	Nature of Knowledge
Hard Pure (e.g., Physics, Chemistry)	cumulative, atomistic structure, concerned with universals, simplification and a quantitative emphasis; resulting in discovery/explanation
Soft Pure (e.g., History, Literature)	reiterative, holistic, concerned with particulars and having a qualitative bias; no sense of superseded knowledge; resulting in discovery/interpretation
Hard Applied (e.g., Mechanical Engineering)	purposive; pragmatic (know-how via hard knowledge); concerned with mastery of the physical environment; resulting in products/techniques
Soft Applied (e.g., Education, Business Studies)	functional; utilitarian (know-how via soft knowledge); concerned with the enhancement of (semi-) professional practice; resulting in protocols/procedures

In this study, a large corpus consisting of 640 RAs across four disciplines and two historical periods (1985-1989 vs 2015-2019) was complied. The four disciplines selected are Biological Sciences, Mechanical Engineering, History, and Applied Linguistics. In line with Becher's (1989) typology, these disciplines representing natural science, technology, humanities, and social sciences were sampled to operationalize the two broad disciplinary distinctions: hard vs soft and pure vs applied. The corpus represents the disciplinary spectrum, as presented in Table 3.2. Hard disciplines aim to explore the workings of the natural world and are generally characterized by falsifiable predictions, controlled experiments, quantifiable data, cumulativeness, and replicability. In contrast, soft disciplines primarily study human behaviors, interactions, or thoughts. The natural sciences such as Physics, Chemistry, and Biology are referred to as "hard," whereas the humanities and social sciences such as Sociology, Anthropology, and Applied Linguistics are considered as "soft." Disciplines can also be classified as pure and applied ones. The pure fields are more theoretical and reflective, in contrast with the applied fields, which are more practical and active. The broad groupings of hard vs soft and pure vs applied disciplines were adopted because they are the traditional divisions of academic scholarship in many cross-disciplinary variation studies (e.g. Hyland, 2010; Jiang & Hyland, 2016a, 2016b, 2017; Zou & Hyland, 2020).

Table 3.2 The four disciplines represented in the corpus

Hard Science		Soft Science	
Pure	Applied	Pure	Applied
Biology	Mechanical Engineering	History	Applied Linguistics

To trace changes occurring over 30 years in the employment of knowledge emotion markers in RAs, I chose 1985 as a starting point. For one thing, a large number of academic journals moved toward electronic publishing due to the effects of the Worldwide Web. Thus, the e-version of scholarly publications became available and accessible online around 1985 (Peek & Pomerantz, 1998). For another, Hyland and Jiang (2016b), focusing on stance features in three periods (1965, 1985, 2015), found that disciplines of biology and sociology exhibited a notable decline in the use of stance markers over this time period. They also reported that academic writers in the soft knowledge fields (i.e. Applied Linguistics) tended to adopt a less visible stance, in contrast with those from the hard sciences (particularly Electrical Engineering), who seemed to show greater visibility. In addition, they detected an overall decline in signaling explicit affective responses using attitude markers in the soft disciplines (e.g. Sociology and Applied Linguistics), in contrast to the opposite trend in Electrical Engineering. Based on these findings, Hyland and Jiang (2018a) remarked that the year 1985 was "a turning point in the use of a number of stance features in different fields" (p.144). Thus, it was posited that possible changes in the employment of knowledge emotion markers in RAs might have also occurred around 1985.

The selection of journals for inclusion in the corpus was, to some extent, constrained by the fact that journals may undergo drastic changes in terms of scope, target audience, and journal-title. For example, some journals that enjoyed international prestige and reputation in the 1980s can be eliminated from the current list of high-ranking journals. Nevertheless, efforts were made to choose the top journals (defined by Web of Science indexing and impact factors) (Garfield, 2006) in each field with a long history. Four top peer-reviewed (English-medium) international journals were selected from each discipline according to journal rankings and the impact factors provided by ISI Web of Science (2019). Furthermore, disciplinary experts were consulted to nominate and recommend six reputable journals in their respective fields. The journals nominated by experts and with a high impact factor were selected. The journals included in the corpus are listed in Table 3.3.

Table 3.3 Selected top journals in the corpus

Discipline	Time	Journal
Biology	Time 1	*Biological Reviews*
		Bioscience
		Journal of Extracellular Vesicles
		PLOS Biology
	Time 2	*Biological Reviews*
		Bioscience
		Journal of Biological Chemistry
		Journal of Cell Biology

(*to be continued*)

Discipline	Time	Journal
Mechanical Engineering	Time 1	*International Journal of Machine Tools and Manufacture*
		International Journal of Plasticity
		Proceedings of the Combustion Institute
		Progress in Energy and Combustion Science
	Time 2	*Aerosol Science and Technology*
		Journal of Engineering Mechanics
		Proceedings of the Combustion Institute
		Progress in Energy and Combustion Science
History	Time 1	*Journal of Global History*
		The American Historical Review
		The Economic History Review
		The Journal of American History
	Time 2	*Agricultural History*
		The American Historical Review
		Journal of Contemporary History
		International Review of Social History
Applied Linguistics	Time 1	*Applied Linguistics*
		Language Learning
		TESOL Quarterly
		The Modern Language Journal
	Time 2	*Applied Linguistics*
		Language Learning
		Foreign Language Annals
		The Modern Language Journal

For inclusion in the corpus, only full-length empirical RAs from all the issues of the chosen source journals were downloaded from the periods of 2015-2019 (Time 1) and 1985-1989 (Time 2) across the four disciplines. Brief reports, research reviews, book reviews, and other non-empirical items were excluded.

Research Randomizer, a free online resource, was used to randomly sample 160 research articles from each discipline to enhance the representativeness of the corpus.

For the inclusion of the gender-based corpus, downloaded RAs from the four disciplines were coded with the gender of the author(s). If the article was co-authored or multi-authored, the gender of the first author was identified because the first author is usually the most significant intellectual contributor to the research work in terms of research design, data analysis, and manuscript writing. Multiple sources of information were checked to determine the author's gender. First, where bio information was attached to a paper, that information was utilized to identify the gender of the (first) author. If such information was not available, the official university webpage of the (first) author was located by googling his/her name and his/her affiliation to check if a photo of the researcher was included in the faculty profile. If no photo was placed in the researcher's profile details, various academic websites and social networks such as Academia.edu, Researchgate, Google Scholar, academic blogs, Facebook, and LinkedIn were searched to obtain the information. If the gender of the first author could still not be determined by the described efforts, this publication was eliminated. In about 6% of the publications, the first author's gender could not be identified.

As regards the variable of geo-academic location, downloaded RAs from the four disciplines were coded for the academic affiliations of the single or the first author. The geo-academic location of the researcher in terms of his/her institutional affiliation was roughly divided into two broad regions: Anglophone countries + other Western and Northern European countries (Core) vs the remaining countries (Periphery). This division was informed by Canagarajah (2002) and Kieńć (2017). The former study that examined inequalities in academic publishing referred to the West as center academic communities and those colonized by European invasion, i.e. the Third World, as periphery ones. The latter one defined scholars' core and periphery status according to whether they were "based in countries with a gross domestic product (GDP) per capita less or greater than US$18,000" (p.125). Kieńć (2017) used this classification because there was a strong co-relation (0.84) of a country's publication output and GDP per capita according to World Bank Data on academic journal articles (Kieńć, 2017). The list of core countries provided by

Kieńć's study mainly consisted of Anglophone countries, other Western countries such as Australia and New Zealand, and European countries that exclude Central and Eastern Europe. Informed by these studies, Core regions in the present study refer to Anglophone countries as well as other Western and North European countries, such as the United States, Canada, Britain, Australia, Belgium, Czech Republic, Finland, Germany, and France. Periphery regions consist of those areas that do not fall into the Core category, such as Asian countries, Latin America, and Caribbean countries. The geographical location of the singe- or the first author's research affiliation was checked and categorized into Core-based academics or Periphery-based academics.

All the chosen RAs were cleaned up. For each RA, only the main text was kept. Titles, authors, abstracts, tables, figures, footnotes/endnotes, acknowledgments, reference lists, and appendices were removed. Then, the texts were converted to text format for corpus analysis. The 640 articles sampled totaled 4,049,956 running words. Table 3.4 shows descriptive information of the compiled corpora.

Table 3.4　Sizes in tokens of the compiled corpora

Discipline	Time	Geo-academic Location	Gender	No. of RAs	Total Words	Average Words/RA
Biology	Time 1	Core-based academics	Male	20	161,580	8,079
			Female	20	163,496	8,175
		Periphery-based academics	Male	20	165,440	8,272
			Female	20	165,600	8,280
	Time 2	Core-based academics	Male	20	94,720	4,736
			Female	20	93,760	4,688
		Periphery-based academics	Male	20	96,640	4,832
			Female	20	98,060	4,903

(to be continued)

Discipline	Time	Geo-academic Location	Gender	No. of RAs	Total Words	Average Words/RA
Mechanical Engineering	Time 1	Core-based academics	Male	20	168,400	8,420
			Female	20	165,940	8,297
		Periphery-based academics	Male	20	168,420	8,421
			Female	20	164,100	8,205
	Time 2	Core-based academics	Male	20	84,200	4,210
			Female	20	80,160	4,008
		Periphery-based academics	Male	20	85,600	4,286
			Female	20	88,020	4,401
History	Time 1	Core-based academics	Male	20	144,620	7,231
			Female	20	145,580	7,279
		Periphery-based academics	Male	20	143,140	7,157
			Female	20	148,780	7,439
	Time 2	Core-based academics	Male	20	80,140	4,007
			Female	20	82,520	4,126
		Periphery-based academics	Male	20	82,380	4,119
			Female	20	84,420	4,221
Applied Linguistics	Time 1	Core-based academics	Male	20	175,840	8,792
			Female	20	173,860	8,693
		Periphery-based academics	Male	20	171,840	8,592
			Female	20	174,740	8,737
	Time 2	Core-based academics	Male	20	98,640	4,932
			Female	20	102,120	5,106
		Periphery-based academics	Male	20	97,880	4,894
			Female	20	99,320	4,966

3.2.2 Methods of data coding and analysis

3.2.2.1 Analytical procedures for identifying frame elements

Hu and Chen (2019) developed a Surprise frame in RAs in the two disciplines of

Psychological Counseling and Applied Linguistics. The present study constituted a continuing effort to generalize semantic frames of knowledge emotions, particularly those for interest and confusion markers in academic discourse, and in the meanwhile to testify the proposed Surprise frame in other disciplines (Hu & Chen, 2019).

Following similar steps taken by Hu and Chen (2019) for generating the Surprise frame, this study adopted FrameNet's lexical approach to take lexical units as the focus of analysis. First, I compiled a comprehensive list of synonyms and antonyms (in case of negation) and all the derivative forms of *surprise, interest*, and *confusion* from reputable online resources, including *Thesaurus.com* and *Thesaurus by Merriam-Webster*. The listed words were used as search terms to identify surprise, interest, and confusion markers in the corpus of research articles. The complete lists of search words are presented in Tables 3.5-3.7.

Table 3.5 The complete list of search words used to identify surprise markers

Category	Part of Speech	Search Word
Surprisingness	Verb	*surprise, amaze, astonish, astound, shock, startle, flabbergast, floor, marvel, stun, strike, impress, ball over, explode a bombshell, blow out, take aback*
	Noun	*surprise, astonishment, amazement, admiration, bombshell, stupefaction, shock, surprisingness, unexpectedness, inexpectation, wonder, wonderment*
	Adjective	*surprising, surprised, amazed, amused, amused, astonishing astounding, alarming, amazing, astonished, disconcerting, disturbing, intriguing, remarkable, startled, startling, astounded, shocked, shocking, unusual, uncommon, exceptional, incredible, extraordinary, stunning, staggering, unforeseen, unpredictable, sudden, unannounced, striking,unheralded, unpredicted, unanticipated, uncharacteristic, unlooked-for, unhoped, unthought, jolting unprovided for*

(*to be continued*)

Category	Part of Speech	Search Word
	Adverb	*surprisingly, abnormally, alarmingly, amazingly, astonishingly, exceptionally, extraordinarily, incredibly, remarkably, suddenly, uncommonly, uncharacteristically, unexpectedly, unusually*
Unsurprisingness	Verb	*expect, await, anticipate, assume, foresee, foretell, hypothesize, predict, presume, reckon, suppose, theorize, take for granted*
	Noun	*anticipation, expectation, expectancy, prospect*
	Adjective	*anticipated, assumed, awaited, expected, expectable, hoped-for, foretold, foreseeable, predicted, predictable, matter-of-course, normal, supposed, usual, common, unsurprising*
	Adverb	*commonly, expectedly, expectably, predictably, supposedly, unsurprisingly, usually*

Table 3.6 The complete list of search words used to identify interest markers

Category	Part of Speech	Search Word
Interestingness	Verb	*interest, attract, absorb, captivate, entertain, fascinate, grip, intrigue, involve, rivet, appeal to, arouse, curiosity, draw attention, grab attention, hold the attention of, catch one's eye*
	Noun	*absorption, attentiveness, attention, attraction, appeal, captivation, curiosity, engrossment, heed, inquisitiveness, fascination*
	Adjective	*interesting, interested, appealing, absorbing, arresting, attractive, attracted, beguiling, captivating, curious,compelling, engaging, engrossing, entertaining, enthralling, enthusiastic, fascinated, gripping, intriguing, involving, noteworthy, entrancing, enchanting, riveting, riveted, stimulated, stimulating, spellbinding, tantalizing, obsessed, keen, eye-catching*

(*to be continued*)

Category	Part of Speech	Search Word
	Adverb	*interestingly, appealingly, attractively, enthusiastically, keenly, fascinatingly, intriguingly, inquisitively, noticeably, obsessively, tantalizingly*
Uninterestingness	Verb	*bore, disinterest, disregard*
	Noun	*boredom, disinterestedness, unconcern, indifference*
	Adjective	*boring, dull, dreary, monotonous, tiresome, tedious, weary, uninteresting, indifferent, unattractive, unconcerned, uninterested, unexciting, unexciting, wearied*
	Adverb	*uninterestingly, unattractively, indifferently, monotonously, tediously, wearily*

Table 3.7 The complete list of search words used to identify confusion markers

Category	Part of Speech	Search Word
Confusion	Verb	*confuse, becloud, bewilder, bemuse, befuddle, blur, complicate, confound, disorient, disturb, distract, equivocate, misinform, muddle, puzzle, baffle, perplex, mystify, flummox, nonplus, obscure, lead astray, mix up with, mistake for*
	Noun	*confusion, ambiguity, bafflement, befuddlement, bemusement, bewilderment, bewilderedness, discombobulation, maze, disorientation, distraction, disturbing, mystification, puzzle, puzzlement, perplexity, tangle*
	Adjective	*confusing, confused, ambiguous, baffling, baffled, bewildering bewildered, blurring, complicated, complicating, complex, confounding, cryptic, discombobulated, enigmatic, equivocal, elusive, enigmatic, disorientated, disconcerting, puzzling, misleading, flummoxed, ill-informed, incomprehensible, inexplicable, muddling, muddled, muzzy, mysterious, mystified, nonplussed, ambiguous, inconsistent, perplexing, perplexed, puzzled, unclear, vague, weird, unaccountable, unfathomable, uncertain, unknown, unanswered*

(*to be continued*)

Category	Part of Speech	Search Word
	Adverb	*bewilderingly, ambiguously, confusingly, incomprehensibly, equivocally, elusively, confusedly, mysteriously, vaguely, misleadingly, unclearly*
Clarity	Verb	*clarify, enlighten, illuminate, make sense, straighten out, unscramble, untangle*
	Noun	*awareness, enlightenment, clarification, clarity, understanding, comprehension*
	Adjective	*aware, clear, enlightened, easy, informed, simple, plain, understandable, uncomplicated, explicable, unambiguous, intelligible, understandable, understanding, enlightening, fathomable, undisturbed, comprehensible, straightforward*
	Adverb	*clearly, understandably, intelligibly, unambiguously*

Second, all the hits in the corpus were manually checked to remove those lexical items irrelevant to the expressions of surprise, interest, and confusion, such as interest in raising interest rates. Third, surprise, interest, and confusion markers identified in the corpus were categorized according to the semantic frames they were assigned to in FrameNet. If a particular surprise, interest, or confusion marker could not be found on the list of FrameNet's lexical units, these markers were grouped to a frame according to their semantic similarity to other surprise, interest, and confusion markers listed in FrameNet. Fourth, a coding scheme was developed based on the distinct frame elements associated with the semantic frames identified in the corpus. Then, the coding scheme was used to identify and classify all the frame elements occurring in the instances of the surprise, interest, and confusion semantic frames found in the corpus. In addition, the relations among the identified surprise, interest, and confusion semantic frames were examined and determined by checking the "frame-frame relations" documented in FrameNet. In this way, semantic frames of surprise, interest, and confusion markers were identified and generated for the sampled research articles (see Figure 3.1).

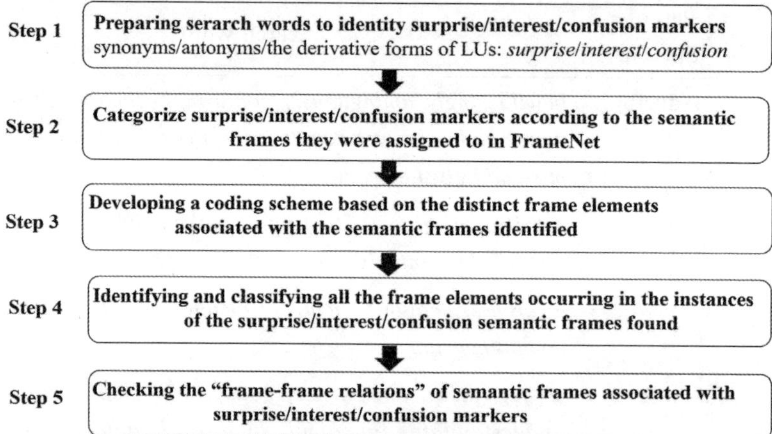

Figure 3.1 The analytical procedure for identifying frame elements associated with surprise/interest/confusion markers

3.2.2.2 Inter-rater reliability checking of data-coding

To ensure inter-rater reliability of the coding of frame elements identified, one coder, a full-time associate professor with a Doctorate in Applied Linguistics, was trained to use the coding scheme to ensure the consistency of coders in the interpretation of the coding scheme. Both coders (the author and trained coder) co-coded 30% of the total number of knowledge emotions markers found for an inter-rater reliability check. When the co-coding exercise was completed, the author discussed with the trained coder and resolved all disagreement cases before the comprehensive implementation of the coding. Results for inter-rater reliability showed Cohen's Kappa values of 0.71 with a 95% confidence interval (CI) from 0.64 to 0.78 for the coded frame elements of *surprise* markers, of 0.72 with a 95% confidence interval (CI) from 0.61 to 0.83 for *interest* markers, and of 0.74 with a 95% confidence interval (CI) from 0.69 to 0.79 for *confusion* markers, respectively. These values indicated good inter-coder reliability (Landis & Koch, 1977; Hallgren, 2012).

3.2.2.3 Data analysis

For RQ1, the software package MAXQDA 2018 Pro was utilized for lexical search and text annotation based on the coding scheme designed for the text. Moreover, quantitative calculations were performed to identify frame elements and their distributive features associated with knowledge emotion markers. For the RQs that aimed to identify discipline-, gender-, location- and time-related differences in the use of knowledge emotions, binary logistical regression analyses were conducted using SPSS 23.0. Such analyses were intended to determine whether predictor variables (i.e. discipline, gender, location of academics' affiliations, and time) could predict the absence or presence of a particular type of knowledge emotion markers in research articles. Given the binominal measures in this study, the outcome variables were coded as dichotomous variables, i.e. the absence or presence of a knowledge emotion marker and its frame elements. The reasons for using logistical regression analyses were twofold: 1) there were not many instances of knowledge emotion markers across the data; 2) the knowledge emotion markers that occurred multiple times in the corpus, for example, surprise markers, shared the same source of incongruence.

While a binary logistical regression can provide the statistical results related to the choice of knowledge emotion markers and their frame elements, Nagelkerke's adjusted R^2 and odds ratio indicators can index the proportion of variance explained by the predictor variable. The odds ratio indicating the likelihood of the occurrence of one event compared to another assumes a positive relationship between the two events if it is greater than 1. By contrast, a negative relationship can be assumed if an odds ratio is smaller than 1.

In the binary logistical regressions, hard discipline, male, Core-based academics, and the first period (2015-2019) were set as the reference value. Bonferroni correction was applied to adjust the alpha value because multiple statistical tests were conducted on the subframes of knowledge emotion markers.

3.3 Interviews

The ethnographic inquiry that allows for the exploration of situated meanings of a text (Lillis, 2008) can provide insights into academic writers' motivations and intentions behind their choice of a particular type of knowledge emotion markers in RAs. As Gardner (2012) argued, "without developing an emic (participant) understanding... the analyst risks imposing classifications from the contexts that are inadequate for the texts being described" (p.61). In this study, text-based interviews in a semi-structure format were conducted with disciplinary specialists. I drew on a "text-based" interview format because it uses interviewees' textual product to elicit their accounts of the underlying considerations for their linguistic choice. This method would "enable researchers to compare participants' stated perspectives and beliefs about writing with actual discursive strategies evident in texts" (Lillis & Curry, 2010, p.21). The semi-structured format was chosen because it guides the interview with prepared prompts and gives the interviewee freedom to "follow up interesting development and let the interviewee elaborate on certain issues" without going astray (Dörnyei, 2007, p.136). In other words, the academic authors were asked to explain why they employed a particular type of knowledge emotion markers and comment on other scholars' use of these markers. They were also allowed to raise any relevant issues regarding the use of knowledge emotion markers in scholarly communication. The interviews were conducted in English or Chinese, depending on the participants' preference.

3.3.1 Participants

Potential interviewees, identified based on the corpus constructed for this study, were first contacted via e-mail. Those who expressed their interest in participating in the study were provided with details concerning the interview, including information related to the purpose of the study, their rights, and their expected role in the interview. When the written consent was obtained, each interviewee was contacted to schedule an interview in person. A copy of RAs with highlighted texts written by them and other academics using surprise, interest, and confusion markers and interview questions were sent to them in advance. They were encouraged to think about these questions before the interview.

Ideally, informants need to be enlisted from a pool of academic writers whose RAs were included in the corpus. In addition, four informants from each discipline should be enlisted with balanced distribution by gender (two males and two females), affiliations (two from the Core and two from the Periphery regions), and time (two from the earlier period and two from the more recent period). However, it was not easy to contact authors who published from 1985 to 1989 since the authors' contact information included in the RAs in that period was usually the postal address rather than an e-mail address. I searched the authors' names and their institutions online, using Google Scholar, LinkedIn, Facebook, or institutional websites, only to find that some information was no longer accurate due to increasing academic mobility. Although some potential informants' contact information was identified, they were not available for the interview because of health problems, a busy schedule, or a lack of confidence to provide valuable responses. Therefore, except for the discipline of applied linguistics, three disciplinary experts (History, Mechanical Engineering, and Biology) whose RAs were not included in the corpus but who had international publications containing the use of knowledge emotion markers in the earlier period were enlisted. In total, 16 recognized experts across four disciplines, i.e. Biology, Mechanical Engineering, History, and Applied Linguistics, were invited to be the participants. They represented both genders, two geographically defined research sites, and the two periods of publication time. For preserving anonymity, the interviewees were referred to as Informant 1, 2, and so on. Eight participants were full professors, six were associate professors, and two were assistant professors (see Table 3.8). All of them had a considerable number of English publications in prestigious journals.

Table 3.8 Demographic information of participants for the interview

Informant	Discipline	Gender	Geo-academic Location	Time	Academic Rank
I-1	APL	Male	Core (UK)	1985-1989	Professor
I-2		Male	Periphery (China)	2015-2019	Associate professor
I-3		Female	Core (UK)	2015-2019	Associate professor
I-4		Female	Periphery (Brazil)	2015-2019	Assistant professor
I-5	HIS	Female	Periphery (China)	1985-1989	Professor
I-6		Male	Core (USA)	2015-2019	Professor
I-7		Male	Periphery (Thailand)	2015-2019	Assistant professor
I-8		Female	Core (USA)	2015-2019	Associate professor
I-9	BIO	Female	Core (USA)	1985-1989	Professor
I-10		Female	Periphery (China)	2015-2019	Professor
I-11		Male	Periphery (Russia)	2015-2019	Professor
I-12		Male	Core (UK)	2015-2019	Associate professor

(*to be continued*)

Informant	Discipline	Gender	Geo-academic Location	Time	Academic Rank
I-13	MEE	Male	Periphery (South Korea)	1985-1989	Professor
I-14		Female	Core (USA)	2015-2019	Professor
I-15		Female	Periphery (Egypt)	2015-2019	Associate professor
I-16		Male	Core (Canada)	2015-2019	Associate professor

3.3.2 Interview schedule

An interview guide (see the Appendix) was developed corresponding to the mediating variables for academics' use of knowledge emotion markers in RAs, including discipline, gender, academic affiliation location, and time of publication. The interview guide included general questions and text-based questions. The general questions revolved around 1) the interviewees' discipline characteristics, their intentions, and anticipation of potential readers' response for their use of knowledge emotion markers and 2) the interviewees' perception of discipline-, gender-, academic location-, and time-specific style of academic writing. The more specific questions mainly dealt with eliciting the interviewees' responses concerning the variables under investigation based on an extract containing the use of surprise/interest/confusion markers. Before the semi-structured interviews were conducted, the interview guide was piloted and modified. Each interview lasted approximately 30-40 minutes. The transcripts were sent to the informants to check for accuracy after the interviews were transcribed.

3.3.3 Data analysis

For the qualitative data, a thematic analysis procedure was adopted. Thematic analysis, as a type of qualitative analysis, is used to analyze classifications and present themes (patterns) that relate to the data. It illustrates the data in great detail and addresses diverse subjects via interpretations (Boyatzis, 1998). As such, an in-depth analysis with the main focus either on the perspectives of separate or groups of individuals can be achieved by investigating the observational data emanating from participants' opinions or feedback (Creswell, 2017). All the transcribed data were uploaded to MAXQDA Pro (version 2018) and read through to generate prominent themes related to the research questions of this study. First, initial codes were generated, grouped, and described using headings. Second, these codes were compared to coded extracts, reexamined, and revised iteratively to capture the most relevant elements of the data (Braun & Clarke, 2021). Next, the themes that emerged were constantly compared and defined to truly reflect the data. This recursive process helped identify, refine and finalize the themes. Interview extracts were selected, translated into English (if the interviews were done in Chinese), and included in the study.

Chapter Four

Semantic Frames of Knowledge Emotion Markers

4.1 Surprise markers

4.1.1. Frames and frame elements evoked by surprise markers

Using the lexical search function of MAXQDA with the list of search words presented in the preceding section, 66 distinct surprise markers in different categories were found. They included nouns (e.g. *astonishment, surprise*, and *shock*), verbs (e.g. *strike, amaze*, and *surprise*), adjectives (e.g. *remarkable, unexpected* and *striking*), adverbs (e.g. *surprisingly, remarkably*, and *extraordinary*), and phrases/structures (e.g. *expectation not met, deviate from... assumed*, and *not as expected*). Notably, a small number of surprise markers (i.e. *surprise, impressive, striking, surprising, unexpected, surprisingly, unusual, discrepancy*) occurred more than 30 times. Altogether, they constituted about 80% of all the occurrences of surprise markers. Table 4.1 provides the list of surprise markers identified and their frequency in the present corpus.

Table 4.1 Categories and frequencies of surprise markers found in the corpus

Category	Surprise Marker
Noun	discrepancy (62), shock (8), surprise (44), astonishment (9)
Adjective	amazing (11), amazed(5), astonishing (23), astonished (12), discrepant (2),
	extraordinary (15) , impressive (38), remarkable (64), staggering (2),
	startling (18), striking (69), strange (19), sudden (24), surprising (91),
	unanticipated (11), uncommon (18), unexpected (81), unpredictable (16),
	unusual (57)
Adverb	amazingly (10), exceptionally (6), extraordinary (14), incredibly (9),
	impressively (9), suddenly (15), remarkably (28), strikingly (8),
	surprisingly (67), uncharacteristically (1), unexpectedly (9), unusually (8)
Verb	amaze (8), astonish (6), shock (6), strike (2), surprise (18)
Phrase/structure	against assumption (2), anticipate... but... (3), assumption... not met (3)
	assumption of... violated... (2), comparative+ than anticipated (3)
	comparative than expected (4), contradict expectation (2)
	contrary to expectation... (1), deviate from assumed (3)
	deviation from observed (1), differ from the expectations... (2)
	does not expect that... (3), expectation not met... (5), expectation not born out (2), go beyond expectations... (2), in contrast to assumption of ... (2)
	inconsistent to assumption (1), not align with expectation (2)
	not as expected (5), not conform to expectation (1)
	not expect (3), not predict (1), run counter to prediction... (1)
	though someone expect... (2), unlike assumption of (1)

The 846 instances of surprise markers were examined against FrameNet's lexical units and found to evoke eight semantic frames. The frames evoked by these surprise markers and their distributions are presented in Table 4.2.

Table 4.2 Frequency distributions of surprise markers in terms of frames

Frame	Number of Surprise Markers	Percentage of All Frames
Expectation	287	33.92
Stimulate_focus	211	24.94
Typicality	186	21.99
Similarity	63	7.45
Just_found_out	59	6.97
Desirability	21	2.48
Stimulate_emotion	11	1.3
Emotion_directed	8	0.95
Total	846	100

4.1.1.1 The Expectation frame

As shown in Table 4.2, the Expectation frame was the most frequently occurring one, accounting for more than one-third of the surprise markers found in the corpus. As shown in FrameNet, "words in this frame have to do with a Cognizer (the person) believing that some Phenomenon (what) will take place in the future" (FrameNet). This frame was evoked by lexical units such as *unexpected, unpredictable*, and a variety of phrases or structures such as *contrary to expectation and differ from expectation* (see Examples1-4 below①).

(1) [$_{\text{Phenomenon}}$ That most work has treated the rural as an undifferentiated whole and very little has been published about variation in IMR between rural places] is UNEXPECTED^{Target}. [$_{\text{Cognizer}}$INI] (History)

(2) [$_{\text{Phenomenon}}$ The peak soot thus occurs at a higher temperature than found in this study], but this is UNEXPECTED^{Target} since pure ethylene has a higher flame temperature than the mixture (50% C2H4) used in the current study. [$_{\text{Cognizer}}$INI] (Mechanical Engineering)

(3) CONTRARY TO [$_{\text{Cognizer}}$ OUR] EXPECTATIONS^{Target}, [$_{\text{Phenomenon}}$ invertebrate

① All the examples taken from the corpus were presented in the annotation format adopted in FrameNet. INI in the examples stands for Indefinite Null Instantiation (FrameNet), suggesting the omission of the Cognizer, which is conceptually salient (Ruppenhofer et al., 2016).

engineers had stronger effects on species richness at higher latitudes than vertebrate engineers, and both invertebrate and vertebrate engineers were similarly important in the tropics]. (Biology)

(4) [$_{Phenomenon}$ Such a process] is nonlinear and indeed UNPREDICTABLE^{Target} in that it is constructed on a moment-by-moment basis, as the students adapt to the unfolding circumstances of each other's actions and their displayed orientations to their situated participation frameworks. (Applied Linguistics)

4.1.1.2 The Stimulus_focus frame

The Stimulus_focus frame was another frequently occurring frame in the corpus, accounting for approximately 23% of the surprise markers found in the data. This frame "brings about a particular emotion or experience in the Experiencer or saliently fails to bring about a particular experience" (FrameNet). According to FrameNet, Stimulus refers to "the object or event which brings about the emotion," the Experiencer relates to the person who experiences the emotion brought about by the Stimulus," and Degree is defined as the extent to which the Stimulus evokes the emotion in the Experiencer and Circumstances "marks expressions that indicate a set of conditions under which the Stimulus is able to bring about the emotion." Also as described in FrameNet, the Experiencer is "rarely present when the Stimulus is characterized by the experience likely to be evoked in an Experiencer." The Stimulus_focus frame, in the present corpus, was typically evoked by lexical units such as *striking, surprising, startling, astonishing,* and *impressive*, as shown in Examples 5-8.

(5) [$_{Degree}$ More] SURPRISING^{Target} was [$_{Stimulus}$ the Mandarin listeners' inability to use stress in word recognition when the first syllable of the target and competitor words differed in both segmental and suprasegmental cues (unlike English listeners)]. (Applied Linguistics)

(6) As has been noted, [$_{Stimulus}$ the evidence for a metazoan phylotypic stage] is [$_{Degree}$ very] IMPRESSIVE^{Target}. (Biology)

(7) [$_{Stimulus}$ The time it took to close the education gap between Ireland women and men is] ASTONISHING^{Target}, [Circumstances given the size of women initial disadvantage]. (History)

(8) [$_{Degree}$ Somewhat] SURPRISINGLY^{Target}, [Stimulus the process was reported

to be more sensitive to CO_2 in the feed than it was to CO in the feed]. (Mechanical Engineering)

4.1.1.3 The Typicality frame

The Typicality frame, evoked by lexical units such as *strange*, (not) *common*, and *unusual*, refers to "a State_of_affairs [which] is generally, or with regard to a particular Feature, representative of its class, which may be narrowed to a specific Comparison_set" (FrameNet). In FrameNet, the Comparison_set describes "the set of individuals, which are of similar kind to the Entity, and to which the Entity is compared," and the state of affairs is "evaluated concerning whether it exhibits the essential characteristics of a Comparison_set." This frame occurred with approximately 23% of the surprise markers. Examples of this frame are shown as follows.

(9) The last two components contribute an extremely small proportion of the total variance, and indeed [$_{\text{State\_of\_affairs}}$ items with these double links] were NOT COMMON^{Target} in the data. (Applied Linguistics)

(10) This is important as it confirms that the UNUSUAL^{Target} [$_{\text{State\_of\_affairs}}$ preservation at the base of sandstone beds] is due to particular taphonomic conditions rather than unique organism properties. (Biology)

(11) In exceptional cases it is even possible to determine the count of yarn spun, although [$_{\text{State\_of\_affairs}}$ this level of detail] is [$_{\text{Degree}}$ quite] UNUSUAL^{Target}. (History)

(12) This predicted an UNCOMMON^{Target} [$_{\text{State\_of\_affairs}}$ behavior of the variation of pressure exponent b] as shown in Fig. 102 following the trend of the experimental results. (Mechanical Engineering)

4.1.1.4 The Similarity frame

The Similarity frame, evoked by lexical units such as *discrepancy and deviation from someone assumed* in the corpus, involves "Two or more distinct entities, which may be concrete or abstract objects or types, are characterized as being similar to each other" (FrameNet). According to FrameNet, the frame element of Differentiating_fact reveals how one Entity is the same or different from other Entities. FrameNet states that "influenced by figure/ground relations, the entities may be expressed in different frame elements and constituents respectively" such as Entity_1 and Entity_2 (Examples 13 and 14) or "jointly as one single frame element and constituent" (Examples 15 and 16) (FrameNet). As illustrated in Example 13, two roles, i.e. Entity_1 and Entity_2 describe two entities that are similar to each other possibly due to "appearance, physical properties, or other characteristics" (FrameNet). As shown in Example 15, Entities, expressed as one constituent, denote the similarities between two entities. In Examples 13 and 14, Entity_1 is foregrounded, while in Examples 15 and 16, the two entities are perceived as being in the foreground.

(13) Of note, [Entity_1 the single-channel Ca$_2$+ conductance of the dOrai-P288L channel] in our study [Differentiating_fact is approximately 20 pS (Fig 1D), which has a 40-fold greater unitary Ca$_2$+ conductance (approximately 0.5 pS)] than [Entity_2 a mutant hOrai1 channel]. We think that the DISCREPANCY^{Target} may be due to the different methodology used to measure single-channel conductance. (Biology)

(14) One is that [Entity_1 the intercity real wage gap in 1935 as indicated by welfare ratios] are [Differentiating_fact considerably narrower] than [Entity_2 the income gap as suggested by per capita output estimates in Table 2]. The DISCREPANCY^{Target} is consistent with the tendency for wages to improve more slowly than non-wage incomes at early stages of economic development, which results in rising inequality. (History)

(15) Notwithstanding, the DISCREPANCY^{Target} between [Entities biotic divergence time estimations and Tethyan closure] could indicate earlier vicariant events, as well as selective extinction or errors of calibration. (Biology)

(16) The DISCREPANCY^{Target} between [Entities predicted exothermic peak temperature and experimental ignition temperature] is hard to understand without introducing additional processes not detected by TA measurements. (Mechanical Engineering)

4.1.1.5 The Just_found_out frame

FrameNet defines the Just_found_out frame as "an Experiencer, Expressor, or State having a surprised emotion as evoked by a Stimulus or concerning a Topic," as illustrated by Examples 17-20. This frame was realized by lexical units such as *surprised, surprise* and *shock*. It occurred with approximately 7% of the surprise markers found in the corpus.

(17) It is [Degree quite] a SURPRISE^{Target} that [Stimulus learner motivation in the experimental group did not improve in motivational intensity as one important aspect

of motivation]. (Applied Linguistics)

(18) The [$_{\text{Experiencer}}$ authors] interpreted their results as indicating that behavioural plasticity was quite evolutionarily variable, and appeared SURPRISED^{Target} [Stimulus by this finding]. (Biology)

(19) [$_{\text{Degree}}$ Much] to [$_{\text{Experiencer}}$ her] surprise, [$_{\text{Stimulus}}$ the event was extremely well attended], despite the lack of publicity and her fear that Gandhi was already forgotten. (History)

(20) Taken by SURPRISE^{Target}, [Stimulus many whites living at isolated farms and mines were killed]. (History)

4.1.1.6 The Desirability frame

Evoked by lexical units such as *extraordinary* and *amazing*, the Desirability frame "concerns an Evaluee being judged for its quality, i.e. how much it would probably be liked," and "often times, the Evaluee is implicitly judged good or bad relative to other instances of its type" (FrameNet). As defined by FrameNet, the frame element Evaluee refers to the entity "being judged for its quality," the Parameter "marks expressions that denote a scalar property of the Evaluee with respect to which the Evaluee is judged," and the Affected_party indicates "entities that benefit or suffer from the good or bad quality of the Evaluee." These frame elements of the Desirability frame can be seen in the examples below.

(21) The premise behind this idea is that empires were not at all monolithic entities, and that, on the contrary, they possessed an EXTRAORDINARY^{Target} [$_{\text{Evaluee}}$ capacity for resilience]. (History)

(22) The idea of the Fantic provided the conceptual framework for the establishment and implementation of an EXTRAORDINARY^{Target} [$_{\text{Evaluee}}$ legal system] [$_{\text{Affected\_party}}$ on Indian northwest frontier]. (History)

(23) It was also [$_{\text{Degree}}$ rather] EXTRAORDINARY^{Target} [$_{\text{Parameter}}$ in terms of its language and provisions]. (History)

(24) Furthermore, the peptide Met307-Met322 covering the O-loop was identified to be capable of disrupting liposomes but AMAZINGLY^{Target} [$_{\text{Evaluee}}$ the deletion of Met307-Met311 completely eliminated the membrane-damaging capacity of the peptide Asn312-Met322]. (Biology)

4.1.1.7 The Stimulate_emotion frame

Evoked by verbs such as *surprise, startle, shock*, the Stimulate_emotion frame, describes "some phenomenon (the Stimulus) provokes a particular emotion in an Experiencer" (FrameNet). Examples of its frame elements are presented as follows.

(25) [$_{\text{Stimulus}}$ The finding] STARTLED^{Target} [$_{\text{Experiencer}}$ us], because, as one of the anonymous reviewers pointed out, one would not generally expect to find much variation between individuals with an AO of D4; indeed, most early starters within this span are expected to become native like speakers. (Applied Linguistics)

(26) [$_{\text{Stimulus}}$ These initiatives] SURPRISED^{Target} [$_{\text{Experiencer}}$ those who had thought him a moderate for having championed "socialism in one country" against Trotsky's "permanent revolution."] (History)

4.1.1.8 The Emotion_directed frame

The Emotion_directed frame describes "an Experiencer who is feeling or experiencing a particular emotional response to a Stimulus or about a Topic" (FrameNet). It was evoked in the corpus by lexical units such as astonish (see Examples 27 and 28). This frame occurred infrequently in the corpus.

(27) [$_{\text{Experiencer}}$We] were ASTONISHED^{Target} by [Stimulus the ecological literature which contains different terms for environmental heterogeneity, with often undefined or even conflicting underlying concepts]. (Biology)

(28) At that time, [$_{\text{Experiencer}}$ Spanish scholars visiting Salonica] were ASTONISHED^{Target} to [Stimulus find something akin to medieval Iberia flourishing under the Ottoman rule of Sultan Abdul Hamid II]. (History)

With respect to the distribution of frames evoked by surprise markers, it could be seen that the most frequently occurring frames (i.e. the Expectation frame, the Stimulate_ emotion frame, and the Typicality frame) accounted for almost 80% of all frame instances. This finding corroborated the relevant distributions reported by Hu and Chen (2019) who maintained that these distributions related to the sources of surprise. Teigen and Keren (2003) observed that although a high contrast or a significant disparity between one's expectation and reality could trigger surprise, the low probability of an event also constituted a source of this emotive response. Thus, the Expectation frame and the Typicality frame occurred more frequently than the other frames in the corpus.

4.1.2 Interconnections among the identified frames of surprise markers

Frame-frame relations documented in FrameNet allow "frames (and thus their lexical units) to be associated despite being separated" (Ruppenhofer et al., 2016, p.79), thereby connecting frames to constitute a network of their concepts. Given this, interconnections among the eight identified frames of surprise markers were investigated, drawing on the network of frame-frame relations documented by FrameNet.

The findings demonstrated that while the Expectation frame is not connected with any other frame, the other seven frames are connected with one or more frames. As demonstrated in Figure 4.1, the Typicality frame and the Similarity frame are connected via the frame relation of Use. Furthermore, the other five frames identified are interconnected through different kinds of frame-frame relations, including Use, Inheritance, and Perspective_on. The Emotions frame serves to connect all five frames. For instance, the Just_found_out frame is connected with the Emotion_directed and stimulate_emotion frames via the Emotions_by stimulus and Emotions frames. Likewise, the Desirability frame relates to the Stimulate_focus frame via the Experience_focused_emotion frame and the Emotions frame through the frame relation of Inheritance and Perspective_on: the Desirability frame inherits the Experience_focused_emotion frame, and the latter provides a perspective on the Emotions frame, which is perspectivized in the Stimulate_focus frame. In addition, the Stimulate_focus frame is connected with the Stimulate_emotion and the Emotion_directed frame by the Emotions frame via the frame relation of Use.

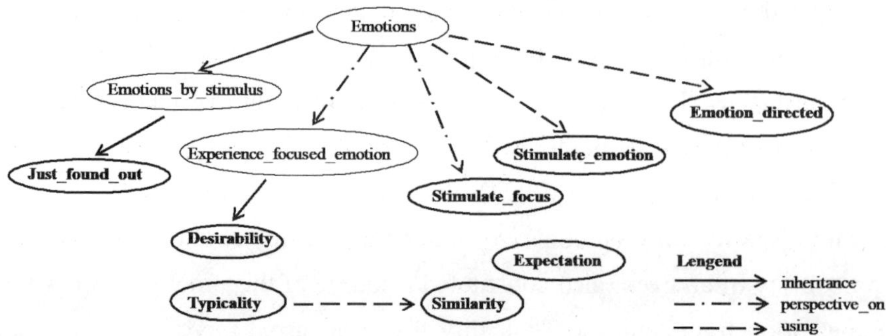

Figure 4.1 Frame interconnections of identified frames of surprise markers

As revealed, the Expectation frame is not connected with the other identified frames. However, it should be noted that this frame is central to the source of surprise, i.e. inconsistency or disparity between prior expectations and the current situation.

4.1.3 Coded frame elements and their distributions

As shown in Table 4.3, a coding scheme was developed based on the distinct frame elements of the semantic frames identified in the corpus that FrameNet categorizes. This coding scheme was used to code and identify all the frame elements that occurred in the instances of the surprise-related frames found in the corpus. The coding scheme of frame elements and distributions of coded frame elements are shown in Table 4.3 and Table 4.4.

Table 4.3 Coding scheme of frame elements

Frame	Frame Elements (Core)*	Frame Elements (Non-Core)*	Lexical Unit Example
Stimulate_ emotion	Experiencer; Stimulus	Circumstances; Degree Explanation; Result	*amaze*
Stimulus_focus	Stimulus	Circumstances; Degree; Experiencer	*surprising*
		Comparison_set; Property, Parameter	
Desirability	Evaluee; Parameter (unexpressed)	Affected_party; Circumstances Comparison_set; Degree	*extraordinary*
Just_found_out	experiencer; Expressor; State Stimulus; Topic	Circumstances; Degree; Experiencer; Parameter	*shock*
Similarity	Differentiating fact; Dimension Entities	Circumstances; Degree; Explanation Depictive	*discrepconcy*
Emotion_directed	Stimulus; Topic; Experiencer; Eevent; Reason; Expressor, State	Circumstances; Degree; Parameter Empathy_target	*astonished*

(*to be continued*)

Frame	Frame Elements (Core)*	Frame Elements (Non-Core)*	Lexical Unit Example
Typicality	Feature; State_of_affairs	Comparison_set; Degree	unususal
Expectation	Phenom; Topic; Cognizer	Degree; Evidence; Depictive	unexpected

Table 4.4 Distributions of frame elements

Frame	Raw Frequency	Percentage of All Frame Instances
Stimulus	846	100
Result	305	36.9
Explanation	286	34.62
Degree	106	12.83
Experiencer	88	10.65
Entities	53	6.3
Comparison_set	19	2.3
Topic	11	1.33
Feature	8	0.97

*Frame elements are extracted from FrameNet.

Stimulus was present in all surprise-related frame instances. Result and Explanation were the second and third most frequently occurring frame elements, accounting for almost 70% of all frame instances. Degree, Experiencer, and Entities frame elements occurred much less frequently, only accounting for about 13%, 11%, and 6%, respectively. The remaining frame elements (i.e. Comparison_set, Feature, and Topic) were rare in the corpus. These distributions were consistent with Hu and Chen's (2019) findings.

Notably, FrameNet names frame elements differently in different semantic frames. For example, what is named Stimulus in the Stimulate_emotion frame is renamed Phenomenon in the Expectation frame, Evaluee in the Desirability frame, and State_of_affair in the Typicality frame, respectively. Obviously, according to the annotation examples of these frames from FrameNet, they all relate to what triggers the feelings of surprise. Likewise, what is referred to as Explanation in the Stimulate-emotion frame is called Reason in the Emotion_directed frame and Circumstance in the Stimulus_focus frame. As a matter of fact, these frames all pertain to the source of incongruence. By the same token, Experiencer is referred to as Cognizer in the Expectation frame and Affected_party in the Desirability frame, which all indicate who experiences this emotive response. Given the conceptually overlapping frame elements in different semantic frames and the interconnections among different frames of surprise markers, it was possible to generate a Surprise frame, which could add to our understanding of how academics expressed their surprise linguistically.

4.1.4 The Surprise frame in RAs

Given the high similarities in the surprise-related frames, their frame elements, and distributions in the present corpus and Hu and Chen's (2019) corpus, the Surprise frame developed by Hu and Chen (2019) was employed to code all instances of the surprise markers found in the present corpus. This endeavor was intended to test the applicability of the Surprise frame to RAs from disciplines (i.e. History, Biology, and Mechanical Engineering) not investigated in Hu and Chen (2019) and compare the resultant patterns across the four disciplines examined in this study.

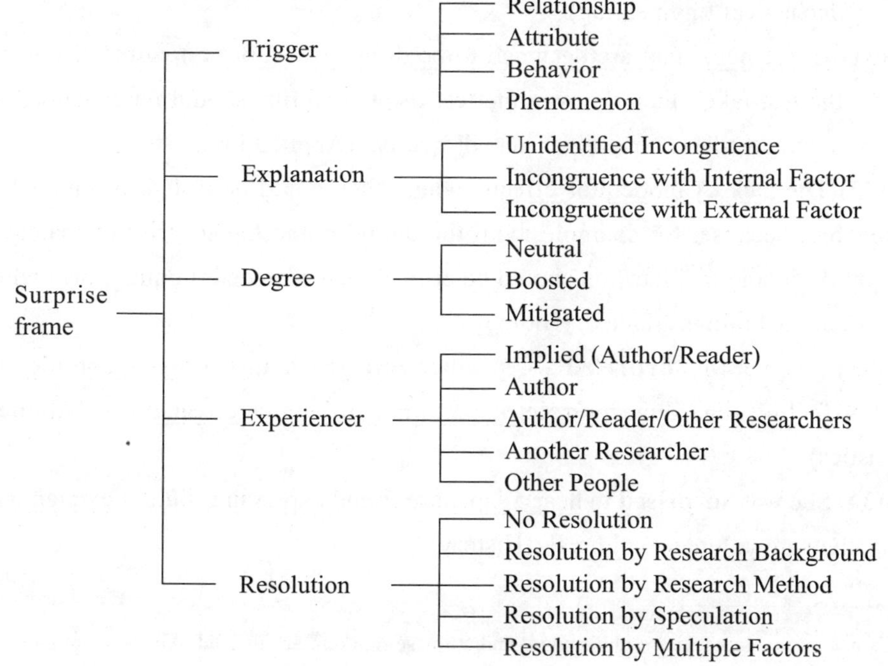

Figure 4.2 The surprise frame from Hu and Chen (2019)

4.1.4.1 Trigger

In the Surprise frame generated by Hu and Chen (2019), Trigger refers to the cause of surprise. The four types of Trigger include relationship, attribute, behavior, and phenomenon. The first type of Trigger describes "relationships between research variables, between findings yielded by the same study or between findings from different studies that evoke the emotive response" (p.162), as illustrated by Examples 29-30.[②] Attribute, the second type of Trigger, defines "characteristics of research participants, research methods or research objects" (Hu & Chen, 2019, p.126), as illustrated in Examples 31-32. The third type of Trigger, behavior, relates to "physical, verbal, and mental behaviors" (Hu & Chen, 2019, p.163), as shown in Examples 33-34. The last type of Trigger, phenomena, pertains to "all happenings and entities that do not belong to the first three types of Trigger" (Hu & Chen, 2019, p.163), as presented in Examples 35-36.

(29) The finding that Pronounced sexual dimorphism in cervical muscles is **surprising** given that humans do not fight by biting with the jaws. (Biology)

(30) The results were **surprising** in that they demonstrated that altering the refractive index of the accumulation mode particles had little effect on the overall S, value. (Mechanical Engineering)

(31) If test items that are designed to be difficult turn out **unexpectedly** to be easy for the test-taker, then the way the test-taker performs should be explained in relation to perceived easiness rather than difficulty. (Applied Linguistics)

(32) The lack of moderator effects, where they could be tested, is somewhat **unexpected**, because, for example, both the duration and the severity of maternal under nutrition and malnutrition should be critical factors in determining how and to what extent the brain is affected. (Biology)

(33) Yet we are **surprised** when other ESL teachers express a completely different feeling regarding the role of grammar in language teaching. (Applied Linguistics)

(34) She was **surprised** to hear a Japanese friend expressing similar excitement, saying, they are volunteer soldiers! (History)

---

② Target frame elements are underlined, and surprise markers are in bold. All the examples are from the present corpus.

(35) **Impressively**, rapamycin treatment starting at 600 days in mice, an age analogous to 50 years in human, can extend lifespan up to 14% in female and 9% in male mice (Harrison et al., 2009). (Biology)

(36) Most work, unfortunately, has treated the rural as an undifferentiated whole and very little has been published about variation in IMR between rural places[5]. This is **surprising** because the evolution of rural IMR in the second half of the nineteenth century shows distinctive patterns which offer insight into infant mortality more generally. (History)

For the distributions of these four types of Trigger, phenomenon accounted for 43% of the frame instances across the data, relationship occurred in 31% of the instances, attribute was found in 22% of the frame instances, and the least occurring type, behaviors, accounted for only 4%. These distributions were largely consistent with those reported in Hu and Chen (2019), although their corpus comprised research articles from the disciplines of Applied Linguistics and Counseling Psychology.

4.1.4.2 Degree

As a frame element, Degree concerns the intensity of an expressed surprise and describes how strongly it is felt (Hu & Chen, 2019). In the present corpus, a large proportion of surprise markers (85%) were neutral ones, being neither softened nor intensified, as shown in Examples 37-38. Mitigation or weakening of the expressed surprises (see Examples 39-40) occurred in 9% of the frame instances while boosting or intensifying the expressed emotion (see Examples 41-42) occurred in 6% of the cases. *Somewhat* and *perhaps* were the top two most frequently used modifiers to mitigate the emotive response. When boosters were employed to tone up the feeling, *most* and *very* were the preferred choices.

(37) The pattern of CNV resolution when the anticipated event was **unexpectedly** omitted provides an apparent neural correlate for the extra cost of unexpected events (Fig. 3). (Biology)

(38) **Remarkably**, the TDP-43 sequence forming the O-loop appears to be extremely critical for manifesting its neurotoxicity. (Mechanical Engineering)

(39) Generally, and somewhat **surprisingly**, we detected less variability across these moderators than for others we examined. (Applied Linguistics)

(40) Perhaps *surprisingly*, the process was reported to be more sensitive to CO_2 in the feed than it was to CO in the feed. (Mechanical Engineering)

(41) Very **unexpectedly**, as shown in Fig. 3A, unlike the wild type, all three mutants finally transformed into the conformations which have CD spectra typical of the amyloid oligomers, as previously well-documented. (Biology)

(42) Much to her **surprise**, the event was extremely well attended, despite the lack of publicity and her fear that Gandhi was already forgotten. (History)

4.1.4.3 Explanation

Surprise, which interrupts ongoing thoughts, is informational and motivational (Reisenzein, 2000). When surprise arises, it informs us of the schema discrepancy and motivates us to figure out the reasons to revise our relevant cognitive schemata (Reisenzein, 2000). According to Hu and Chen (2019), Explanation identifies why the feeling of surprise is triggered and can be categorized into three types: unidentified incongruence, external factors, and internal factors. Unidentified incongruence, found in 79% of the frame instances, refers to the absence of an explanation for why something is surprising, as shown in Examples 43-44. External factors, found in 15% of the cases, relate to discrepancies identified "between findings of previous studies or characteristics of the research context" (Hu & Chen, 2019, p.164), as illustrated by Examples 45-46. Internal factors that occurred in 6% of the cases refer to incongruence between one's expectation and "other findings obtained in the same study and attributes of research participants" (p.164), as shown in Examples 47-48.

(43) Results showed **remarkable** similarities to the findings of the high school LLS training study described just above. (Applied Linguistics)

(44) Our measurements show **surprisingly** good agreement between the measured lattice rotations and strains, and those predicted by CPFE (Fig. 6), inspiring some confidence in the use of this combination of techniques for analysing crystal scale deformation. (Mechanical Engineering)

(45) This degree of conservation may be **surprising**, since S6 phosphorylation is such a widely conserved response to mitogenic stimulation in many species (Samways & Kreuzinger, 2011; Warui et al., 2005). (Biology)

(46) This absence is **striking** for two reasons. First, early modern Spain has long been interpreted from the perspective of its interactions and exchanges with Europe, America, and Asia... Second, historical works on nineteenth-century

Spain tend to adopt local and regional frames of analysis, or, at best, national ones. (History)

(47) Owing to its complex tectonichistory, the IT floristic region displays **striking** geological and lithospheric heterogeneity. (Biology)

(48) In view of the fact that this duct has a roughly oval cross section, it is **surprising** that the m=2 term contributes strongly to the wall displacement. (Mechanical Engineering)

4.1.4.4 Resolution

Confronted with cognitive incongruity due to the lack of alignment between what is expected to occur and what occurs, people are motivated to resolve the discrepancy so that the knowledge gap may be closed and new understandings may be cultivated. In the present corpus, most of the expressed surprises (77%) were not resolved, while 23% were resolved in different ways. Moreover, it was noted that of the cases where a resolution was provided, 92% were done extra-sententially. That is, the resolutions could stretch across two or more sentences or even paragraphs.

The types of resolutions found in the present corpus were basically consistent with those reported by Hu and Chen (2019). Thus, their terms for resolutions were borrowed. First, an expressed surprise could be resolved with the research context or findings generated in previous studies (4%), as shown in Examples 49 and 50. As demonstrated by Examples 51-52, the second type of resolution describes the situation when the surprising result could be explained by the research methods employed in the current study (7%). In addition, researchers could offer a new hypothesis, speculative interpretations, or tentative explanations for the surprising findings (9%), as seen in Examples 53-54. Arguably, by advancing hypothetical propositions or providing speculations in scholarly writing, the author invests in effortful cognitive processing of the current knowledge, thus fostering knowledge production. Finally, approximately 3% of the cases of incongruence were resolved by multiple factors, as shown in Examples 55-56. Notably, there were cases where surprise expressed was just used to provide background information or point to a knowledge gap that may motivate further research, as seen in Examples 57-58. Compared with the ways to resolve surprise identified in Hu and Chen (2019), no instance of resolution by another finding in the same study was found in the present corpus.

(49) Although this result is **surprising**, because the participants were not novice L2 readers, the result resembles that of Haynes and Carr (1990), which also tested university students in an EFL context. Overall, the result corroborates the findings of a meta-analysis (Jeon and Yamashita, 2014) by showing that components related to L2 language accounted for L2 reading variance to a considerably larger extent than did L1 reading. (Applied Linguistics)

(50) The most massive tissues sampled (i.e. adipose and skeletal muscle tissues) that grow the most throughout the lifetime of have **unexpectedly** low mass specific metabolic rates. This observation is consistent with similar patterns observed in fish (Itazawa & Oikawa, 1986) and birds (Scott & Evans,1992). (Biology)

(51) This **discrepancy** probably happened because the recall score reflected participants' sight vocabulary and not comprehension vocabulary. The recognition test did not overestimate learners' vocabulary, but measured a different type of vocabulary than the recall test. (Applied Linguistics)

(52) Although climate is considered in many ecological studies (Field et al., 2009), climatic EH was **surprisingly** scarce in our dataset. Studies with a focus on climatic or soil EH only constituted 5.7 and 8.3% of the whole dataset, respectively, and mostly analysed effects on plant richness (54.5 and 56.3% of the respective studies; Fig. 3). Again, this bias might be partly due to our selection criteria, as more soil studies may be found at smaller spatial scales, for instance. (Biology)

(53) This **unexpected** result led the authors to hypothesize that Chinese parents were more focused on print identification than conversing in English. (Applied Linguistics)

(54) However, we also found that rhythm-based predictions resulted in slower responses to **unexpected** targets than memory-based predictions and in immediate resolution of the CNV when a temporal prediction was **unexpectedly** violated. These possibly reflect a resonance mechanism compatible with entrainment. (Biology)

(55) Two factors could contribute to this **unusual** phenomenon, namely, the high cholesterol concentration and the very high protein concentration in the AcChRrich membranes. (Biology)

(56) **Contrary to our prediction**, the finding is inconsistent with the hypothesis that the trans-Atlantic slave trade promoted local political fragmentation. One possible explanation is that some communities were already more politically

fragmented and this prior fragmentation enabled them to export more slaves. Another explanation could be that there is some other factor which influenced both the slave export intensity and the level of political fragmentation. (History)

(57) Perhaps **surprisingly**, there was no neat East/West or what one might today call global North/South divide in the discussions. (History)

(58) **Surprisingly**, despite their predaceous nature, we never observed larvae attacking conspecific eggs, even upon starvation. (Biology)

4.1.4.5 Experiencer

This frame element refers to the person who experiences the emotion of surprise. In the corpus, implied Experiencers made up the majority of cases (86%), as exemplified by Examples 59-60. Of the cases where an Experiencer was provided explicitly, five types of Experiencer were identified, including the author(s) of the research article (8%), as can be seen in Examples 61-62, another researcher (2%), as illustrated by Examples 63-64, research participant(s) (1%), as can be seen in Examples 65-66, and other people (3%), as shown in Examples 67-68. This observation was consistent with Hu and Chen's (2019) finding that implied Experiencers occurred in most expressed surprises in their corpus. This finding also supported Tutin's (2015) observation that Experiencers are often not explicitly identified but implied in research articles.

(59) The premise behind this idea is that empires were not at all monolithic entities and that, on the contrary, they possessed an **extraordinary** capacity for resilience. (History)

(60) The pattern of CNV resolution when the anticipated event was **unexpectedly** omitted provides an apparent neural correlate for the extra cost of unexpected events (Fig. 3). (Biology)

(61) Generally, and somewhat **surprisingly**, we detected less variability across these moderators than for others we examined. (Applied Linguistics)

(62) **Remarkably**, the authors detected an unexplained 'shift' of the subcellular localization of DCXR in cancerous cells compared to healthy tissue. (Biology)

(63) One of the most illuminating episodes of enculturation through language is shown in this example by Rich (2009), **surprised** by the sight of a 'Western woman on the street'. (Applied Linguistics)

(64) Rivers used the diary approach to present a personalized view of the LLSs used while learning Spanish in South America. Although she recorded a wide range of conscious strategies, she also noted her **surprise** at her unconscious strategy use. (Applied Linguistics)

(65) A dramatic instance of someone losing deliberate control over their writing production occurred when Denise, while grappling with a personally challenging point in the argument task, wrote several sentences in French mid way through her English text. She was **astonished** to realize, a few minutes later, that she had been doing this: Ah, #empecher#? I, ah, switch in French. I'm writing in French now. (Applied Linguistics)

(66) With his remaining followers starving and desperate to plant crops for the coming season, Mapondera returned to Negomo territory, where in September 1903 he surrendered, much to the **surprise** of the Chartered Administration (see Figure 7). (History)

(67) Visitors are **surprised** when they encounter Nana Tabir, perhaps because he does not appear in any museum plans or programs; hence his presence is **unexpected**. (History)

(68) The learner is called on to repeat structure and lexicon in ways that either **strike** the **native speaker** as unnatural, or create implicatures unintended by the authors. (Applied Linguistics)

4.2 Interest markers

4.2.1 Frames and frame elements evoked by interest markers

In total, 36 unique interest markers in different categories were identified in the present corpus, including nouns (e.g. *interest* and *fascination*), verbs (e.g. *intrigue* and *fascinate*), adjectives (e.g. *interesting, appealing*, and *curious*), adverbs (e.g. *interestingly* and *intriguingly*), and phrases/structures (e.g. *attract attention, attract interest in...*, and *spark interest in...*). *Interest, interesting*, and *interestingly* were the most frequently occurring interest markers, making up 67% of all occurrences. Table 4.5 lists the interest markers and their frequency in the present corpus. The 1,099 tokens of interest markers were scrutinized and found to evoke six semantic frames listed by FrameNet. These frames and their distributions are presented in Table 4.6.

Table 4.5 Categories and frequencies of interest markers found in the corpus

Category	Interest Marker
Noun	interest (316), attraction (2), fascination (7), curiosity (12)
Adjective	attractive (18), appealing (10), arresting (2), compelling (10)
	curious (17), fascinating (11), fascinated (4), interested (50)
	interesting (202), intriguing (52), obsessed (1)
Adverb	interestingly (187), intriguingly (17), curiously (8)
Verb	interest (45), fascinate (4), intrigue (6)
Phrase/structure	appeal to (2), arouse interest in (2), attract attention (15)
	attract interest in (10), be of interest (56), draw attention (6)
	have an interest in (7), hold interest in (1), not a lack of interest (3)
	not unattractive (1), not uninteresting (1), profess interest in (1)
	show an interest in (4), spark interest in (1), take an interest in (8)

Table 4.6 Frequency distributions of interest markers in terms of frames

Frame	Number of Interest Markers	Percentage of All Frames
Emotion_directed	386	35.12
Mental_stimulus_stimulus_focus	264	24.02
Experiencer_focused_emotion	186	16.92
Stimulus_focus	134	12.19
Stimulate_emotion	87	7.92
Mental_stimulus_exp_focus	42	3.82
Total	1,099	100

4.2.1.1 The Emotion_directed frame

As shown in Table 4.6, the Emotion_directed frame was the most frequently occurring one in the corpus, accounting for about 35% of the interest markers. The Emotion_directed frame, as discussed previously, characterizes an Experiencer's emotional response to a particular Stimulus or about a certain topic (FrameNet). This type of frame was evoked by *interest* used as a noun. Its frame elements are illustrated in Examples 69-71.

(69) During the last two decades there has been a [Degree great] INTEREST[Target] in [Stimulus the study of fascism] - indeed within Italy it has become one of the most productive fields of historical research]. (History)

(70) [Stimulus The stochastic finite element method] has recently attracted considerable INTEREST[Target] among [Experiencer researchers] [Reason for its obvious safety and other implications]. (Mechanical Engineering)

(71) [Stimulus The application of this concept], which is gaining INTEREST[Target] among [Experiencer scientists and policymakers], can facilitate collaboration between them and relevant practitioners and reduce conflicts among stakeholders (Tallis et al., 2012, Kelble et al., 2016). (Biology)

4.2.1.2 The Mental_stimulus_stimulus_focus frame

Evoked by adjectives (e.g. *interesting* and *fascinating*) and adverbs (e.g. *interestingly*), the Mental_stimulus_stimulus_focus frame describes a situation where the "Stimulus serves to bring about an emotion of mental stimulation in an Experiencer" (FrameNet). This frame was the second most frequently occurring one (accounting for 25% of the cases) in the corpus, as manifested in the following examples.

(72) Another INTERESTING[Target] finding is [Stimulus that some of the learners' favourite bundles were actually not used appropriately]. (Applied Linguistics)

(73) INTERESTINGLY[Target], [Stimulus the transcription of TFAM itself is regulated by PGC-1α and NRF1], suggesting a central role of PGC-1α in mitochondrial biogenesis. (Biology)

(74) Some also believed, INTERESTINGLY[Target], [Stimulus that the "people's militia" (mintuan) in the villages, an age old institution in China, could be utilized fruitfully both in carrying out and in defending the revolution]. (History)

4.2.1.3 The Experiencer_focused_emotion frame

The Experiencer_focused_emotion frame pertains to "an Experiencer's emotions with respect to some Content" (FrameNet). As explained by FrameNet, Content, which refers to "what the Experiencer's feelings or experiences are directed toward or based upon", is different from a Stimulus because the latter is construed as being directly responsible for causing the emotion, but Content is not (FrameNet). This frame, often evoked by *interested*, accounted for approximately 18% of all frame instances in the corpus. See the following examples.

(75) [$_{\text{Experiencer}}$ researchers in language and education policy] have long been INTERESTED^{Target} in [Content the theories and literature of LI to explain and even to predict the effectiveness of language policy in society]. (Applied Linguistics)

(76) In addition, [$_{\text{Experiencer}}$ we] were INTERESTED^{Target} in [$_{\text{Content}}$ comparing the relative importance of each predictor across our publication/authorship categories rather than specifying a precise regression model through model fitting]. (Biology)

(77) [$_{\text{Experiencer}}$ We] are INTERESTED^{Target} in [$_{\text{Content}}$ determining the intrinsic failure response at a material point which is assumed to depend on the history of the local mechanical field variables only]. (Mechanical Engineering)

4.2.1.4 The Stimulus_focus frame

The Stimulus_focus frame accounted for approximately 13% of frame instances in the corpus. As noted previously, this frame has to do with causing or failing to cause a particular emotion or experience in the Experiencer (FrameNet). In the present corpus, the frame was typically evoked by lexical units such as *intriguing, fascinating*, and *intriguingly*, as illustrated by Examples 78-80.

(78) He also found an INTRIGUING^{Target} [Stimulus sex difference in LLS use, with females showing a greater propensity than males to engage in out-of-class social interactions]. (Applied Linguistics)

(79) INTRIGUINGLY^{Target}, recent studies have shown [Stimulus that fathers can affect their offspring's behaviour via epigenetic pathways even if those fathers have no contact with their offspring]. (Biology)

(80) A FASCINATING^{Target} but little-understood aspect of aggregation spawning is [$_{\text{Stimulus}}$ how migrating young fish know where spawning sites are located, their degree of site fidelity, and what happens if migrations are disrupted]. (Biology)

4.2.1.5 The Stimulate_emotion frame

The Stimulate_emotion frame, evoked by verbs such as *interest, fascinate, appeal*, and adjectives such as *appealing*, describes a situation where "some phenomenon (the Stimulus) provokes a particular emotion in an Experiencer" (FrameNet), as demonstrated by Examples 81-83.

(81) [$_{\text{Stimulus}}$ Two themes] INTEREST^{Target} [Experiencer the authors of this

volume]. (History)

(82) [Stimulus The concept of Circulation] may APPEAL[Target] to [Experiencer practitioners of global history] [Explanation because it implies a vision of their terrain as a closed system, but also, in connection therewith, because it evokes a peculiar form of transmission or passage within that system, along given infrastructures, a system of "veins" or vessels]. (History)

(83) [Stimulus EVs] FASCINATE[Target] [Experiencer researchers] in basic science and translational applications alike, but our understanding of EV biogenesis, secretion, tissue retention and potential therapeutic use depends on the ability to isolate and characterize specific, well-defined populations of vesicles. (Biology)

4.2.1.6 The Mental_stimulus_exp_focus frame

Evoked by words such as *fascinated* and *curious*, the Mental_stimulus_exp_focus frame pertains to "an Experiencer [having] an emotion as caused by a Stimulus or concerning a Topic" (FrameNet). This frame was, comparatively speaking, rare in the corpus, as exemplified by Examples 84-86.

(84) [Experiencer Historians] have long been FASCINATED[Target] with [Stimulus the families that women and men built under slavery]. (History)

(85) However, these studies also reveal some CURIOUS[Target] [Stimulus inconsistencies indicative of a nascent drive toward vindication of English spoken with Chinese accents]. (Applied Linguistics)

(86) As with all Ediacara-type fossils a critical question is whether to look for similarities or differences with living animals; taken to extremes these may lead to radically different conclusions. For example, there is a CURIOUS[Target] [Stimulus similarity of some elongate Kimberella to fronds] (Fig. 5B). (Biology)

4.2.2 Interconnections among the identified frames of interest markers

Drawing on the frame-frame relations network found in FrameNet, the interconnections of the six identified frames were examined. It was shown in Figure 4.3 that the six frames are all connected via different kinds of frame relations. For example, the Emotions frame uses the Emotion-directed frame and the Stimulate_emotion frame; in the meanwhile, it provides a perspective on the Experience_focused_emotion frame and the Stimulate_focus frame. In addition, the Experience_ focused_emotion frame inherits from the Mental_stimulus_exp_focus frame, which, in turn, provides a perspective on the Emotions_of_mental_activity frame. Finally, the Mental_stimulus_stimulus_focus frame provides a perspective on the Emotions_of_mental_activity frame and thus is connected with the Mental_stimulus_exp_focus frame.

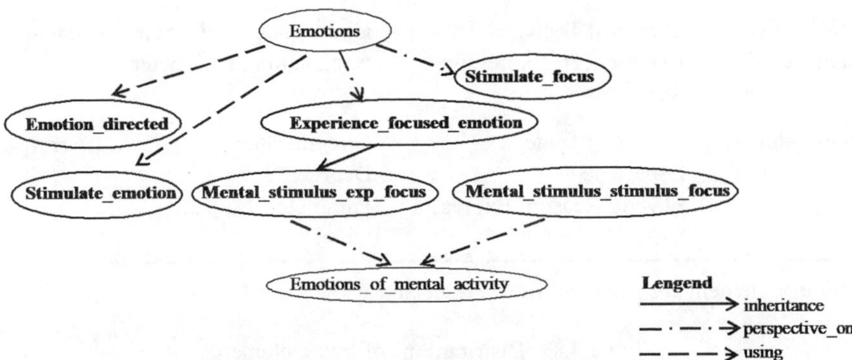

Figure 4.3 Frame interconnections of identified frames of interest markers

4.2.3 Coded frame elements and their distributions

Taking a similar approach to generating the Surprise frame (Hu & Chen, 2019), a coding scheme (see Table 4.7) was developed based on the distinct frame elements of the semantic frames identified in the corpus that FrameNet lists. The coding scheme was used to code and identify all the frame elements of the interest markers that occurred in the corpus. The coded frame elements and their distributions are summarized in Table 4.8.

Table 4.7 Coding scheme of frame elements

Frame	Frame Elements (Core)*	Frame Elements (Non-Core)*	Lexical Unit Example
Stimulate_ emotion	Experiencer; Stimulus	Circumstances; Degree Explanation; Result	*interest (verb)*
Mental_ stimulus_ stimulus_focus	Experiencer; Stimulus	Circumstances; Degree; Explanation; Parameter	*interesting*

(*to be continued*)

Frame	Frame Elements (Core)*	Frame Elements (Non-Core)*	Lexical Unit Example
Experiencer_ focused_emotion	Content; Event; Experiencer topic; Expressor, State	Circumstances; Degree; Explanation	*interested*
Stimulus_focus	experiencer, Expressor; State Stimulus; Topic	Circumstances; Degree Experiencer, Parameter	*intriguing*
Mental_ stimulus_exp_ focus	Stimulus; Topic; Experiencer; Expressor; State	Circumstances; Degree Explanation, Parameter	*fascinated*
Emotion_directed	Stimulus; Topic; Experiencer Eevent; Reason; Expressor State	Circumstances; Degree; Parameter; Empathy_ target	*interest(noun)*

*Frame element are extracted from FrameNet.

Table 4.8 Distributions of frame elements

Frame Elements	Raw Frequency	Percentage of All Frame Instances
Stimulus	934	87.95
Degree	321	30.22
Experiencer	156	14.69
Explanation	103	9.69
Content	63	5.93
Topic	11	1.03
Parameter	9	0.85
Circumstances	7	0.66
Event	4	0.38

4.2.4 The Interest frame in RAs

As illustrated in Table 4.8, Stimulus was found to be the most saliently occurring frame element (almost 88%) among all frame instances identified in the corpus. Degree, Experiencer, and Explanation accounted for approximately 30%, 15%, and 10% of the frame instances, respectively. As noted earlier, there are some conceptual overlaps of frame elements listed in FrameNet. For example, Content in the Experiencer_focused_emotion frame is named Topic in the Mental_stimulus_exp_ focus frame but is renamed Stimulus in the Stimulate_emotion frame. However, they all relate to what makes us feel interesting. Similarly, Circumstance in the Stimulus_focus frame, Reason in the Emotion_directed frame, and the Explanation in the Stimulate_emotion frame all indicate why we find something interesting. Therefore, given the distributions of the interest-related frame elements, the interconnections among the identified frames of interest, and the conceptual overlapping of frame elements in different frames, an Interest frame was generated for research articles based on the key frame elements, as shown in Figure 4.4. To avoid terminological complexity, Trigger refers to the causes of this emotive response, and Explanation gives information about why this emotive response is induced.

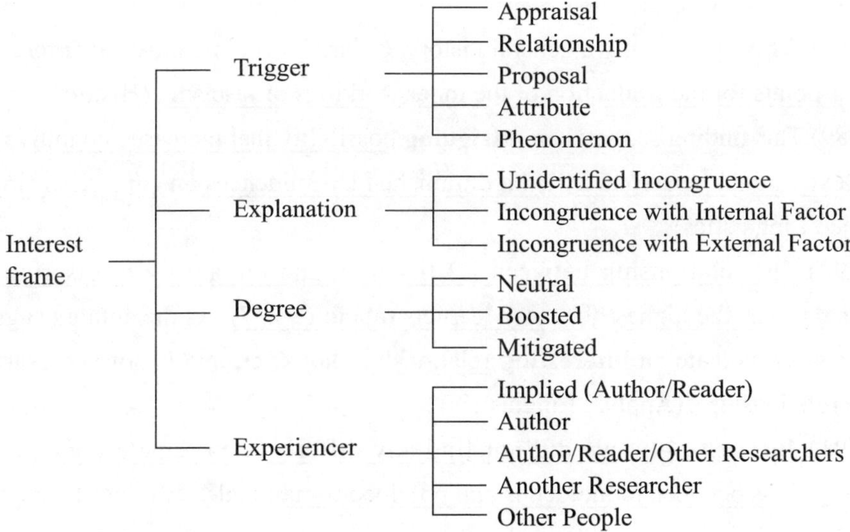

Figure 4.4 The interest frame

4.2.4.1 Trigger

The first type of Trigger, termed appraisal, refers to evaluations of the value, significance, or implications of the findings or results of the current study or previous studies, as illustrated by Examples 87-89. The second type of Trigger includes relationships between different research variables or objects, between results obtained in the current study or from different studies, as shown in Examples 90-92. The third type of Trigger is named proposal, which includes hypotheses, viewpoints or potential research trends suggested or proposed (Examples 93-95). Attribute, as another type of Trigger, concerns the distinctive features, characteristics, and qualities of research methods, research objects, research variables, or participants, as seen in Examples 96-98. Finally, as a Trigger for the emotion of interest, phenomenon refers to experiences, entities, and happenings that do not fall into the categories mentioned above, as illustrated by Examples 99-101. In the present corpus, the five categories of Trigger (in the order presented above) accounted for 27%, 24%, 19%, 8%, and 22% of the frame instances, respectively.

(87) Naturally, the evolution of the aforementioned plastic regions in Figs. 4(b), 5(b) and 6(b) give **interesting** insights into the microstructural events arising under macroscopic loading of the types pure shear, uniaxial tension, and uniaxial compression. (Biology)

(88) Whilst principally a general history, Colarizi's volume provides **interesting** starting-points for the evaluation of the inner workings of fascism. (History)

(89) This finding suggests an **intriguing** possibility that increased cognitive task complexity might be associated with diminished L1 influences on comprehensibility. (Applied Linguistics)

(90) The relationship between L2 listening and the ability to discriminate consonants was the highest for these learners (about r = .37). As the authors suggest, these results indicate an **interesting** relationship; however, this is not necessarily a causal relationship. (Applied Linguistics)

(91) **Interestingly**, we did not find any difference in female allocation to offspring mass between monotocous and polytocous mammals. (Biology)

(92) This is another **interesting** result, given the significance of fertility in ecological studies of IMR determinants, such as that of Woods et al. (2010). (History)

(93) Examining learners' motivations for maintaining the gains made abroad as well as their self-perceptions of language maintenance would be **interesting** areas to explore in future research to better understand to what extent we are meeting the needs of these students in order to maintain the gains they made while abroad. (Applied Linguistics)

(94) It is an **intriguing** question whether the phylogeny of the three proline biosynthetic enzymes is homeomorphic with the phylogeny of the organisms in which they are found, or whether the genes for these enzymes may have followed different evolutionary paths from each other. (Biology)

(95) It is of **interest** to investigate how much it contributes to the vibration, for if it could be neglected, then the analytical model would be considerably simplified. (Mechanical Engineering)

(96) This study has clear limitations: due to space constraints, many **interesting** data episodes are omitted. (Applied Linguistics)

(97) This **interesting** feature of the rice futures markets before the Second World War in Japan reflects the fact that the futures markets provided settlement on the balance and delivery of physical rice to clear the nearest month transactions. (History)

(98) Another **interesting** approach would be to use novel technology combining both micro-fluidics, which facilitate concentration of the EVs in the micro-environment, and organoid cultures, which have been highly recommended to mimic in vivo cellular organisation. (Biology)

(99) **Interestingly**, no work of which we are aware has focused on the relationship between mammalian LonP2 and aging. (Biology)

(100) What is particularly **interesting**, however, is the choice of name for the new British company. (History)

(101) **Interestingly**, no mention is made of any difficulty in learning two typologically different languages concurrently. (Applied Linguistics)

4.2.4.2 Degree

Similar to the emotion of surprise, the strength of the expressed interest can also be modulated. The emotion could be boosted (Examples 102-103) or mitigated (see Examples 104-105). Most of the frame instances (i.e. 64%), however, fell into the "neutral" category, with the expressed interest being neither boosted nor weakened (Examples 106-107), compared with the 29% that were boosted and the 7% that were mitigated. Notably, when expressed interest was boosted, various boosting devices were employed, for example, *very, certainly, keenly*, and *particularly*. When expressed interest was hedged, *perhaps* was preferred.

(102) As I talked with the participants in interviews and group discussions, I became very **interested** in questions of agency and emotion in the narrated accounts. (Applied Linguistics)

(103) The observations that mTOR-regulated apoptosis can selectively target

cancerous cells are particularly **interesting**, because this has direct relevance to the effect of rapamycin on delaying aging (Harrison et al., 2009). (Biology)

(104) Another possibility is provided by the slight, but perhaps **intriguing** similarity of the supposed 'pharynx' region of Dickinsonia to the terminal structure of Kimberella (Figs 4E and 5A), suggesting that a perhaps also possessed an introvert-like structure. (Biology)

(105) Circulation may **appeal** to global historians because it suggests a vision of their object of study as a closed system. (History)

(106) Despite their very different personalities, careers, and political and ethical commitments, these three figures shared **intriguing** commonalities in their relationship as Brazilians to India. (History)

(107) Shape memory alloys (SMAs) exhibit **interesting** properties when subjected to thermo-mechanical loadings, such as pseudoelasticity, shape memory effect, actuation and damping, which are owing to a first-order diffusionless solid-solid transformation between austenite and martensite phases. (Mechanical Engineering)

4.2.4.3 Explanation

Explanation concerns the reason for the evoked feeling of interest. Some research has shown that people find something interesting when they appraise events as more relevant to them (Connelly, 2011) or perceive an event as novel, unexpected, complex, yet potentially comprehensible (Reeve, Lee, & Won, 2015; Silvia, 2008, 2019). The factors contributing to feeling interested could be signaled explicitly or implicitly in scientific communication. When an Explanation is provided explicitly, the elicited interest could be ascribed to external or internal factors. The external factors refer to hypotheses, results, and findings of previous research or characteristics of the research background or context, as illustrated by Examples 108-110. The internal ones relate to results or findings from the current study or characteristics of research objects, variables or participants, as shown in Examples 111-113. In the corpus, most frame instances (82%) did not explain why something was interesting (see Examples 114-115), while 12% provided explanations related to external factors, and 6% gave explanations related to internal factors.

(108) In this regard, aphids represent an **interesting** exception among insects since their 18S, 5.8S and 28S rDNA genes are usually arranged as tandemly repeated

clusters atone telomere of each X chromosome, as revealed by silver staining (Fig. 1B) (Blackman & Hales, 1986; Hales, 1989; Manicardi et al., 2003). (Biology)

(109) The observations that mTOR-regulated apoptosis can selectively target cancerous cells are particularly **interesting**, because this has direct relevance to the effect of rapamycin on delaying aging (Harrison et al., 2009). (Biology)

(110) This is another **interesting** result, given the significance of fertility in ecological studies of IMR determinants, such as that of Woods et al. 2010. (History)

(111) These results are especially **interesting** given the assumption behind the combustion models (Section 4.3), namely that the structure of the turbulent flame is the same as that of a laminar flame. (Mechanical Engineering)

(112) The latter finding is particularly **interesting**, as the vocabulary test was very easy (see Appendix C): Learners who failed to achieve the maximum score on L1 vocabulary were likely to be among the weakest FL readers. (Applied Linguistics)

(113) The area is all the more **interesting** for scholars in that it was the site of an out-burst of grower militancy in 1939, an outburst that quickly became known as "the apricot war." (History)

(114) EVs **fascinate** researchers in basic science and translational applications alike, but our understanding of EV biogenesis, secretion, tissue retention and potential therapeutic use depends on the ability to isolate and characterize specific, well-defined populations of vesicles. (Biology)

(115) **Appealing** though the concept is, there are no data, however, on whether starvation signals, via leptin-dependent mechanisms, induce reductions in body core temperature in large mammals, especially in free living mammals in their natural habitats. (Biology)

4.2.4.4 Experiencer

Experiencer concerns who feels interested. Experiencers can either be stated or implied in research articles. As found earlier for the Surprise frame, the omission of the Experiencers was salient, occurring with a majority of cases of expressed interest (77%), as shown in Examples 116-117. When the Experiencers were explicitly provided, five different categories were identified, including author(s) (12% of instances of expressed interest), as seen in Examples 118-119, author/reader/other researchers (6%), as shown in Examples 120-121, another researcher (3%), as illustrated by Examples 122-123, and other people (2%), as illustrated by Examples 124-125.

(116) The assumption of a phonological core deficit in FL, though **appealing**, has to be evaluated with further investigation. (Applied Linguistics)

(117) With regard to the formation of water waves and bubbles in the typical underwater ablation technique, it is **interesting** to note that the condition of water layer is of importance and needs to be properly controlled to make the laser ablation process in water more efficient and reliable for enhancing the process performance and quality of cut accordingly. (Mechanical Engineering)

(118) Very **interestingly**, we found the phosphorylation of ezrin is increased and the attenuation of phosphorylation is delayed in Rictor KO B cells and that Latrunculin B treatment can rescue the defect of BCR signaling and internalization as well as the FO differentiation. (Biology)

(119) We are particularly **interested** in explaining how the protectionist turn of the 1930s and the great contraction of trade in cereals, and especially wheat, were mainly caused by self-sufficiency policies developed by European importers, in addition to general policies arising from the Depression. (History)

(120) It is obvious that they must draw on the insights and methodologies of anthropologists, sociologists, and practitioners of other disciplines who have long been **interested** in the phenomenon of cultural diffusion and transformation. (History)

(121) Various alcohol fuels, particularly first four aliphatic compounds (methanol, ethanol, propanol and butanol) are of significant **interest** to combustion research community as future renewable fuels because these alcohols can be synthesized chemically or biologically. (Mechanical Engineering)

(122) Wicherts et al. (2006) were **interested** in reanalyzing data from published research in psychology to examine the sensitivity of reported findings to outliers. (Applied Linguistics)

(123) However, as this researcher was only **interested** in two ranks, the fact that 50 instead of 57 judges participated in the test did not detract from the power of the test or the validity of the conclusion. (Applied Linguistics)

(124) Always more **interested** in agricultural policy than the problems of industry, and dependent on southern congressional support for passage of New Deal legislation, Roosevelt refused to intervene. (History)

(125) If <u>Weber</u> could have returned to New York City twenty years later, and James also could have lived longer (he died in 1910), perhaps <u>they</u> would have been **fascinated** by the ways institutionalized religion and modernizing religious institutions thrived in this capital of American secularism. (History)

4.3 Confusion markers

4.3.1 Frames and frame elements evoked by confusion markers

A total of 59 distinct confusion markers were identified in the corpus, including nouns (e.g. *confusion, puzzle*, and *complexity*), verbs (e.g. *confound* and *obscure*), adjectives (e.g. *confusing, misleading*, and *complicated*), adverbs (e.g. *confusingly* and *mistakenly*), and phrases/structures (e.g. *be mistaken as...* and *lead astray...*). Notably, *complex, complicated, misleading, confound, unknown*, and *unclear* occurred more frequently, accounting for 76% of all occurrences of confusion markers. Table 4.9 lists all the confusion markers identified in the corpus and their frequencies. These confusion markers occurred 924 times and evoked 10 semantic frames listed by FrameNet. These frames and their distributions are summarized in Table 4.10.

Table 4.9 Categories and frequencies of confusion markers found in the corpus

Category	Confusion Marker
Noun	ambiguity (3), confusion (15), complexity (15)
	disorientation (1), puzzle (10), uncertainty (14),
Adjective	ambiguous (18), bewildered (1), bewildering (1)
	complicated (86), confounding (18), cryptic (2)
	complex (243), confused (2), confusing (7)
	disconcerting (1), disturbing (6), enigmatic (5)
	equivocal (10), inexplicable (1), misleading (27)
	muddled (1), mystifying (1), obscure(5), perplexing (5)
	puzzling(13), tricky (3), unanswered (15), uncertain (4)

(*to be continued*)

Category	Confusion Marker
	unclear (79), unexplored (8), unknown (72)
	unresolved (23), unsettled (2), not clear (46)
Adverb	mistakenly (2), equivocally (1), enigmatically (1)
	obscurely (1), confusingly (2), misleadingly (1), puzzlingly (2)
Verb	baffle (1), bewilder (1), blur (1), complexify (3), complicate (73)
	confuse (5), confound (24), disorient (1), misinform (1)
	obscure (27), perplex (1), puzzle (2)
Phrase/structure	be mistaken as (1), be mistaken with (1), incomplete understanding (1)
	lead astray (1), there is no unequivocal evidence that (1)
	remain to be clarified (1), not make sense of (1), hard to understand (2)
	have no explanation for (1), require clarification (1)

Table 4.10 Frequency distribution of confusion markers in terms of frames

Frame	Number of Confusion Markers	Percentage of All Frame Instances
System_complexity	275	31.43
Stimulate_ emotion	181	20.68
Obviousness	163	18.62
Awareness	82	9.37
Prevarication	65	7.43
Stimulus_focus	45	5.14
Eclipse	24	2.74
Resolve_problem	18	2.28
Certainty	12	1.37
Emotion_directed	10	0.94
Total	875	100

4.3.1.1 The System_complexity frame

The System_complexity frame, evoked by lexical units such as *complex, complicate, complexify, complexity* and *complicated*, captures perceptions of a System (the complete entity or system) "as complex depending on the intricacy of the interconnectivity of its parts or components" (FrameNet). This frame was the most frequently occurring one, accounting for about 31% of the confusion frame instances in the corpus. Its distinct frame element, i.e. System, is shown in Examples 126-128.

(126) Between Israel's establishment in 1948 and the 1967 War, the Wall was, of course, in Jordanian territory, and the lack of access to it by Jews led to a COMPLICATED^{Target} [system reshaping of the imagery, memories, and longings associated with it], and to the establishment of substitute sites of national sacrality. (History)

(127) [$_{\text{system}}$ Identifying the transitions in sex-determining systems and their directions in squamates] is also COMPLICATED^{Target} by the complete lack of any information on sex determination in many species. (Biology)

(128) The findings reinterpret and COMPLEXIFY^{Target} Ruusuvuori's (2013) conclusion [$_{\text{system}}$ that emotion can serve as an affordance in institutional talk]. (Applied Linguistics)

4.3.1.2 The Stimulate_emotion frame

Evoked by words such as *confuse, perplex, puzzle, bewilder, mystify, enigmatic*, and confound, the Stimulate_emotion frame, as noted previously, relates to "some phenomenon (the Stimulus) [provoking] a particular emotion in an Experiencer" (FrameNet). It was the second most frequently occurring frame in the corpus, present in 21% of the frame instances identified. Examples of this frame are presented as follows.

(129) The colonized subject position of the Welsh, which travelled with them around the world, invites us to [$_{\text{Stimulus}}$ unpack the settler as an analytical category, a move which reveals assumptions within conventional approaches], opening spaces which CONFUSE^{Target} but also enrich, [$_{\text{Experiencer}}$ our] understandings. (History)

(130) Nevertheless, [$_{\text{Stimulus}}$ the lack of a significant path between metacognition and working memory] remains PUZZLING^{Target}. (Applied Linguistics)

(131) It is also ENIGMATIC^{Target} [$_{\text{Stimulus}}$ why under some circumstances proline can provide protection against ROS, but in other situations, ROS, generated by the mitochondrial electron transport chain as a by-product of the catabolism of proline (or ornithine) to P5C is responsible for the activation of programmed cell death]

(Hellmann et al., 2000; Deuschle et al., 2008). (Biology)

4.3.1.3 The Obviousness frame

In this frame, "a Phenomenon (the entity or facts) is portrayed with respect to the Degree of likelihood that it will be perceived and known, given the (usually implicit) Evidence, Perceiver, and the Circumstances in which it is considered" (FrameNet). It was evoked in the present corpus by words like *unclear* and *cryptic* (see Examples 132-134).

(132) At present, however, it is UNCLEAR^{Target} [$_{\text{Phenomenon}}$ how to characterize the relative plasticity of different individuals in the same sample, if their reaction norm slopes vary with respect to sign as well as magnitude]. (Biology)

(133) However, [$_{\text{Phenomenon}}$ the detailed catalytic mechanism of Hg0 oxidation by oxygen species over MnO_2 catalysts] is still UNCLEAR^{Target}. (Mechanical Engineering)

(134) During the innovation phase, we suggest that small, soft-bodied biota acquired morphological novelties in variably oxic and dynamic settings and that [Phenomenon this record would remain CRYPTIC^{Target}, i.e. not represented in the fossil record. (Biology)

4.3.1.4 The Awareness frame

Evoked by the word *unknown* in the present corpus, the Awareness frame characterizes "A Cognizer [as having] a piece of Content (the object of the Cognizer's awareness) in their model of the world" (FrameNet), as can be seen in Examples 135-137.

(135) Additionally, because most studies follow a pretest-posttest design and lack a delayed posttest, it is also currently UNKNOWN^{Target} [Content to what extent gains made in L2 fluency are maintained once learners are no longer living in a target language environment but are still enrolled in language programs back in their home universities]. [$_{\text{Cognizer}}$ INI] (Applied Linguistics)

(136) However, it was thought that, analogous to the high temperature flame dominated by small radical chemistry, the nonpremixed cool flames were sustained by a single tage mode of burning, and it was UNKNOWN^{Target} as to [Content whether coexistent multistage burning, analogous to that of the premixed flames, was possible for nonpremixed flames]. [$_{\text{Cognizer}}$ INI] (Mechanical Engineering)

(137) Notwithstanding the enormous output of books and articles on the second world war, [content one of its most successful intelligence networks] still remains UNKNOWN^{Target}. [Cognizer INI] (History)

4.3.1.5 The Prevarication frame

This frame, evoked by lexical units such as *misleading, equivocal* and *ambiguous*, refers to a situation where "a Speaker communicates about a Topic in such a way as to mislead an Addressee" (FrameNet), as illustrated by Examples 138-140.

(138) AR signalling is vital in both the development of the prostate and the progression of prostate cancer (Heinlein & Chang, 2004), but [Topic the regulatory role of AR in the autophagic process] has been EQUIVOCALLY^{Target} reported and not adequately investigated. (Biology)

(139) The paucity of studies has led to some MISLEADING^{target} [Topic generalisations in the earlier literature about the structure, function and behaviour of holocentric chromosomes] based on very little work on very few species. (Biology)

(140) However, a significant barrier to progress in this area is [Topic that many of the terms used to describe within-individual behavioural variability] are AMBIGUOUS^{Target}. (Biology)

4.3.1.6 The Stimulus_focus frame

In this frame, "a stimulus brings about a particular emotion or experience in the Experiencer or saliently fails to bring about a particular experience" (FrameNet). The frame did not occur very frequently (about 5%) in the corpus. It was typically evoked by lexical units, such as *confusing, confounding, perplexing, disorienting, bewildering,* and *disturbing*, as seen in Examples 141-143.

(141) Moreover, because of inconsistent and CONFUSING^{Target} [Stimulus use of numerous alternative names for DCXR], other tetrameric enzymes and the closely related carbonyl reductase 2 (Cbr2), we provide an overview of the systematic classification of these proteins. (Biology)

(142) However, it is [Degree somewhat] PEPLEXING^{Target} [Stimulus that the results of the third cohort do not echo the more positive results of the first and second cohorts, even though all three simply represent the same student population sampled at three different calendar times, 2008, 2009, and 2010 but the same curricular time: the beginning of late FI in grade seven]. (Applied Linguistics)

(143) Finally, and perhaps more DISTURBING[Target], is [Stimulus that "factor which fails to produce an effect in the laboratory might work well in the field"] (Phillips, 1981:18). (Applied Linguistics)

4.3.1.7 The Eclipse frame

In this frame, "an Obstruction blocks an Eclipsed entity partially or completely from perception" (FrameNet). As described in FrameNet, the Obstruction refers to "the entity which blocks the Eclipsed entity from view," and the Eclipsed is "the entity which is blocked from view." This frame was evoked by words such as *obscure* and *obscured*, as illustrated by Examples 144-146.

(144) [Obstruction This conceptual and methodological variability] may OBSCURE[Target] [Eclipsed our understanding of the role and importance of environmental heterogeneity on species diversity]. (Biology)

(145) Unlike Phanerozoic trace fossils that are typically found in environments that do not preserve body fossils, the Ediacaran traces are found in beds that also contain Ediacara-type biota, even if [Eclipsed this relationship] is sometimes OBSCURED[Target] by [Obstruction differential preservation] (see e.g. comments about deeper-water 'Fermeuse-style preservation' in Narbonne, 2005). (Biology)

(146) Metghalchi and Keck [158] reported that, [Obstruction the correlation parameters vary erratically with equivalence ratio], which makes [Eclipsed physical significance] OBSCURE[Target] and produces difficulties in smooth interpolation and extrapolation. (Mechanical Engineering)

4.3.1.8 The Resolve_ problem frame

Evoked by words such as *unanswered* and *unresolved* in the corpus (see Examples 147-149), this frame describes a situation where "an Agent resolves an outstanding Problem by finding its solution, explanation, answer, etc." (FrameNet).

(147) To date no study has examined how the sub-dimensions of utterance fluency develop over time, leaving UNRESOLVED[Target] [Problem the question whether there are different developmental paths for the three sub-domains of utterance fluency]. (Applied Linguistics)

(148) UNRESOLVED[Target], however, is [Problem whether a simple rise in oxygenation was the major control on taxonomic diversification during this interval, or whether the key factor was the spatial heterogeneity produced by isolation of

multiple shallow-water basins by anoxic barriers]. (Biology)

(149) Inevitably, given how these records were produced, [$_{\text{Problem}}$ many questions] have to remain UNANSWERED^{Target}, and any interpretations and conclusions must be, even more so than in most histories, tentative. (History)

4.3.1.9 The Certainty frame

This frame, evoked by the word *uncertainty*, concerns "a Cognizer's certainty about the correctness of beliefs or expectations" (FrameNet). The frame element Content "denotes the mental content that the Cognizer is certain or uncertain about" (FrameNet). The following examples illustrate the frame elements.

(150) In addition to the above limitations, some more UNCERTAINTIES^{Target} require clarification in future research. They include [$_{\text{Content}}$ (i) Does coupling comprehension with production always bring about alignment? (ii) If it does, is the effect of alignment long-lasting or temporary? (iii) Do the continuation task features such as the text genre or the topic affect the manner or strength of alignment?]. [$_{\text{Cognizer}}$ INI] (Applied Linguistics)

(151) There is also UNCERTAINTY^{Target} [$_{\text{Content}}$ in whether the available fossils represent the whole organismor only a part. [$_{\text{Cognizer}}$ INI] (Biology)

(152) If Fi 0 and i < n, the trial stress is out of the field but it is UNCERTAIN^{Target} [$_{\text{Content}}$ whether it lies within the yield surface (Case II)]. [$_{\text{Cognizer}}$ INI] (Mechanical Engineering)

4.3.1.10 The Emotion_directed frame

The Emotion_directed frame, as noted in the earlier discussions on surprise and interest markers, refers to "an Experiencer who is feeling or experiencing a particular emotional response to a Stimulus or about a Topic" (FrameNet). This frame was evoked by lexical units such as *perplexed*, *bewildered*, and *unsettled* (see Examples 153-154). This frame was rare and accounted for about 1% of the confusion-related frame instances found in the corpus.

(153) The UNSETTLED^{Target} [$_{\text{Stimulus}}$ issues] for simple two species predator-prey systems include: (1) how common is predator dependence; (2) what is the range of functional forms and underlying mechanisms of predator dependence. (Biology)

(154) Jiang Tingfu was rather PERPLEXED^{Target} [$_{\text{Stimulus}}$ by the same issue that many others of his and Fairbank's generation: Could China modernize?] (History)

4.3.2 Interconnections among the identified frames of confusion markers

The interconnections of the 10 identified frames were examined in accordance with the frame-frame relation network found in FrameNet. Similar to surprisc and interest markers, the interconnections among the identified frames of confusion markers made it possible to generate a Confusion frame.

As shown in Figure 4.5, except for the Prevarication, Eclipse, and Resolve_problem frames, all the frames are connected in some way. For example, the Emotions frame connects with the Emotion_directed frame, the Stimulate_focus frame, and the Stimulate_emotion frame by either using or providing a perspective on the three frames. Moreover, the System_complexity frame, the Obviousness frame, and the Certainty frames are interconnected via the Gradable_attributes frame by the relationship of Inheritance. Furthermore, the System_complexity frame is connected with the Awareness frame by inheriting from the Gradable_attributes frame, which, in turn, is inherited by the Certainty frame, with the latter using or seeing also the Awareness frame. Although the frames of Prevarication, Eclipse, and Resolve_problem are independent of other frames, they constitute important sources of confusion since the misleading information, the blocking of understanding, or the unresolved problems will probably make us feel mentally challenged or confused.

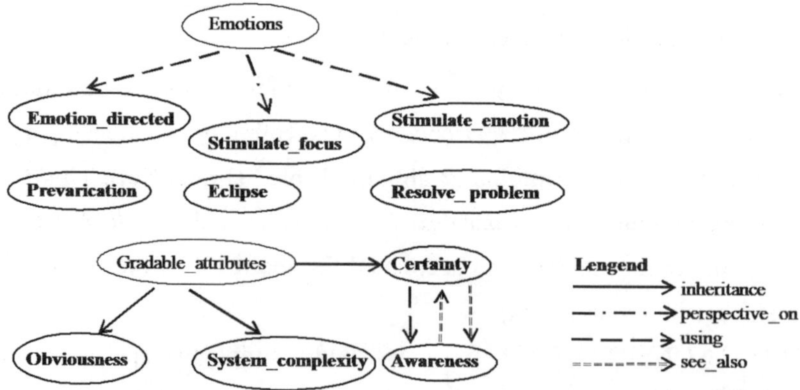

Figure 4.5 Frame interconnections of identified frames of confusion markers

4.3.3 Coded frame elements and their distributions

As with the generation of the Surprise and the Interest frame, a coding scheme was developed based on the distinct frame elements of the confusion-related frames classified by FrameNet (see Table 4.11). This coding scheme was employed to identify all the frame elements that occurred in the instances of confusion-related frames in the corpus. The coded frame elements and their distributions are shown in Table 4.12.

Table 4.11 The coding scheme for confusion-related frame elements

Frame	Frame Elements (Core)*	Frame Elements (Non-Core)*	Lexical Unit Example
Stimulate_ emotion	Experiencer; Stimulus	Circumstances stances; Degree Explanation; Result	*confuse*
System_ complexity	System	Degree; Dimension	*complicated*
Prevarication	addressee; speaker; topic	Degree; Means; Purpose	*equivocate*
Stimulus_focus	experiencer; Expressor; State Stimulus; Topic	Circum stances; Degree; Experiencer; Parameter	*confusing*
Eclipse	Eclipsed; Obstruction	Degree; Vintage point	*obscure*
Emotion_directed	Stimulus; Topic; Experiencer	Circum stances; Degree; Parameter	*bewildered*
Obviousness	Attribute; Degree; Phenomenon	Circum stances; Evidence; Group	*unclear*
Resolve_problem	Agent; Cause; Problem	Circum stances; Degree; Instrument Containing_event; Means	*unresolved*
Awareness	Cognizer; Expressor; Content; Topic	Degree; Explanation; Paradign	*unkown*
Certainty	Cognizer; Expressor, Conten; Topic	Degree; Explanation	*uncertain*

*Frame elements are extracted from FrameNet

Table 4.12 Distributions of the confusion-related frame elements

Frame Elements	Raw Frequency	Percentage of All Frame Instances
Phenomenon	721	82.4
System	375	42.86
Content	187	21.37
Degree	87	9.94
Experiencer	71	8.11
Explanation	64	7.31
Topic	32	3.66
Problem	24	2.74
Eclipsed	10	1.14
Circumstances	7	0.8
Dimension	6	0.67

4.3.4 The Confusion frame in RAs

As shown in Table 4.12, Phenomenon was found in 82% of the confusion-related frame instances and was thus the most frequently occurring frame element. As noted previously, there are conceptual overlaps among some identified frame elements. For instance, although Phenomenon, System, Content all refer to the cause of feeling confused, they are distinguished by FrameNet depending on what semantic frames they are involved in. Likewise, Cognizer in the Awareness frame is conceptually equivalent to Experiencer in the Stimulate_emotion frame because both indicate who experiences this emotive reaction. Thus, based on the conceptual overlap and interconnections of confusion-related frames and distributions of the main frame elements of these frames, a Confusion frame was generated for research articles in the corpus, as shown in Figure 4.6.

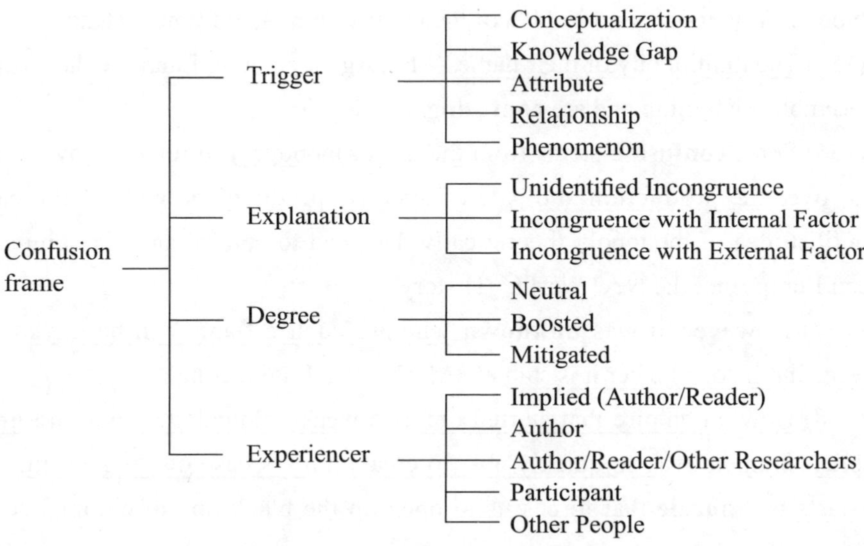

Figure 4.6 The confusion frame

4.3.4.1 Trigger

This element concerns what evokes the emotive response of confusion. In the present corpus, five types of Trigger were identified. The first type of Trigger, conceptualization, refers to terms, concepts, or definitions provided in previous research or extant literature. This type of Trigger appeared in 8% of the frame instances, as shown in the Examples 155-156. The second type of Trigger describes a knowledge gap identified in a given field of study, that is, the missing piece in the literature, an area that has not been addressed adequately or a specific hypothesis formulated in the field of study, as can be seen in Examples 157-158. This type of Trigger occurred in 32% of the frame instances. Attribute, as another type of Trigger, pertains to the properties or characteristics of research objects, research instruments, research variables, research methods, or research participants (see Examples 159-160). This type of Trigger was found in 21% of the confusion-related frame instances. As illustrated by Examples 161-162, another type of Trigger describes relationships or interactions between research variables or objects, between observations, results, or findings generated by the same research or from different research. This type of Trigger occurred in 28% of the confusion-related frame instances. Finally, as the fifth type of Trigger, phenomenon refers to an existing situation that can be observed or experienced, as illustrated by Examples 163-164.

This type of Trigger occurred in 11% of the confusion-related frame instances.

(155) The multiplicity of their names—F2, Agency Tudor, Interallie, la Famille, etc., resemble a labyrinth and are **confusing**. (Biology)

(156) Some **confusion** stems from the use of monopoly to refer to government control over the production and sale of specific products, as well as the early mercantilist idea of monopoly theoretically designed to control and tax commerce between Europe and the New World. (History)

(157) However, it was **unknown** whether such a flame can be physically observed, and if so, whether it is stable. (Mechanical Engineering)

(158) How an empire that started out as a weak colonial state with no grasp of public sentiment was so quickly able to create a mass base of national imperial enthusiasts is a **puzzle** that forces us to open up the black box of colonial social dynamics. (History)

(159) Revision is a rather **complex** activity that involves the reading, evaluation, and internal or external alteration of text representation and production (Alamargot & Chanquoy, 2001; Broekkamp & van den Bergh, 1996; Chanquoy, 2001, 2009; Hayes, 1996; Stevenson et al., 2006). (Applied Linguistics)

(160) Alignment of the trnH-psbA spacer can be highly **ambiguous** because of its complicated molecular evolution, considerable length variation (Chang et al., 2006), and high rates of insertion/deletion in larger families of angiosperms (Chase et al., 2013). (Biology)

(161) All variables were positively related to L2 listening ability. However, it is somewhat **perplexing** that the results of the third cohort do not echo the more positive results of the first and second cohorts, even though all three simply represent the same student population sampled at three different calendar times, 2008, 2009, and 2010 but the same curricular time: the beginning of late FI in grade seven. (Applied Linguistics)

(162) This seems plausible, but as I pointed out earlier in this section, evidence for a faster metabolic rate increasing reproductive output is highly **equivocal**. (Biology)

(163) These concepts have provided tools for analyzing the seemingly **puzzling** phenomena of widespread popular support during even the most brutal regimes. (History)

(164) This bird joins mixed-species flocks of birds (A. Gamero, personal communication) and could potentially follow primate groups. The reason why it has not been observed in PNPAs remains **obscure**. (Biology)

4.3.4.2 Degree

Concerning the degree to which confusion was expressed, authors in the present corpus maintained a "neutral" stance in most cases (88%), as seen in Examples 165-166. The emotive responses were boosted in 8% of the cases (Examples 167-168) and mitigated in another 4% of the instances (Examples 169-170). It was noted that researchers often opted for *highly* and *completely* when the emotive response was toned up but preferred *somewhat* and the modal verb *may* to tone down the expressed confusion.

(165) We propose that it is for this reason that these L1 studies also present **equivocal** findings. (Applied Linguistics)

(166) It is also **enigmatic** why under some circumstances proline can provide protection against ROS, but in other situations, ROS, generated by them itochondrial electron transport chain as a by-product of the catabolism of proline (or ornithine) to P5C is responsible for the activation of programmed cell death (Hellmann et al., 2000). (Biology)

(167) We propose that it is perhaps for this reason that these L1 studies also present highly **equivocal** findings. (Applied Linguistics)

(168) Statistical tests based on assumed probability distributions, primarily Gaussian, provided quite **ambiguous** information about the calculated results. (Mechanical Engineering)

(169) This conceptual and methodological variability may **obscure** our understanding of the role and importance of environmental heterogeneity on species diversity. (Applied Linguistics)

(170) In the case of interior walls, the pores pass through the entire thickness of the wall, whereas in exterior walls they pass through the calcified layers only and are covered by the cuticle, hence the name 'pseudopore' (note that this term is used inconsistently across the Bryozoa as certain complete pores incheilostome frontal walls are somewhat **confusingly** referred to as pseudopores because they connect the hypostegal and visceral coeloms of the zooid. (Biology)

4.3.4.3 Explanation

No explanation was provided for the confusion experienced in 83% of the confusion-related frame instances, as seen in Examples 171-172. Among the remaining cases, 10% contained an Explanation related to internal reasons, namely, factors that are internal to the current or previous research. These internal factors relate to the research itself, such as the methodology employed, the interpretations of findings, or the attributes of research objects, as seen in Examples 173-175. In another 7% of the cases, the Explanation provided pertains to some external factors that may impact the current or previous research, such as the characteristics of the larger research context (Examples 176-178).

(171) The transition from a Proterozoic world with benthic communities consisting of microbial mats and algae, and phytoplank tonic communities with no zoo plankton into a Cambrian world with thriving benthic and planktonic animal communities raises **puzzling** questions about cause and effect. (Biology)

(172) The findings reinterpret and **complexify** Ruusuvuori's (2013) conclusion that emotion can serve as an affordance in institutional talk. (Applied Linguistics)

(173) Much of this **confusion** can be attributed to the fact that this research has not adequately distinguished writing expertise from second-language proficiency. (Applied Linguistics)

(174) It is also possible that patterns regarding the relationship between participants' initial proficiency level and gain scores were **obscured** because this study measured change in macrolevel constructs that consist of many sub-components. (Applied Linguistics)

(175) The situation is highly **complicated** for the case of general orthotropic materials, for which Equations (35) do not apply, and arbitrary orientations of the voids, which are within the scope of the analytical model, though not analyzed in detail here. (Mechanical Engineering)

(176) The federal government was **confused** whether this development was a boon or a tragedy, as world war gave way to cold war, which only increased the need for good capitalist citizens on the margin of American territory. (History)

(177) The vast geographic scope of the construct **complicated** litigation suits such as Diego since it was often difficult to prove who was an Indio from Spanish or Portuguese contested territories. (History)

(178) However, human adaptation to resource decline is likely to be additionally **complicated** by increased frequency of biophysical tipping points, because of global environmental changes and increasingly prevalent human pressure (table 1; Rocha et al., 2015a). (Biology)

4.2.4.4 Experiencer

The Experiencers of expressed confusion were not stated but implied in 91% of the relevant frame instances found in the corpus (see Examples 179-180). Where the Experiencers were explicitly identified, they could be classified as author(s) (4%), as shown in Examples 181-182, author(s)/reader/other researchers (3%), as illustrated by Examples 183-184, research participant (1%), as can be seen in Examples 185-186, and other people (1%), as shown in Examples 187-188.

(179) Lately, however, connectedness has become a sprawling word; border crossing became an exemplar and an explanation at the same time. And this has led to some **muddled** thinking. (History)

(180) Consequently, the boundary conditions to be applied at the outer surface are somewhat **ambiguous**. (Biology)

(181) Although this nuclear location of the binding site could provide a rationale for its RNA cargo, the biogenesis and the biological significance of ST-EVs, its cargo of relatively short and seemingly non-functional RNAs, and its cargo of fibronectin, an extracellular protein, are rather **enigmatic** from our present perspective of EV biogenesis and functions. (Biology)

(182) It is still **unknown** to us whether CSF-cNs also differentiate through a process of apical domain loss and polarity re-establishment or not. (Biology)

(183) The thesis is, though, **misleading** for whomsoever wishes to understand the nature of fascism and its meaning in Italian history. (History)

(184) If one attempts to correct it by the grid reference, one is **mistakenly** assuming that the rapid growth is due to the spatial effect, and the correction introduces a bias, making the corrected neighboring genotypes of growth rates even lower than the true values. (Biology)

(185) Given such conflicting professional advice, many ESL teachers are understandably **confused** and frustrated. (Applied Linguistics)

(186) Interlocutors are far more likely to lose their conversational footing as a result of **confusing** aspects of the discourse as a whole. (Applied Linguistics)

(187) Evidence for the three famines, although possibly **ambiguous** for Bengal, points to FAD2 famines, as in Vietnam. (History)

(188) Especially **perplexing** for Jews were Christian attempts to renounce or sublimate sexuality. (History)

4.4 Comparison among the three knowledge emotion frames

4.4.1 Trigger as a core frame element for the three knowledge emotion frames

Trigger, which elicits the emotive response (i.e. feeling surprised, interested or confused), is a core frame element that "instantiates a conceptually necessary component of the frame" (Ruppenhofer et al., 2016, p.23). Although FrameNet gives it different names in different semantic frames (e.g. stimulus in the Stimulus_focus frame, Phenomenon in the Expectation frame, Evaluee in the Desirability frame), this frame element is fundamental to what is surprising, interesting, and confusing.

As noted earlier, surprise is induced when our held expectation is contravened by an actual event we have experienced. This kind of conceptual incongruence not only informs us of the discrepancy (Kövecses, 2015), but also motivates us to find reasons for the discrepancy (Tsang, 2013). Concerning what may cause the feeling of surprise, the data revealed that phenomenon (43%) was the most frequently occurring type, followed by relationship (31%) as a type of Trigger. In scholarly communication, academics are more likely to be surprised by a phenomenon or an event that contradicts what they expected to perceive or experience. This finding corroborated what was reported by Hu and Chen (2019) and Tutin's (2015) observation that in scientific writing, surprise is in general articulated when expectations ran counter to observed facts. Furthermore, academics' surprise was also evoked by the different findings from previous research. Arguably, the unexpected results obtained in the current research or contradictory findings inconsistent with the extant research were deemed valuable in scientific communication because they might add a different perspective or shed new light on the topic under investigation. By highlighting the "surprising findings" of their studies, academic writers could promote the uniqueness and significance of their research, i.e. extending the extant literature and producing new knowledge on a topic.

Unlike surprise, interest that arises from heightened attention sparked by external stimuli reflects a particular relationship between the individual concerned and some content or activity (Hidi & Renninger, 2006). The distributions of the different types of Trigger indicated that interest was primarily aroused by evaluating prior work done by other researchers or the current research done by the author(s) (27%). As the second most frequent type of Trigger (24%), relationship is centrally concerned with the novelty of observations or findings obtained in one's study. Understandably, scholars who compete for academic visibility and recognition tend to promote their research to a wider readership (Berkenkotter & Huckin, 2016), including fellow researchers in their own and other disciplines, policy-makers, or even the general public (Rakedzon et al., 2017). Giving credit to previous studies demonstrates the authors' membership in a particular academic community and enables them to claim the centrality of the topic discussed. Explaining the novelty and originality of one's study by highlighting the interestingness of his or her findings helps grab readers' attention, signals the study's contributions to disciplinary knowledge, and, above all, communicates the message that this research is well worth reading (Hyland, 2011). Thus, characterizing data and results as interesting could be viewed as an eye-catching and promotional strategy deployed by academic authors to accommodate the increased competition of globalized academia.

With regard to what may cause the feeling of confusion, the distributions of the different types of Trigger revealed that this emotive response was more likely to be elicited by a knowledge gap (the most frequently occurring type of Trigger accounting for 34% of all the instances). This finding is not surprising since this feeling occurs when we are confronted with a novel and complex situation beyond our capacity to understand (Silvia, 2013, 2019) or when the incongruence of prior knowledge and new information cannot be resolved immediately (Pekerun & Stephens, 2012). Reflecting on the confusion we experience about scientific research, we could modify our emotion-action link, thereby resolving the cognitive conflict (Silvia, 2013, 2019). In scientific writing, confusion is an essential motivator for the creation and growth of knowledge because expressed confusion indicates a potentially unresolved issue or a potential research topic worth exploring.

Particularly, when an academic author's confusion stems from the reported data, ambiguous methods employed, or equivocal interpretations of findings given by previous studies, the necessity of conducting the current study is accentuated and justified.

4.4.2 Explanation as a core frame element for the three knowledge emotion frames

While a Trigger captures the cause of an emotive reaction, an Explanation tells us why the Trigger evokes feelings of surprise, interest, and confusion. According to Ruppenhofer et al.'s (2016) criteria, this frame element essentially distinguishes the knowledge emotion frames from other frames. Thus, it is central to the semantic frames associated with the knowledge emotions. Originally, FrameNet assigns conceptually overlapping frame elements with different core or non-core statuses. For example, the frame element of Reason in the Emotion_directed frame is defined as a core frame element, but Explanation (the conceptual equivalent frame element of Reason) in the Stimulate_emotion frame is characterized as a peripheral one. In the generated frames for expressions of the three knowledge emotions, Explanation is considered as a core frame element because it helps to trace the sources of the evoked feelings in scholarly communication. In other words, Explanations could tell us why the Trigger is surprising, interesting, or confusing.

As can be seen in the present corpus, most instances of expressed surprise, interest, and confusion were not provided with an explanation. It suggests that epistemological assumptions and scientific beliefs are, to a large extent, shared by the academic community as a whole. Since members of a disciplinary community may share the same expectations and references, choosing not to explain why the author(s) feel surprised, interested, or confused can be viewed as a strategic manipulation of language in writer-reader interaction. It could be surmised that discipline-specific norms and conventions may impact the extent to which shared scientific knowledge among community members can be assumed. Clearly, this assumption needs to be tested empirically.

4.4.3 Resolution as a core frame element for the Surprise frame

When we are confronted with cognitive incongruity due to the lack of alignment between what we expect to occur and what we encounter, our feelings of surprise will be induced. Driven by the psychological need to resolve the discrepancy, we are motivated to find a resolution through which the knowledge gap may be closed, and new understandings may be developed. This frame element is a core one to the Surprise frame and deals with how our epistemic incongruity is resolved. In scientific communication, the resolved surprise becomes an important means to construct, create and generate new scientific knowledge, particularly for the experiencers of this emotion. The unresolved surprise could direct the readers' attention to the discrepant event or the divergent stimulus (Topolinski & Strack, 2015) and engage them in the scientific dialogue by motivating them to process, interpret, and explore the incongruence.

Different from feeling surprised that arises from cognitive incongruence (Kövecses, 2015), feeling interested and confused arise from different appraisals of events (Silvia, 2019). According to Silvia (2010, 2019), interest stems from two appraisals: one is the evaluation of the novelty of an event; the other is the comprehensibility of an event. When we have coping potential (e.g. knowledge, skills, and resources) to deal with an unexpected experience or event (Lazarus, 1991), we are capable of understanding it. In other words, the emotive response of interest will be induced if we appraise an event as novel, comprehensible and manageable (Silvia, 2010, 2019). When the new information helps bridge the gap between our current and desired knowledge, we probably have already understood the discrepant situation relevant to interest, expanded the scope of knowledge with new information, and gained the anticipated satisfaction.

While we find something interesting when we can understand, we feel confused when we appraise events as unfamiliar, novel, complex, and beyond our capacity to comprehend (Silvia, 2013, 2019). Confusion may also occur when the contradiction between new information and our prior knowledge cannot be assimilated and accommodated into our schema immediately (Nerantzaki et al., 2021; Pekrun et al., 2017). As confusion is "indicative of a meaning-making process that failed and needs effort and time to be restored" (Nerantzaki et al., 2021, p.3), experiencing confusion could be particularly productive if it could be ultimately resolved (D'Mello et al., 2014). During scientific communication, what triggers confusion primarily centers around the scientific knowledge gap that needs to be bridged through scholarly inquiries. Hence, academics' unresolved confusions are the potential research areas that warrant more investigations. By addressing those issues worth exploring, new knowledge can be generated. This is why confusion belongs to the family of knowledge emotions (Silvia, 2013, 2019).

4.4.4 Degree as a peripheral frame element for the three knowledge emotion frames

Degree concerns the extent of the elicited emotive responses. This frame element is peripheral because it does not "introduce additional, independent or distinct events from the main reported event" (Ruppenhofer et al., 2016, p.24). The data in the present corpus showed that boosters and hedges could modulate the degree of feeling surprised, interested, or confused to demonstrate how confident the author is toward advanced propositions and opinions (Hyland, 2005a). This suggested that the expressed emotive responses are negotiable since emotions are elicited from people's subjective appraisals of an event rather than the event itself (Ellsworth & Scherer, 2003; Silvia, 2008). In other words, people may have different responses and interpretations of a similar situation. How surprising, interesting or confusing the Trigger is may be perceived differently by different individuals. Thus, the strategic choice of modulated linguistic expressions by the author(s) serves to align with readers and establish solidarity with members in the shared disciplinary community and helps to maintain an image of an authoritative discipline insider (Hyland, 2009) privy to what is truly surprising, interesting or confusing (Hu & Chen, 2019). Furthermore, presenting scientific claims objectively and prudently through the use of hedges and boosters may reflect a "shift in rhetorical ethos" (Gillaerts & Van de Velde 2010, p.137). In other words, academic writing appears to be moving away from academic "omniscience" to favor a more dialogic way of projecting a credible and persuasive authorial persona to the disciplinary discourse community by balancing conviction and caution as well as assertiveness and modesty (Dontcheva-Navratilova, 2016; Hyland, 2010).

4.4.5 Experiencer as a peripheral frame element for the three knowledge emotion frames

This frame element concerns who experiences the emotive responses. In research articles, as found for all the three knowledge emotion frames, the omission of the Experiencers was salient and found in a great majority of cases (86% for surprise, 77% for interest, 91% for confusion). Some research showed that the Experiencer was, in most cases, not present in the frame instances of surprise markers found (Hu & Chen, 2019; Tutin, 2015) because surprise is "more source-oriented than experiencer-oriented" (Tutin, 2015, p.431). The present corpus further revealed that apart from Experiencers of surprise, Experiencers of interest and confusion were often not explicitly identified but implied. The omission of Experiencers suggests the existence of knowledge shared between authors and readers in the research community. To leave Experiencers unstated also conforms to academic conventions that value objectivity anchored in empirical observations and processes rather than the researchers themselves. As it does not "uniquely characterize a frame, and can be instantiated in any semantically appropriate frame" (Ruppenhofer et al., 2016, p.24), Experiencer is a peripheral frame element for all three knowledge emotions.

4.5 A generic frame for knowledge emotions in RAs

As made clear by the comparisons above, the three knowledge emotion frames share similar semantic features manifested by the core or peripheral frame elements. In addition, current literature has evidenced that surprise, interest, and confusion are triggered by cognitive states involving discrepancies between novel information and activated schemata, the interruption of information processing, or a gap in prior knowledge (Muis et al., 2018; Nerantzaki & Efklides, 2019; Nerantzaki et al., 2021; Silvia, 2019; Vogl et al., 2021). These emotions prompt us to focus on the new information and motivate our knowledge-seeking endeavors for resolving a potential problem (Muis et al., 2018; Silvia, 2010, 2019).

Therefore, it is possible and plausible to propose a generic knowledge emotion frame given the shared semantic and cognitive properties of these emotions, as presented in Figure 4.7. The frame element or a subtype of a frame element (e.g. Resolution) specific to one of the knowledge emotions is indicated in the parentheses.

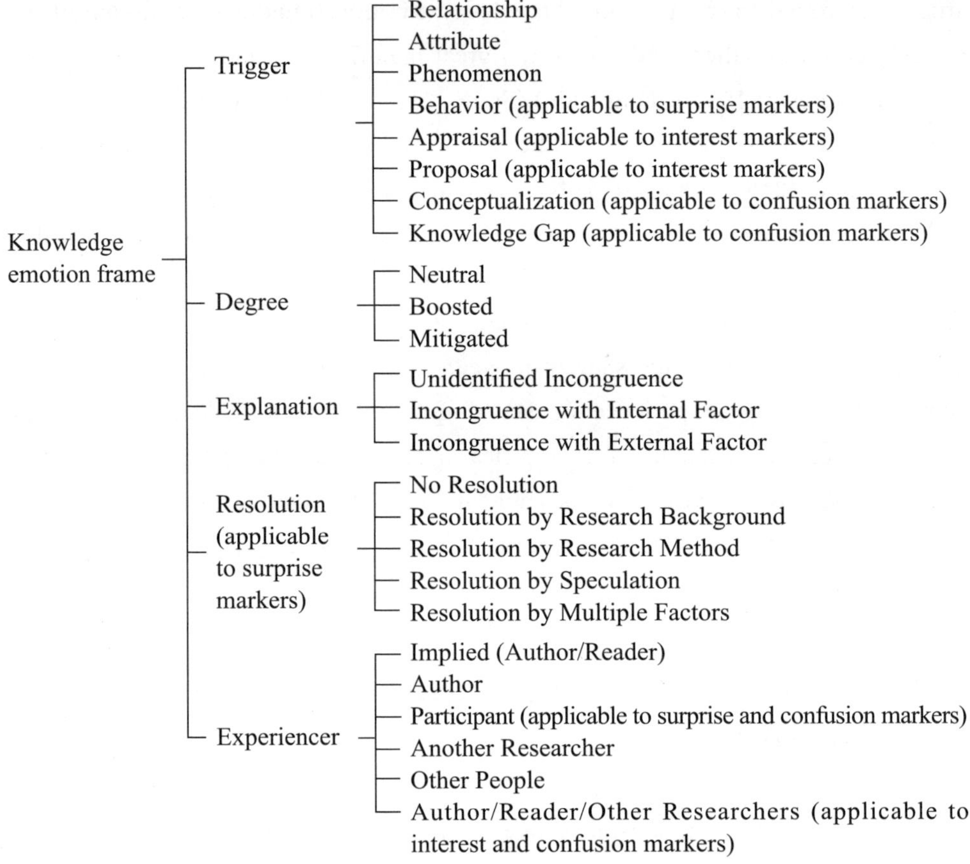

Figure 4.7　The knowledge emotion frame

Apparently, the generic frame could shed light on the studies that attempt to uncover interrelations of surprise, interest, and confusion in psychology (Nerantzaki & Efklides, 2019; Muis et al., 2015; Vogl et al., 2021). Moreover, it helps to reveal the most salient semantic properties, particularly the shared and distinct cognitive characteristics of knowledge emotion markers employed by academics for scholarly communication. More importantly, this conceptual framework could facilitate comparisons of academics' use of knowledge emotion markers based on one coherent frame because scholars may choose to associate their expressed surprise, interest and confusion with the same trigger as illustrated by the example: *Perhaps **surprisingly** but **interestingly**, why some metabolites produced by bacterial species displayed anti-tumorigenic activities remains a **mystery**.*

As noted in the previous sections, the knowledge emotions of surprise, interest, and confusion, as specific evaluative attitude markers in RAs, are important linguistic resources to communicate scientific ideas. Thus, there is good reason to expect that the proposed frame for knowledge emotions can provide a useful conceptual tool for analyzing how discipline, gender, the researcher's geo-academic location, and time may affect the use of knowledge emotion markers. Answers to these questions could contribute to a more comprehensive and nuanced understanding of deep-seated knowledge-making practices and knowledge construction instantiated in the linguistic expressions of knowledge emotions.

Chapter Five

Use of Knowledge Emotion Markers in Research Articles: Quantitative Findings

5.1 Cross-disciplinary differences in the use of knowledge emotion markers

To address RQ2 concerning possible cross-disciplinary differences in the use of knowledge emotion markers in RAs, the proposed knowledge emotion frame was used to code all instances of knowledge emotion markers found in the corpus. Binary logistical regression analyses were then run to identify if there were cross-disciplinary differences. The findings are presented as follows.

5.1.1 Use of surprise markers

5.1.1.1 Overall distributions of surprise markers by discipline

The binary logistic regression analysis run on the overall use of surprise markers across the disciplines did not show a statistically significant difference (Nagelkerke R^2 = 0.018, p = 0.043), as reported in Table 5.1. The result indicated that scholars from the four disciplines grouped on two dimensions did not differ in the use or non-use of surprise markers in their RAs.

Table 5.1 Results of the binary logistic regression on the use of surprise markers (disciplinary groupings as predicators)

Outcome	Predictor	*B*	*SE*	*Wald*	*p*	Odds Ratio (OR)	95% CI for OR	
							Lower	Upper
Surprise markers	Hard vs Soft	0.774	0.478	0.676	0.548	2.424	0.550	2.030
	Pure vs Applied	0.422	0.478	0.282	0.755	1.867	0.493	1.887
	Constant	0.647	0.224	0.053	0.684	1.051	1.910	
	R^2 = 0.021 (Cox & Snell); R^2 = 0.018 (Nagelkerke)							
	Model $\chi^2(2)$ = 5.420, p = 0.043							

However, significant disciplinary differences were observed when binary logistic regression analyses were run on the frame elements of the Surprise frame. In what follows, the detailed statistical results are reported.

5.1.1.2 Distributions of the frame elements of surprise markers by discipline

Core frame element: Trigger

As summarized in Table 5.2, the logistic regressions run on the frame element of Trigger found that the pure/applied distinction was a significant predictor of the frame element subcategory of Relationship (B=2.231, p<0.001, Nagelkerke R^2=0.41, OR=3.237) and that the hard/soft distinction significantly predicted Attribute (B=0.784, p<0.001, Nagelkerke R^2=0.239, OR=2.341) and Behavior (B=−2.789, p<0.001, Nagelkerke R^2=0.068, OR=0.237). As indicated by the Nagelkerke R^2 statistics, 4.1%, 23.9%, and 6.8% of the variance in the outcome variable were explained by the full model. The odds statistics indicated that researchers from the pure disciplines were 3.24 times more likely than those from the applied ones to express their surprises triggered by Relationship. In addition, scholars from the hard disciplines were 2.34 times more likely to express surprises triggered by Attribute than their counterparts from the soft disciplines were. In addition, linguistic expressions of surprise caused by Behavior were 4.22 times (the result of dividing one by the odds ratio) more likely to be found in RAs written by scholars from the soft disciplines than those written by the hard-discipline academics.

Table 5.2 Results of binary logistic regressions on the frame element of Trigger (disciplinary groupings as predicators of surprise markers)

Outcome	Predictor	*B*	*SE*	*Wald*	*p*	Odds Ratio	95% CI for Odds Ratio	
							Lower	Upper
Relationship	Hard vs Soft	0.818	0.529	5.573	0.214	2.655	0.885	3.094
	Pure vs Applied	2.231	0.324	4.259	0.000	3.237	2.78	6.551
	Constant	1.130	0.332	9.321	0.142	1.120		
	R^2=0.029 (Cox & Snell); R^2=0.041 (Nagelkerke)							
	Model $\chi^2(2)$ = 17.4123, p<0.001							
Attribute	Hard vs Soft	0.784	0.619	5.321	0.001	2.341	0.024	4.231
	Pure vs Applied	0.236	0.441	2.237	0.423	1.072	0.528	1.526
	Constant	−3.567	0.453	11.582	0.000	0.243		
	R^2=0.051 (Cox & Snell); R^2=0.239 (Nagelkerke)							
	Model $\chi^2(2)$=11.432, p<0.001							
Behavior	Hard vs Soft	−2.789	0.619	10.634	0.000	0.237	0.512	6.486
	Pure vs Applied	0.65	0.712	5.73	0.341	1.801	0.120	2.451
	Constant	−2.944	0.513	32.945	0.213	0.473		
	R^2=0.008 (Cox & Snell); R^2=0.068 (Nagelkerke)							
	Model $\chi^2(2)$=23.889, p<0.001							
Phenomenon	Hard vs Soft	−1.842	0.256	7.213	0.521	0.478	0.177	5.229
	Pure vs Applied	−0.821	0.421	13.521	0.156	0.312	0.293	0.828
	Constant	−4.264	0.616	22.172	0.251	0.782		
	R^2=0.102 (Cox & Snell); R^2=0.031 (Nagelkerke)							
	Model $\chi^2(2)$=12.506, p=0.029							

Core frame element: Explanation

As shown in Table 5.3, the binary logistic regressions run on Explanation found that the hard/soft distinction significantly predicted the incidence of unidentified sources of expectation (B=0.226, p<0.001, Nagelkerke R^2=0.089, OR=1.655). By contrast, no significant relationship was observed for the source of incongruence, suggesting that either of the two disciplinary distinctions was significantly associated with the presence of the identified sources of expectation. The odds ratios indicated that scientists from the hard disciplines were 1.66 times more likely than their soft-discipline counterparts to leave the expressed surprises unexplained. Table 5.3 presents the detailed statistics for the frame element of Explanation.

Table 5.3 Results of binary logistic regressions on the frame element of Explanation (disciplinary groupings as predicators of surprise markers)

Outcome	Predictor	*B*	*SE*	*Wald*	*p*	Odds Ratio	95% CI for Odds Ratio	
							Lower	Upper
Unidentified	Hard vs Soft	0.226	0.277	4.842	0.000	1.655	0.775	5.125
	Pure vs Applied	−1.278	0.324	7.259	0.712	0.474	1.78	3.551
	Constant	−2.530	0.452	1.372	0.442	0.922		
	R^2=0.039 (Cox & Snell); R^2=0.089 (Nagelkerke)							
	Model $\chi^2(2)$=10.413, p< 0.001							
Internal factor	Hard vs Soft	0.513	0.629	3.143	0.843	1.341	0.176	6.422
	Pure vs Applied	0.725	0.227	6.188	0.275	2.151	0.028	2.118
	Constant	2.213	2.163	17.582	0.321	1.143		
	R^2=0.091 (Cox & Snell); R^2=0.316 (Nagelkerke)							
	Model $\chi^2(2)$=11.432, p=0.021							
External factor	Hard vs Soft	−4.612	0.843	11.311	0.621	0.123	0.915	4.723
	Pure vs Applied	0.554	0.215	7.141	0.822	1.892	0.770	8.821
	Constant	−2.632	0.573	21.34	0.000	0.723		
	R^2=0.012 (Cox & Snell); R^2=0.038 (Nagelkerke)							
	Model $\chi^2(2)$=21.341, p=0.055							

Core frame element: Resolution

Table 5.4 shows that the variable of hard vs soft discipline only significantly predicted expressed surprises resolved by speculation ($B=-2.142$, $p<0.001$, Nagelkerke $R^2=0.176$, OR=0.367). Specifically, RAs written by authors from the soft disciplines were 2.72 times more likely than those from the hard disciplines to provide speculative resolutions to the feeling of surprise. The Nagelkerke R^2 statistics indicated that the full model explained about 18% of the variance in the outcome variable. For this frame element, the disciplinary distinctions did not predict the presence of Unresolved surprises, Resolution by context, method, and multiple factors.

Table 5.4 Results of binary logistic regressions on the frame element of Resolution (disciplinary groupings as predicators of surprise markers)

Outcome	Predictor	*B*	*SE*	*Wald*	*p*	Odds Ratio	95% CI for Odds Ratio Lower	Upper
Unresolved	Hard vs Soft	0.115	0.462	3.215	0.616	1.267	1.264	7.237
	Pure vs Applied	−0.383	0.611	4,523	0.103	0.451	0.667	2.421
	Constant	−5.931	0.226	0.351	0.042	0.922		
	R^2=0.021 (Cox & Snell); R^2=0.008 (Nagelkerke)							
	Model $\chi^2(2)$=14.225, p=0.062							
Resolution by context	Hard vs Soft	0.728	0.443	1.214	0.089	1.773	0.668	4.582
	Pure vs Applied	−0.226	0.821	4.266	0.251	0.951	0.028	2.118
	Constant	−1.378	3.255	12.112	0.421	0.143		
	R^2=0.064 (Cox & Snell); R^2=0.411(Nagelkerke)							
	Model $\chi^2(2)$=9.432, p=0.055							
Resolution by method	Hard vs Soft	2.631	0.773	5.521	0.774	3.123	0.915	4.723
	Pure vs Applied	0.523	0.667	2.256	0.316	1.131	1.687	6.211
	Constant	2.632	0.874	15.343	0.071	0.115		
	R^2=0.009 (Cox & Snell); R^2=0.022 (Nagelkerke)							
	Model $\chi^2(2)$=8.521, p=0.022							

(*to be continued*)

Outcome	Predictor	B	SE	$Wald$	p	Odds Ratio	95% CI for Odds Ratio	
							Lower	Upper
Resolution by speculation	Hard vs Soft	−2.142	0.622	8.544	0.000	0.367	0.224	3.734
	Pure vs Applied	1.623	0.443	4.216	0.737	1.372	1.642	8.557
	Constant	−1.332	0.225	14.315	0.000	0.624		
	R^2=0.042 (Cox & Snell); R^2=0.176 (Nagelkerke)							
	Model $\chi^2(2)$=17.524, p<.001							
Resolution by multiple factors	Hard vs Soft	−2.433	0.667	10.256	0.845	0.647	0.732	3.147
	Pure vs Applied	1.775	0.524	6.289	0.667	1.627	1.774	6.536
	Constant	−1.473	0.684	10.334	0.000	0.557		
	R^2=0.022 (Cox & Snell); R^2=0.015 (Nagelkerke)							
	Model $\chi^2(2)$=8.452, p=0.258							

Peripheral frame element: Degree

As for the occurrence of the frame element of Degree, the statistical analyses did not yield a significant association between the disciplinary distinctions and the subcategories of neutral and mitigated surprises. However, the hard/soft distinction reliably predicted the presence or absence of boosted surprises expressed (B= −2.463, p<0.001, Nagelkerke R^2=0.112, OR=0.346). The Nagelkerke R^2 statistics showed that the full model explained about 11% of the variance in the outcome variable. Notably, scholars from the two soft disciplines were 2.9 times more likely than their counterparts from the two hard sciences to tone up their expressed surprises in their RAs. Table 5.5 gives the detailed statistics for the frame element of Degree.

Table 5.5 Results of binary logistic regressions on the frame element of Degree (disciplinary groupings as predicators of surprise markers)

Outcome	Predictor	B	SE	$Wald$	p	Odds Ratio	95% CI for Odds Ratio	
							Lower	Upper
Neutral	Hard vs Soft	0.682	0.054	0.032	0.881	1.935	0.559	2.584

(*to be continued*)

Outcome	Predictor	B	SE	$Wald$	p	Odds Ratio	95% CI for Odds Ratio Lower	Upper
	Pure vs Applied	−1.115	0.573	3.257	0.612	0.274	0.456	3.581
	Constant	−1.546	0.884	2.347	0.741	0.673		
	$R^2=0.021$ (Cox & Snell); $R^2=0.069$ (Nagelkerke)							
	Model $\chi^2(2)=2.413$, $p=0.375$							
Mitigated	Hard vs Soft	0.526	0.479	2.421	0.314	0.779	0.247	4.247
	Pure vs Applied	0.225	0.169	4.257	0.568	1.151	0.458	1.225
	Constant	2.213	0.163	17.582	0.321	1.143		
	$R^2=0.022$ (Cox & Snell); $R^2=0.489$ (Nagelkerke)							
	Model $\chi^2(2)=5.467$, $p=0.194$							
Boosted	Hard vs Soft	−2.463	0.483	6.578	0.000	0.346	1.256	6.357
	Pure vs Applied	0.689	0.389	2.427	0.521	1.035	0.627	4.638
	Constant	−1.347	0.491	11.357	0.013	0.468		
	$R^2=0.042$ (Cox & Snell); $R^2=0.112$ (Nagelkerke)							
	Model $\chi^2(2)=10.369$, $p<0.001$							

Peripheral frame element: Experiencer

As indicated in Table 5.6, binary logistical regressions run on the frame element of Experiencer did not find a significant relationship between the disciplinary distinctions and the incidence of implied experiencers, authors, or another researcher. Nevertheless, the statistical results did yield a significant association between the hard/soft distinction and the presence of Participants as the people who experienced surprises ($B=-1.346$, $p<0.001$, Nagelkerke $R^2=0.411$, OR$=0.215$). RAs in the soft disciplines were more likely (i.e. 4.65 times) to describe the surprise of participants in the study than those in the hard disciplines.

Table 5.6 Results of binary logistic regressions on the frame element of Experiencer (disciplinary groupings as predicators of surprise markers)

Outcome	Predictor	*B*	*SE*	*Wald*	*p*	Odds Ratio	95% CI for Odds Ratio Lower	Upper
Implied	Hard vs Soft	0.241	0.347	0.755	0.457	1.742	0.689	3.489
	Pure vs Applied	−2.245	0.326	2.362	0.567	0.256	0.369	4.563
	Constant	−2.424	0.457	1.457	0.251	0.889		
	R^2=0.033 (Cox & Snell); R^2=0.031 (Nagelkerke)							
	Model $\chi^2(2)$=4.357, p=0.346							
Author	Hard vs Soft	0.421	0.865	1.359	0.579	1.426	1.579	6.369
	Pure vs Applied	0.854	0.780	2.479	0.313	2.369	1.113	4.426
	Constant	2.213	2.163	17.582	0.321	1.143		
	R^2=0.011 (Cox & Snell); R^2=0.313 (Nagelkerke)							
	Model $\chi^2(2)$=8.441, p=0.121							
Participant	Hard vs Soft	−1.346	0.526	8.532	0.000	0.215	1.256	6.357
	Pure vs Applied	0.779	0.225	1.246	0.946	1.156	0.892	2.458
	Constant	−1.347	0.491	11.357	0.013	0.468		
	R^2=0.021 (Cox & Snell); R^2=0.041 (Nagelkerke)							
	Model $\chi^2(2)$=8.341, p<0.001							
Another researcher	Hard vs Soft	−1.442	0.441	4.462	0.236	0.336	0.257	4.479
	Pure vs Applied	−0.336	0.226	0.947	0.853	0.672	0.346	6.679
	Constant	−1.357	0.464	9.414	0.046	0.787		
	R^2=0.035 (Cox & Snell); R^2=0.084 (Nagelkerke)							
	Model $\chi^2(2)$=18.256, p=0.237							
Other people	Hard vs Soft	−1.425	0.361	2.209	0.135	0.581	0.083	2.581
	Pure vs Applied	0.346	0.224	1.421	0.632	1.361	0.125	1.467
	Constant	−2.236	0.863	21.472	0.011	0.892		
	R^2=0.067 (Cox & Snell); R^2=0.241 (Nagelkerke)							
	Model $\chi^2(2)$=7.835, p=0.020							

5.1.2 Use of interest markers

5.1.2.1 Overall distributions of interest markers by discipline

As shown in Table 5.7, the binary logistic regression run on the overall distribution of interest markers did not return a significant relationship (Nagelkerke R^2=0.004, p=0.020). The statistics suggested that academic writers from the different disciplinary groupings did not differ in their use of interest markers in their RAs. However, as in the case of surprise markers, some significant disciplinary differences were detected when binary logistic regressions were run on the frame elements of the Interest frame. The detailed statistical results are presented in the following subsections.

Table 5.7 Results of the binary logistic regression on the use of interest markers

Outcome	Predictor	*B*	*SE*	*Wald*	*p*	Odds Ratio (OR)	95% CI for OR Lower	Upper
Interest markers	Hard vs Soft	0.101	0.318	0.101	0.688	1.107	0.593	2.065
	Pure vs Applied	−0.202	0.318	0.404	0.525	0.817	0.731	4.524
	Constant	−1.638	0.276	0.833	0.361	0.241		
	R^2=0.008 (Cox & Snell); R^2=0.004 (Nagelkerke)							
	Model $\chi^2(2)$=3.659, p=0.020							

5.1.2.2 Distributions of the frame elements of interest markers by discipline

Core frame element: Trigger

As can be seen in Table 5.8, the binary logistic regressions run on the frame element of Trigger located statistically significant differences in the subcategories of Appraisal and Proposal in terms of what elicited interest across the disciplines. No such significant relationship was found for the expressed interest triggered by Relationship, Attribute, and Phenomenon. To be more specific, the hard/soft distinction was a reliable predictor of the occurrence of Appraisal (B=−0.231, p<0.001, Nagelkerke R^2=0.61, OR=0.255). The pure/applied distinction significantly predicted the presence of Proposal (B=0.679, p<0.001, Nagelkerke R^2=0.175, OR=2.801). The Nagelkerke R^2 statistics indicated that 13% of the variance in Appraisal was explained by the full model, and about 18% of the variance in Proposal was explained by the full model. The odds statistics revealed that publications in the soft disciplines were 3.92 times more likely to evaluate the value, significance, or implications of the findings of the current study or previous studies than those in the hard sciences. Moreover, expressions of interest triggered by newly proposed hypotheses, viewpoints, or potential research trends were 2.8 times more likely to be found in the pure-discipline research articles than the applied-discipline ones.

Table 5.8 Results of binary logistic regressions on the frame element of Trigger disciplinary groupings as predicators of interest markers)

Outcome	Predictor	*B*	*SE*	*Wald*	*p*	Odds Ratio	95% CI for Odds Ratio Lower	Upper
Appraisal	Hard vs Soft	−0.231	0.729	1.573	0.000	0.255	0.649	1.373
	Pure vs Applied	0.131	0.324	2.216	0.864	1.237	0.782	3.582
	Constant	−0.846	0.275	7.468	0.204	0.418		
	R^2=0.104 (Cox & Snell); R^2=0.133 (Nagelkerke)							
	Model $\chi^2(2)$=13.413, p< 0.001							
Relationship	Hard vs Soft	0.581	0.728	4.248	0.041	1.304	0.853	3.289
	Pure vs Applied	0.433	0.247	6.479	0.532	2.072	0.458	2.492
	Constant	−2.245	0.689	10.542	0.000	0.243		
	R^2= 0.084 (Cox & Snell); R^2= 0.066 (Nagelkerke)							
	Model $\chi^2(2)$=21.416, p=0.017							
Proposal	Hard vs Soft	−1.437	0.268	2.479	0.602	0.427	0.321	2.682
	Pure vs Applied	0.679	0.724	4.247	0.000	2.801	0.228	4.248
	Constant	−2.216	0.358	12.267	0.346	0.854		
	R^2=0.055 (Cox & Snell); R^2=0.175 (Nagelkerke)							
	Model $\chi^2(2)$=13.837, p< 0.001							
Attribute	Hard vs Soft	2.347	0.856	5.246	0.246	1.325	0.436	4.236
	Pure vs Applied	−1.215	0.785	7.368	0.426	0.579	0.316	2.952
	Constant	−2.346	0.536	12.526	0.647	0.357		
	R^2= 0.246 (Cox & Snell); R^2= 0.893 (Nagelkerke)							
	Model $\chi^2(2)$=12.506, p=0.068							
Phenomenon	Hard vs Soft	−2.547	0.568	5.526	0.684	0.889	0.783	2.246
	Pure vs Applied	−0.852	0.245	11.246	0.436	0.558	0.149	0.977
	Constant	−2.424	0.535	12.457	0.535	0.557		

(to be continued)

Outcome	Predictor	*B*	*SE*	*Wald*	*p*	Odds Ratio	95% CI for Odds Ratio Lower	Upper
	R^2=0.543 (Cox & Snell); R^2=0.725 (Nagelkerke)							
	Model $\chi^2(2)$=7.535, p=0.053							

Core frame element: Explanation

As shown in Table 5.9, the binary logistic regressions run on the frame element of Explanation did not identify any significant association between the disciplinary groupings and unexplained expressions of interest. In addition, the statistics did not locate a significant difference in expressed interest elicited by External Factors pertaining to hypotheses, results, and findings of previous research or characteristics of the research background or context. However, notably, the hard/soft disciplinary distinction was a reliable predictor of the incidence of Internal Factors (B=1.656, p<0.001, Nagelkerke R^2=0.058, OR=1.715). The odds ratio indicated that scientists from the hard disciplines were 1.72 times more likely to describe the expressed interest caused by internal factors related to results or findings from the current study or characteristics of research objects, research procedures, and variables than their counterparts from the soft disciplines.

Table 5.9 Results of binary logistic regressions on the frame element of Explanation (disciplinary groupings as predicators of interest markers)

Outcome	Predictor	*B*	*SE*	*Wald*	*p*	Odds Ratio	95% CI for Odds Ratio Lower	Upper
Unidentified	Hard vs Soft	2.467	0.446	3.356	0.072	1.215	0.534	4.424
	Pure vs Applied	−2.426	1.425	4.534	0.235	0.426	1.235	5.454
	Constant	−2.346	0.457	1.425	0.778	0.568		
	R^2=0.021 (Cox & Snell); R^2=0.059 (Nagelkerke)							
	Model $\chi^2(2)$=7.563, p=0.016							
Internal factor	Hard vs Soft	1.656	0.543	2.537	0.000	1.715	2.435	4.543
	Pure vs Applied	0.825	0.425	7.422	0.543	2.432	0.524	3.424
	Constant	1.214	0.153	11.425	0.284	2.163		

(*to be continued*)

Outcome	Predictor	*B*	*SE*	*Wald*	*p*	Odds Ratio	95% CI for Odds Ratio Lower	Upper
	R^2=0.023 (Cox & Snell); R^2=0.058 (Nagelkerke)							
	Model $\chi^2(2)$=9.533, p=<0.0001							
External factor	Hard vs Soft	−3.642	0.475	9.224	0.537	0.654	1.355	6.434
	Pure vs Applied	1.342	0.434	4.434	0.235	2.434	0.896	3.842
	Constant	−1.434	0.575	15.342	0.000	0.323		
	R^2=0.033 (Cox & Snell); R^2=0.048 (Nagelkerke)							
	Model $\chi^2(2)$=13.421, p=0.033							

Peripheral frame element: Degree

Table 5.10 shows that the hard/soft distinction significantly predicted the use of boosted interest in RAs (B=−1.885, p<0.001, Nagelkerke R^2=0.163, OR=0.292). Specifically, researchers from the soft disciplines were 3.42 times more likely than those from the hard disciplines to intensify their feelings of interest in scientific communication. The Nagelkerke R^2 statistics indicated that the full model accounted for about 16% of the variance in the outcome variable. For this frame element, no statistically significant relations could be found between the disciplinary groupings and the presence of neutrally expressed interest and mitigated interest.

Table 5.10 Results of binary logistic regressions on the frame element of Degree (disciplinary groupings as predicators of interest markers)

Outcome	Predictor	*B*	*SE*	*Wald*	*p*	Odds Ratio	95% CI for Odds Ratio Lower	Upper
Neutral	Hard vs Soft	0.682	0.054	0.032	0.881	1.935	0.559	2.584
	Pure vs Applied	−1.115	0.573	3.257	0.612	0.274	0.456	3.581
	Constant	−1.546	0.884	2.347	0.741	0.673		
	R^2=0.021 (Cox & Snell); R^2=0.069 (Nagelkerke)							
	Model $\chi^2(2)$=2.413, p=0.375							
Mitigated	Hard vs Soft	0.526	0.479	2.421	0.314	0.779	0.247	4.247
	Pure vs Applied	0.225	0.169	4.257	0.568	1.151	0.458	1.225

(*to be continued*)

Outcome	Predictor	*B*	*SE*	*Wald*	*p*	Odds Ratio	95% CI for Odds Ratio	
							Lower	Upper
	Constant	2.213	0.163	17.582	0.321	1.143		
	R^2=0.022 (Cox & Snell); R^2=0.489 (Nagelkerke)							
	Model $\chi^2(2)=5.467, p=0.194$							
Boosted	Hard vs Soft	−1.885	0.456	6.442	0.000	0.292	1.113	7.435
	Pure vs Applied	0.553	0.854	1.363	0.224	2.036	0.532	3.422
	Constant	−1.422	0.679	9.534	0.077	0.746		
	R^2=0.044 (Cox & Snell); R^2=0.163 (Nagelkerke)							
	Model $\chi^2(2)=14.259, p<0.001$							

Peripheral frame element: Experiencer

As regards the occurrence of the non-core frame element of Experiencer, the statistical analyses did not locate any significant associations between the disciplinary distinctions and the subcategories of this frame element (see Table 5.11). This result suggested that researchers from the different disciplines did not differ in identifying the people who experienced the feeling of interest.

Table 5.11 Results of binary logistic regressions on the frame element of Experiencer (disciplinary groupings as predicators of interest markers)

Outcome	Predictor	*B*	*SE*	*Wald*	*p*	Odds Ratio	95% CI for Odds Ratio	
							Lower	Upper
Implied	Hard vs Soft	0.556	0.454	0.422	0.345	1.534	0.557	2.534
	Pure vs Applied	−1.434	0.678	2.062	0.534	0.642	0.789	4.114
	Constant	−2.543	0.889	1.974	0.634	0.865		
	R^2=0.023 (Cox & Snell); R^2=0.066 (Nagelkerke)							
	Model $\chi^2(2)=7.634, p=0.224$							
Author	Hard vs Soft	0.634	0.976	1.534	0.884	1.113	0.555	4.523
	Pure vs Applied	0.223	0.423	1.534	0.779	2.523	1.008	5.432
	Constant	2.642	0.889	7.532	0.390	1.753		

(*to be continued*)

Outcome	Predictor	*B*	*SE*	*Wald*	*p*	Odds Ratio	95% CI for Odds Ratio	
							Lower	Upper
	R^2=0.022 (Cox & Snell); R^2=0.54 (Nagelkerke)							
	Model $\chi^2(2)$=6.521, p=0.166							
Author/ reader/ other researchers	Hard vs Soft	−1.254	1.523	5.534	0.064	0.432	0.252	5.363
	Pure vs Applied	0.435	0.666	1.534	0.456	1.534	0.634	2.514
	Constant	−1.423	0.534	7.524	0.055	0.865		
	R^2=0.052 (Cox & Snell); R^2=0.077 (Nagelkerke)							
	Model $\chi^2(2)$=2.541, p=0.066							
Another researcher	Hard vs Soft	−1.423	0.542	4.543	0.532	0.775	0.524	3.643
	Pure vs Applied	−0.535	0.776	0.543	0.235	0.222	1.532	6.641
	Constant	−1.257	0.541	6.462	0.520	0.643		
	R^2=0.063 (Cox & Snell); R^2=0.078 (Nagelkerke)							
	Model $\chi^2(2)$=12.366, p=0.448							
Other people	Hard vs Soft	−2.442	0.442	2.434	0.246	0.662	0.421	1.265
	Pure vs Applied	0.778	0.895	1.523	0.889	1.634	0.523	3.645
	Constant	−1.434	0.633	11.534	0.035	0.754		
	R^2=0.011 (Cox & Snell); R^2=0.533 (Nagelkerke)							
	Model $\chi^2(2)$=6.755, p=0.021							

5.1.3 Use of confusion markers

5.1.3.1 Overall distributions of confusion markers by discipline

As indicated by Table 5.12, the binary logistic regression analysis run on the overall distribution of confusion markers did not yield a statistically significant difference (Nagelkerke R^2=0.004, p=0.055), indicating that academic writers from different disciplinary groupings did not differ in the employment of confusion markers. Nevertheless, significant disciplinary differences were observed when binary logistic regression analyses were run on the subcategories of the Confusion frame. In the subsequent sections, detailed results are reported.

Table 5.12 Results of the binary logistic regression on the use of confusion markers

Outcome	Predictor	*B*	*SE*	*Wald*	*p*	Odds Ratio (OR)	95% CI for OR Lower	95% CI for OR Upper
Confusion markers	Hard vs Soft	0.080	0.429	0.04	0.841	2.083	0.494	2.374
	Pure vs Applied	−2.472	0.877	0.659	0.477	0.817	0.438	1.788
	Constant	−1.427	0.347	11.944	0.000	0.145		
	R^2=0.008 (Cox & Snell); R^2=0.004 (Nagelkerke)							
	Model $\chi^2(2)=3.659$, $p=0.055$							

5.1.3.2 Distributions of the frame elements of confusion markers by discipline

Core frame element: Trigger

As summarized in Table 5.13, the logistic regression analysis run on the frame element of Trigger yielded a statistically significant association for the subcategories of Knowledge Gap and Attribute. By contrast, no such relationship was found for the expressed confusion triggered by Conceptualization, Relationship, or Phenomenon. Specifically, the hard/soft disciplinary distinction was a reliable predictor for the presence of Knowledge Gap ($B=0.846$, $p<0.001$, Nagelkerke $R^2=0.107$, OR=3.741) and Attribute ($B=-2.006$, $p<0.001$, Nagelkerke $R^2=0.097$, OR=0.336). As indicated by the Nagelkerke R^2 statistics, about 11% and 10% of the variance in the outcome variables were explained by the full model. In addition, the odds statistics showed that RAs in the hard disciplines were 3.74 times more likely than those in the soft ones to describe confusion caused by an under-explored hypothesis or an inadequately addressed question. Furthermore, linguistic expressions of confusion triggered by Attribute were 2.98 times more likely to be found in RAs written by scholars from the soft disciplines than those written by their hard-discipline counterparts.

Table 5.13 Results of binary logistic regressions on the frame element of Trigger (disciplinary groupings as predicators of confusion markers)

Outcome	Predictor	*B*	*SE*	*Wald*	*p*	Odds Ratio	95% CI for Odds Ratio Lower	95% CI for Odds Ratio Upper
Conceptualization	Hard vs Soft	0.774	0.894	2.171	0.241	1.025	0.883	4.746

(*to be continued*)

Outcome	Predictor	B	SE	$Wald$	p	Odds Ratio	95% CI for Odds Ratio	
							Lower	Upper
	Pure vs Applied	0.131	0.543	2.216	0.063	1.985	0.553	1.424
	Constant	−1.458	0.275	2.632	0.560	0.553		
	R^2=0.033 (Cox & Snell); R^2=0.075 (Nagelkerke)							
	Model $\chi^2(2)$=16.352, p=0.771							
Knowledge gap	Hard vs Soft	0.846	0.673	1.864	0.000	3.741	1.278	4.650
	Pure vs Applied	−1.235	0.877	3.175	0.781	0.336	0.397	0.779
	Constant	−1.425	0.363	22.421	0.001	0.662		
	R^2=0.031 (Cox & Snell); R^2=0.107 (Nagelkerke)							
	Model $\chi^2(2)$=11.238, p<0.001							
Attribute	Hard vs Soft	−2.006	0.667	4.147	0.000	0.336	0.321	2.682
	Pure vs Applied	0.246	0.445	1.156	0.036	1.324	0.228	4.248
	Constant	−2.216	0.358	12.267	0.346	0.854		
	R^2=0.055 (Cox & Snell); R^2=0.097 (Nagelkerke)							
	Model $\chi^2(2)$=13.837, p<0.001							
Relationship	Hard vs Soft	1.213	0.562	6.378	0.336	1.091	0.236	4.035
	Pure vs Applied	−1.425	0.774	2.013	0.551	0.772	0.734	3.006
	Constant	−2.153	0.883	1.324	0.771	0.211		
	R^2=0.033 (Cox & Snell); R^2=0.059 (Nagelkerke)							
	Model $\chi^2(2)$=12.211, p=0.442							
Phenomenon	Hard vs Soft	0.235	0.338	5.167	0.442	1.241	0.312	4.007
	Pure vs Applied	−2.006	0.668	2.474	0.551	0.443	0.778	6.443
	Constant	−1.335	0.885	6.321	0.000	0.214		
	R^2=0.442 (Cox & Snell); R^2=0.763 (Nagelkerke)							
	Model $\chi^2(2)$=24.521, p=0.211							

Core frame element: Explanation

The results of the binary logistic regressions on the frame element of Explanation are presented in Table 5.14. The hard/soft disciplinary distinction significantly predicted the absence or presence of unidentified sources of confusion (B=0.211, p<0.001,

Nagelkerke R^2=0.076, OR=2.023). However, no such statistically significant relationship was found for the identified sources of confusion. The odds ratio values showed that, similar to surprise markers, researchers from the hard disciplines were two times more likely not to explain the source of confusion than those from the soft ones were.

Table 5.14 Results of binary logistic regressions on the frame element of Explanation (disciplinary groupings as predicators of confusion markers)

Outcome	Predictor	*B*	*SE*	*Wald*	*p*	Odds Ratio	95% CI for Odds Ratio Lower	Upper
Unidentified	Hard vs Soft	0.211	0.331	2.357	0.000	2.023	0.775	2.412
	Pure vs Applied	1.775	0.532	6.006	0.661	2.415	0.314	4.778
	Constant	0.667	0.781	2.647	0.778	1.721		
	R^2=0.044(Cox & Snell); R^2=0.076 (Nagelkerke)							
	Model $\chi^2(2)$=11.024, p=<0.001							
Internal factor	Hard vs Soft	0.331	0.662	1.006	0.207	1.115	0.413	0.989
	Pure vs Applied	1.324	0.774	4.534	0.543	1.667	1.007	4.421
	Constant	0.776	0.866	6.007	0.006	0.205		
	R^2=0.055 (Cox & Snell); R^2=0.074 (Nagelkerke)							
	Model $\chi^2(2)$=19.964, p=0.014							
External factor	Hard vs Soft	−1.222	0.675	6.313	0.073	0.045	0.566	3.451
	Pure vs Applied	0.799	0.431	2.007	0.656	1.113	1.322	6.076
	Constant	−2.336	0.432	10.321	0.010	0.009		
	R^2=0.063 (Cox & Snell); R^2=0.088 (Nagelkerke)							
	Model $\chi^2(2)$=23.102, p=0.026							

Peripheral frame element: Degree

As for the occurrence of the frame element of Degree, the statistical tests did not point to statistically significant cross-disciplinary differences in the subcategories of neutral and mitigated surprises. However, the hard/soft disciplinary distinction reliably predicted the presence or absence of boosted confusion (B=−2.645,

$p<0.001$, Nagelkerke $R^2=0.216$, OR=0.651). The Nagelkerke R^2 statistics showed that the full model explained about 22% of the variance in the outcome variable. As revealed by the odds ratios, scholars from the soft disciplines were 1.53 times more likely than their counterparts from the hard sciences to tone up their expressed confusion in their RAs. Table 5.15 shows the detailed statistics for the frame element of Degree.

Table 5.15 Results of binary logistic regressions on the frame element of Degree (disciplinary groupings as predicators of confusion markers)

Outcome	Predictor	*B*	*SE*	*Wald*	*p*	Odds Ratio	95% CI for Odds Ratio Lower	Upper
Neutral	Hard vs Soft	0.682	0.054	0.032	0.881	1.935	0.559	2.584
	Pure vs Applied	−1.115	0.573	3.257	0.612	0.274	0.456	3.581
	Constant	−1.546	0.884	2.347	0.741	0.673		
	$R^2=0.021$ (Cox & Snell); $R^2=0.069$ (Nagelkerke)							
	Model $\chi^2(2)=2.413$, $p=0.375$							
Mitigated	Hard vs Soft	0.526	0.479	2.421	0.314	0.779	0.247	4.247
	Pure vs Applied	0.225	0.169	4.257	0.568	1.151	0.458	1.225
	Constant	2.213	0.163	17.582	0.321	1.143		
	$R^2=0.022$ (Cox & Snell); $R^2=0.489$ (Nagelkerke)							
	Model $\chi^2(2)=5.467$, $p=0.194$							
Boosted	Hard vs Soft	−2.654	0.525	3.531	0.000	0.651	0.355	0.875
	Pure vs Applied	1.322	0.776	4.882	0.024	1.542	0.854	2.203
	Constant	−2.564	0.876	7.125	0.043	0.046		
	$R^2=0.009$ (Cox & Snell); $R^2=0.216$ (Nagelkerke)							
	Model $\chi^2(2)=4.723$, $p<0.001$							

Peripheral frame element: Experiencer

The binary logistical regressions run on the frame element of Experiencer did not locate any significant differences in the absence or presence of different type of Experiencers (see Table 5.16). These results indicated that, as in the case of interest markers, the authors from the different disciplinary groupings did not differ in identifying who experienced confusion.

Table 5.16 Results of binary logistic regressions on the frame element of Experiencer (disciplinary groupings as predicators of confusion markers)

Outcome	Predictor	*B*	*SE*	*Wald*	*p*	Odds Ratio	95% CI for Odds Ratio	
							Lower	Upper
Implied	Hard vs Soft	0.111	0.085	0.788	0.764	1.865	0.667	3.446
	Pure vs Applied	1.562	0.224	4.451	0.344	2.121	0.435	1.563
	Constant	−1.543	0.324	2.503	0.043	0.008		
	R^2=0.001 (Cox & Snell); R^2=0.004 (Nagelkerke)							
	Model $\chi^2(2)$=2.314, p=0.541							
Author	Hard vs Soft	0.271	0.781	4.007	0.321	2.003	0.752	5.114
	Pure vs Applied	0.142	0.431	0.887	0.057	1.560	0.331	4.787
	Constant	1.268	0.006	3.631	0.519	1.113		
	R^2=0.009 (Cox & Snell); R^2=0.030 (Nagelkerke)							
	Model $\chi^2(2)$=9.436, p=0.559							
Author/	Hard vs Soft	1.006	0.779	3.241	0.531	1.432	0.767	4.327
reader/	Pure vs Applied	0.667	0.874	2.467	0.078	3.213	1.884	6.355
other researchers	Constant	−2.531	0.667	1.345	0.076	0.034		
	R^2=0.006 (Cox & Snell); R^2=0.017 (Nagelkerke)							
	Model $\chi^2(2)$=12.342, p=0.018							
Participant	Hard vs Soft	−2.213	0.546	2.214	0.213	0.008	1.356	7.535
	Pure vs Applied	−1.432	0.535	5.435	0.004	0.035	0.126	1.997
	Constant	−1.257	0.541	6.462	0.520	0.643		
	R^2=0.044 (Cox & Snell); R^2=0.064 (Nagelkerke)							
	Model $\chi^2(2)$=8.168, p=0.559							
Other people	Hard vs Soft	−1.456	0.432	3.657	0.032	0.067	1.536	4.177
	Pure vs Applied	0.234	0.445	0.887	0.082	2.414	2.661	7.114
	Constant	−2.401	0.773	4.431	0.713	0.002		

(*to be continued*)

Outcome	Predictor	*B*	*SE*	*Wald*	*p*	Odds Ratio	95% CI for Odds Ratio Lower	Upper
	$R^2=0.034$ (Cox & Snell); $R^2=0.078$ (Nagelkerke)							
	Model $\chi^2(2)=12.711, p=0.027$							

5.2 Gender-based differences in the use of knowledge emotion markers

In response to RQ3 regarding possible gender-based differences in the use of knowledge emotion markers, binary logistical regression analyses were run to identify whether male and female academics differ in their use of these markers. The findings are presented as follows.

5.2.1 Use of surprise markers

5.2.1.1 Overall distributions of surprise markers by gender

As summarized in Table 5.17, the binary logistic regression run on the overall use of surprise markers by male or female scientists did not return a statistically significant difference (Nagelkerke $R^2=0.047$, $p=0.077$), indicating that gender could not reliably predict the presence or absence of surprise markers. Male and female scholars did not differ in the use or non-use of surprise markers in their RAs. Nevertheless, some significant gender-based differences were detected when binary logistic regression analyses were run on the subcategories of the Surprise frame. In what follows, detailed statistical results are reported.

Table 5.17 Results of binary logistic regression on the use of surprise markers (gender as predictor)

Outcome	Predictor	*B*	*SE*	*Wald*	*p*	Odds Ratio (OR)	95% CI for OR Lower	Upper
Surprise markers	Male vs Female	1.715	0.552	5.571	0.046	1.005	0.674	4.225
	Constant	0.072	0.271	0.029	0.678	1.331	1.910	

(*to be continued*)

Outcome	Predictor	B	SE	Wald	p	Odds Ratio (OR)	95% CI for OR Lower	Upper
	R^2=0.033 (Cox & Snell); R^2=0.047 (Nagelkerke)							
	Model $\chi^2(1)$=6.312, p=0.077							

5.2.1.2 Distributions of the frame elements of surprise markers by gender

Core frame element: Trigger

As shown in Table 5.18, the logistic regressions run on the frame element of Trigger did not locate a statistically significant difference in what caused surprise between RAs written by male and female authors.

Table 5.18 Results of binary logistic regressions on the frame element of Trigger (gender as predictor of surprise markers)

Outcome	Predictor	B	SE	Wald	p	Odds Ratio	95% CI for Odds Ratio Lower	Upper
Relationship	Male vs Female	0.213	0.789	2.346	0.665	1.214	1.643	4.757
	Constant	1.342	0.435	5.321	0.341	2.362		
	R^2=0.055 (Cox & Snell); R^2=0.064 (Nagelkerke)							
	Model $\chi^2(1)$=11.423, p=0.043							
Attribute	Male vs Female	1.432	0.785	4.245	0.444	1.435	0.098	3.356
	Constant	−2.457	0.432	8.551	0.088	0.678		
	R^2=0.088 (Cox & Snell); R^2=0.446 (Nagelkerke)							
	Model $\chi^2(1)$=7.417, p=0.016							
Behavior	Male vs Female	2.332	0.631	6.894	0.088	1.877	0.779	7.753
	Constant	−2.966	0.442	12.456	0.032	0.475		
	R^2=0.012 (Cox & Snell); R^2=0.021 (Nagelkerke)							
	Model $\chi^2(1)$=13.546, p=0.023							
Phenomenon	Male vs Female	−1.358	0.534	8.525	0.896	0.637	0.456	3.424
	Constant	−3.462	0.775	16.354	0.567	0.165		
	R^2=0.294 (Cox & Snell); R^2=0.066 (Nagelkerke)							
	Model $\chi^2(1)$=7.432, p=0.088							

Core frame element: Explanation

As presented in Table 5.19, the binary logistic regressions on the frame element of Explanation subcategory did not identify any significant gender-based difference for the identified sources of incongruence. However, gender significantly predicted the incidence of unidentified sources of expectation (B=0.567, p<0.001, Nagelkerke R^2=0.153, OR=2.752). The odds ratio indicated that male authors were 2.75 times more likely than their female counterparts to leave the expressed surprises unexplained.

Table 5.19 Results of binary logistic regressions on the frame element of Explanation (gender as predictor of surprise markers)

							95% CI for Odds Ratio	
Outcome	Predictor	*B*	*SE*	*Wald*	*p*	Odds Ratio	Lower	Upper
Unidentified	Male vs Female	0.567	0.245	6.221	0.000	2.752	0.896	4.132
	Constant	−1.533	0.456	2.343	0.231	0.789		
	R^2=0.077 (Cox & Snell); R^2=0.153 (Nagelkerke)							
	Model $\chi^2(1)$=15.869, p<0.001							
Internal factor	Male vs Female	0.778	0.456	2.438	0.815	1.312	0.666	4.853
	Constant	1.434	0.785	8.663	0.082	2.154		
	R^2=0.022 (Cox & Snell); R^2=0.657 (Nagelkerke)							
	Model $\chi^2(1)$=8.567, p=0.066							
External factor	Male vs Female	−2.435	0.153	7.534	0.778	0.345	0.789	6.111
	Constant	−1.355	0.556	13.343	0.564	0.113		
	R^2=0.044 (Cox & Snell); R^2=0.035 (Nagelkerke)							
	Model $\chi^2(1)$=16.334, p=0.324							

Core frame element: Resolution

As for the frame element of Resolution, the logistic regressions did not find any statistically significant difference, indicating that gender was not a reliable predictor for the resolved or unresolved surprises in the RAs (see Table 5.20).

Table 5.20 Results of binary logistic regressions on the frame element of Explanation (gender as predictor of surprise markers)

Outcome	Predictor	*B*	*SE*	*Wald*	*p*	Odds Ratio	95% CI for Odds Ratio Lower	Upper
Unresolved	Male vs Female	2.445	0.768	3.453	0.754	2.531	0.897	6.245
	Constant	3.345	2.568	1.457	0.213	1.457		
	R^2=0.033 (Cox & Snell); R^2=0.046 (Nagelkerke)							
	Model $\chi^2(1)$=16.346, p=0.346							
Resolution by context	Male vs Female	0.244	0.435	5.235	0.022	2.533	1.432	5.356
	Constant	−2.113	2.547	8.467	0.779	0.564		
	R^2=0.077 (Cox & Snell); R^2=0.082 (Nagelkerke)							
	Model $\chi^2(1)$=9.568, p=0.066							
Resolution by method	Male vs Female	1.347	0.562	4.553	0.995	1.455	1.457	7.147
	Constant	2.213	0.564	12.121	0.476	2.341		
	R^2=0.016 (Cox & Snell); R^2=0.038 (Nagelkerke)							
	Model $\chi^2(1)$=8.662, p=0.078							
Resolution by speculation	Male vs Female	2.345	0.868	5.132	0.646	3.535	1.568	8.467
	Constant	−1.003	0.657	16.747	0.046	0.561		
	R^2=0.012 (Cox & Snell); R^2=0.232 (Nagelkerke)							
	Model $\chi^2(1)$=11.342, p=0.035							
Resolution by multiple factors	Male vs Female	−1.346	0.223	8.344	0.374	0.456	0.893	6.346
	Constant	−1.112	0.789	13.436	0.464	0.778		
	R^2=0.068 (Cox & Snell); R^2=0.088 (Nagelkerke)							
	Model $\chi^2(1)$=4.562, p=0.331							

Peripheral frame element: Degree

As seen from Table 5.21, the statistical analyses did not locate any significant gender-based difference for the subcategories of neutral and mitigated surprises. However, gender reliably predicted the use of boosted surprises (B=−2.687, p< 0.001, Nagelkerke R^2=0.162, OR=0.321). Nagelkerke R^2 showed that the full model explained about 16% of the variance in the outcome variable. The female scholars were 3.1 times more likely than their male counterparts to scale up their expressed surprises.

Table 5.21 Results of binary logistic regressions on the frame element of Degree (gender as predictor of surprise markers)

Outcome	Predictor	*B*	*SE*	*Wald*	*p*	Odds Ratio	95% CI for Odds Ratio Lower	Upper
Neutral	Male vs Female	0.224	0.086	1.343	0.332	3.435	1.432	6.332
	Constant	1.325	0.456	3.324	0.446	1.324		
	R^2=0.055 (Cox & Snell); R^2=0.078 (Nagelkerke)							
	Model $\chi^2(1)$=12.324, p=0.241							
Mitigated	Male vs Female	0.112	0.535	3.235	0.463	2.413	0.784	5.346
	Constant	1.321	0.234	11.242	0.055	1.488		
	R^2=0.012 (Cox & Snell); R^2=0.034 (Nagelkerke)							
	Model $\chi^2(1)$=6.435, p=0.221							
Boosted	Male vs Female	−2.687	0.436	4.457	0.000	0.321	1.243	8.464
	Constant	−1.003	0.644	14.356	0.043	0.674		
	R^2=0.058 (Cox & Snell); R^2=0.162 (Nagelkerke)							
	Model $\chi^2(1)$=16.668, p<0.001							

Peripheral frame element: Experiencer

As indicated in Table 5.22, the binary logistical regressions run on the frame element of Experiencer found that gender only reliably predicted the frame subcategory of Author (B=−1.689, p<0.001, Nagelkerke R^2=0.168, OR=0.243). The female researchers were more likely (i.e. 4.1 times) to describe the feeling of surprise associated with themselves than the male researchers were.

Table 5.22 Results of binary logistic regressions on the frame element of Experiencer (gender as predictor of surprise markers)

Outcome	Predictor	*B*	*SE*	*Wald*	*p*	Odds Ratio	95% CI for Odds Ratio	
							Lower	Upper
Implied	Male vs Female	0.554	0.785	3.246	0.868	2.432	0.879	5.346
	Constant	−1.342	0.644	2.434	0.452	0.786		
	R^2=0.012 (Cox & Snell); R^2=0.024 (Nagelkerke)							
	Model $\chi^2(1)$=7.437, p=0.778							
Author	Male vs Female	−1.689	0.353	3.231	0.000	0.243	1.521	6.614
	Constant	1.341	0.324	12.532	0.755	1.942		
	R^2=0.044 (Cox & Snell); R^2=0.168 (Nagelkerke)							
	Model $\chi^2(1)$=12.323, p<0.001							
Participant	Male vs Female	−2.303	0.112	6.553	0.324	0.568	1.112	3.536
	Constant	−1.214	0.674	12.413	0.852	0.221		
	R^2=0.004 (Cox & Snell); R^2=0.047 (Nagelkerke)							
	Model $\chi^2(1)$=3.142, p=0.044							
Another researcher	Male vs Female	−0.345	0.778	0.251	0.972	0.323	0.875	7.425
	Constant	−2.414	0.213	4.434	0.033	0.034		
	R^2=0.021 (Cox & Snell); R^2=0.055 (Nagelkerke)							
	Model $\chi^2(1)$=12.226, p=0.034							
Other people	Male vs Female	0.633	0.784	1.3471	0.866	1.073	0.878	1.333
	Constant	−1.633	0.233	1.486	0.774	0.444		
	R^2=0.012 (Cox & Snell); R^2=0.245 (Nagelkerke)							
	Model $\chi^2(1)$=12.323, p=0.023							

5.2.2 Use of interest markers by gender

5.2.2.1 Overall distributions of interest markers by gender

As shown in Table 5.23, the binary logistic regression on the overall distribution of interest markers did not return a significant difference (Nagelkerke R^2=0.021, p= 0.031). The male and female academic authors did not differ in the use of interest markers in their RAs.

Table 5.23 Results of binary logistic regression on the use of interest markers (gender as predictor)

Outcome	Predictor	*B*	*SE*	*Wald*	*p*	Odds Ratio (OR)	95% CI for OR Lower	95% CI for OR Upper
Interest markers	Male vs Female	1.224	0.678	0.234	0.668	1.331	0.981	3.314
	Constant	0.638	0.445	0.213	0.775	1.006		
	R^2=0.011 (Cox & Snell); R^2=0.021 (Nagelkerke)							
	Model $\chi^2(1)$=2.613, p=0.031							

However, similar to what has been found regarding the use of surprise markers, some significant gender-based differences were observed when binary logistic regressions were run on the subcategories of the Interest frame. The detailed statistical results are presented in the following subsections.

5.2.2.2 Distributions of the frame elements of interest markers by gender

Core frame element: Trigger

The logistic regressions run on the frame element of Trigger did not return any statistically significant gender-based difference for the subcategories of this frame element (see Table 5.24).

Table 5.24 Results of binary logistic regressions on the frame element of Trigger (gender as predictor of interest markers)

Outcome	Predictor	*B*	*SE*	*Wald*	*p*	Odds Ratio	95% CI for Odds Ratio Lower	95% CI for Odds Ratio Upper
Appraisal	Male vs Female	−0.754	0.424	1.775	0.562	0.423	0.789	2.214
	Constant	−0.574	0.235	5.344	0.342	0.886		
	R^2=0.056 (Cox & Snell); R^2=0.088 (Nagelkerke)							
	Model $\chi^2(1)$=17.453, p=0.042							
Relationship	Male vs Female	1.103	0.754	5.124	0.079	2.124	1.433	7.675
	Constant	−2.053	0.353	10.232	0.335	0.432		
	R^2=0.012 (Cox & Snell); R^2=0.024 (Nagelkerke)							
	Model $\chi^2(1)$=11.746, p=0.089							

(*to be continued*)

Outcome	Predictor	*B*	*SE*	*Wald*	*p*	Odds Ratio	95% CI for Odds Ratio Lower	Upper
Proposal	Male vs Female	−1.437	0.268	2.479	0.602	0.427	0.321	2.682
	Constant	−2.216	0.358	12.267	0.346	0.854		
	R^2=0.055 (Cox & Snell); R^2=0.175 (Nagelkerke)							
	Model $\chi^2(2)=13.837$, $p=0.021$							
Attribute	Male vs Female	1.342	0.445	4.232	0.896	1.554	0.785	7.454
	Constant	−2.865	0.784	14.353	0.443	0.231		
	R^2=0.331 (Cox & Snell); R^2=0.532 (Nagelkerke)							
	Model $\chi^2(1)=16.512$, $p=0.024$							
Phenomenon	Male vs Female	−1.335	0.755	6.353	0.032	0.321	1.334	7.442
	Constant	−2.535	0.235	14.235	0.644	0.642		
	R^2=0.254 (Cox & Snell); R^2=0.546 (Nagelkerke)							
	Model $\chi^2(1)=12.346$, $p=0.084$							

Core frame element: Explanation

The binary logistic regressions run on the frame element of Explanation did not find a significant difference for the subcategories of Internal and External Factors as Explanations (see Table 5.26). However, gender was a reliable predictor for the subcategory of Unidentified Factors ($B=1.122$, $p<0.001$, Nagelkerke $R^2=0.234$, OR=1.853). The odds ratio indicated that the male authors were 1.85 times more likely not to explain the expressed interest than the female authors.

Table 5.25 Results of binary logistic regressions on the frame element of Explanation (gender as predictor of interest markers)

Outcome	Predictor	*B*	*SE*	*Wald*	*p*	Odds Ratio	95% CI for Odds Ratio Lower	Upper
Unidentified	Male vs Female	1.122	0.646	2.399	0.000	1.853	0.937	7.245
	Constant	−1.532	0.864	1.532	0.032	0.432		

(*to be continued*)

Outcome	Predictor	*B*	*SE*	*Wald*	*p*	Odds Ratio	95% CI for Odds Ratio Lower	Upper
	R^2=0.166 (Cox & Snell); R^2=0.234 (Nagelkerke)							
	Model $\chi^2(1)=16.321, p=<0.001$							
Internal factor	Male vs Female	1.342	0.432	6.363	0.034	1.113	0.688	6.331
	Constant	1.423	0.864	12.322	0.313	3.423		
	R^2=0.044 (Cox & Snell); R^2=0.062 (Nagelkerke)							
	Model $\chi^2(1)=11.231, p=0.074$							
External factor	Male vs Female	−3.642	0.475	7.035	0.242	0.654	1.355	4.322
	Constant	−1.434	0.863	11.422	0.000	0.322		
	R^2=0.033 (Cox & Snell); R^2=0.048 (Nagelkerke)							
	Model $\chi^2(1)=7.321, p=0.036$							

Peripheral frame element: Degree

As for the frame element of Degree, Table 5.26 indicates that gender significantly predicted boosted interest ($B=-2.123$, $p<0.001$, Nagelkerke $R^2=0.234$, OR=0.342). In other words, the female researchers were 2.92 times more likely to tone up their expressed interest than their male counterparts were. Nagelkerke R^2 indicated that the full model explained about 23% of the variance in the outcome variable. No significant gender-based differences were found for neutrally expressed interest and mitigated interest.

Table 5.26 Results of binary logistic regressions on the frame element of Degree (gender as predictor of interest markers)

Outcome	Predictor	*B*	*SE*	*Wald*	*p*	Odds Ratio	95% CI for Odds Ratio Lower	Upper
Neutral	Male vs Female	1.234	0.643	1.743	0.323	1.123	0.964	6.242
	Constant	−1.423	0.324	3.543	0.034	0.231		
	R^2=0.132 (Cox & Snell); R^2=0.332 (Nagelkerke)							
	Model $\chi^2(1)=16.234, p=0.743$							

(to be continued)

Outcome	Predictor	*B*	*SE*	*Wald*	*p*	Odds Ratio	95% CI for Odds Ratio	
							Lower	Upper
Mitigated	Male vs Female	1.742	0.432	2.621	0.022	2.301	0.865	8.342
	Constant	2.123	0.224	12.532	0.863	1.432		
	R^2=0.012 (Cox & Snell); R^2=0.431 (Nagelkerke)							
	Model $\chi^2(1)$=15.324=0.442, p=0.032							
Boosted	Male vs Female	−2.123	0.593	4.424	0.000	0.342	0.658	5.434
	Constant	−1.432	0.221	8.524	0.021	0.843		
	R^2=0.112 (Cox & Snell); R^2=0.234 (Nagelkerke)							
	Model $\chi^2(1)$=12.532, p<0.001							

Peripheral frame element: Experiencer

As regards the non-core frame element of Experiencer, the statistical analyses only located a significant gender-based difference for all the subcategory of Author as Experiencer (B=−2.432, p<0.001, Nagelkerke R^2=0.412, OR=0.342). The female authors were 2.43 times more likely to describe themselves as the Experiencer of expressed interest. Table 5.27 summarizes the detailed statistics.

Table 5.27 Results of binary logistic regressions on the frame element of Experiencer (gender as predictor of interest markers)

Outcome	Predictor	*B*	*SE*	*Wald*	*p*	Odds Ratio	95% CI for Odds Ratio	
							Lower	Upper
Implied	Male vs Female	1.219	0.372	2.429	0.422	1.837	0.869	4.573
	Constant	−1.483	0.733	1.382	0.038	0.483		
	R^2=0.043 (Cox & Snell); R^2=0.076 (Nagelkerke)							
	Model $\chi^2(1)$=11.583, p=0.683							
Author	Male vs Female	−2.432	0.432	3.693	0.000	0.412	0.975	6.634
	Constant	1.784	2.132	6.509	0.063	1.874		
	R^2=0.043 (Cox & Snell); R^2=0.136 (Nagelkerke)							
	Model $\chi^2(1)$=16.443, p<0.001							

(*to be continued*)

Outcome	Predictor	*B*	*SE*	*Wald*	*p*	Odds Ratio	95% CI for Odds Ratio Lower	Upper
Author/reader/	Male vs Female	−2.242	0.234	2.683	0.844	0.633	0.632	3.535
other researchers	Constant	−1.635	0.843	6.564	0.043	0.235		
	R^2=0.011 (Cox & Snell); R^2=0.034 (Nagelkerke)							
	Model $\chi^2(1)$=6.431, p=0.435							
Another	Male vs Female	−1.798	0.242	2.563	0.634	1.632	0.954	7.643
researcher	Constant	−1.453	0.843	7.743	0.736	0.243		
	R^2=0.032 (Cox & Snell); R^2=0.751 (Nagelkerke)							
	Model $\chi^2(1)$=2.426, p=0.036							
Other people	Male vs Female	1.524	0.976	1.754	0.784	2.215	0.868	3.473
	Constant	−1.895	0.642	8.642	0.013	0.533		
	R^2=0.045 (Cox & Snell); R^2=0.782 (Nagelkerke)							
	Model $\chi^2(1)$=4.745, p=0.862							

5.2.3 Use of confusion markers by gender

5.2.3.1 Overall distributions of confusion markers by gender

As shown in Table 5.28, the binary logistic regression run on the overall distribution of confusion markers did not yield a significant difference (Nagelkerke R^2=0.021, p=0.074), suggesting that the male and female authors did not differ in the use of confusion markers in their RAs.

Table 5.28 Results of binary logistic regression on the use of confusion markers (gender as predictor)

Outcome	Predictor	*B*	*SE*	*Wald*	*p*	Odds Ratio (OR)	95% CI for OR Lower	Upper
Confusion markers	Male vs Female	−1.321	0.435	0.875	0.322	0.665	0.789	2.646
	Constant	−1.113	0.342	1.435	0.005	0.452		
	R^2=0.023 (Cox & Snell); R^2=0.021(Nagelkerke)							
	Model $\chi^2(1)$=1.223, p=0.074							

However, when binary logistic regressions were run on the subcategories of the Confusion frame, some significant gender-based differences were observed, exhibiting similar distributional patterns with those of surprise and interest markers.

5.2.3.2 Distributions of the frame elements of confusion markers by gender

Core frame element: Trigger

As summarized in Table 5.29, the logistic regression run on the frame element of Trigger did not yield a statistically significant association between gender and different types of confusion Trigger.

Table 5.29 Results of binary logistic regressions on the frame element of Trigger (gender as predictor of confusion markers)

Outcome	Predictor	*B*	*SE*	*Wald*	*p*	Odds Ratio	95% CI for Odds Ratio Lower	Upper
Conceptualization	Male vs Female	1.869	0.234	2.453	0.674	2.857	1.684	6.124
	Constant	−1.683	0.674	3.573	0.583	0.224		
	R^2=0.042 (Cox & Snell); R^2=0.067 (Nagelkerke)							
	Model $\chi^2(1)$=5.321, p=0.053							
Knowledge gap	Male vs Female	1.445	0.532	3.243	0.074	1.534	0.263	2.655
	Constant	−1.372	0.437	12.482	0.083	0.243		
	R^2=0.043 (Cox & Snell); R^2=0.882 (Nagelkerke)							
	Model $\chi^2(1)$=738,2, p=0.076							
Attribute	Male vs Female	−1.381	0.372	2.947	0.035	0.835	0.895	5.483
	Constant	−2.483	0.475	4.394	0.483	0.735		
	R^2=0.011 (Cox & Snell); R^2=0.024 (Nagelkerke)							
	Model $\chi^2(1)$=3.832, p=0.021							
Relationship	Male vs Female	1.682	0.462	5.353	0.031	2.435	1.493	5.832
	Constant	−2.473	0.331	1.483	0.044	0.583		
	R^2=0.034 (Cox & Snell); R^2=0.077 (Nagelkerke)							
	Model $\chi^2(1)$=7.532, p=0.213							
Phenomenon	Male vs Female	0.849	0.535	4.873	0.536	2.352	0.983	6.975

(*to be continued*)

Outcome	Predictor	*B*	*SE*	*Wald*	*p*	Odds Ratio	95% CI for Odds Ratio Lower	Upper
	Constant	1.533	0.233	1.324	0.042	3.553		
	R^2=0.032 (Cox & Snell); R^2=0.551 (Nagelkerke)							
	Model $\chi^2(1)$=14.483, p=0.037							

Core frame element: Explanation

The results of the binary logistic regressions are presented in Table 5.30. Although gender did not significantly predict the identified sources of confusion, it was a reliable predictor for unidentified confusion (B=1.235, p<0.001, Nagelkerke R^2= 0.221, OR=1.873). Similar to surprise and interest markers, the male authors were 1.87 times more likely to leave the source of confusion unidentified than their female counterparts.

Table 5.30 Results of binary logistic regressions on the frame element of Explanation (gender as predictor of confusion markers)

Outcome	Predictor	*B*	*SE*	*Wald*	*p*	Odds Ratio	95% CI for Odds Ratio Lower	Upper
Unidentified	Male vs Female	1.235	0.573	2.532	0.000	1.873	1.435	5.483
	Constant	0.583	0.221	6.353	0.032	1.124		
	R^2=0.12 (Cox & Snell); R^2=0.221 (Nagelkerke)							
	Model $\chi^2(1)$=14.432, p=<0.001							
Internal factor	Male vs Female	0.893	0.324	1.583	0.066	2.434	0.983	4.235
	Constant	0.242	0.123	2.938	0.482	1.435		
	R^2=0.012 (Cox & Snell); R^2=0.033 (Nagelkerke)							
	Model $\chi^2(1)$=11.434, p=0.076							
External factor	Male vs Female	1.435	0.532	4.533	0.031	1.352	0.673	7.735
	Constant	−1.436	1.593	7.324	0.452	0.535		
	R^2=0.011 (Cox & Snell); R^2=0.029 (Nagelkerke)							
	Model $\chi^2(1)$=13.233, p=0.053							

Peripheral frame element: Degree

As for the frame element of Degree, the statistical analyses did not find statistically significant gender-based differences for the subcategories of Neutral and Mitigated surprise. However, gender reliably predicted boosted confusion expressed ($B=-1.758$, $p<0.001$, Nagelkerke $R^2=0.114$, OR=0.524). The full model explained about 11% of the variance in the outcome variable. The female authors were 1.9 times more likely than their male counterparts to tone up their expressed confusion in the RAs. Table 5.31 shows the detailed statistics for the frame element of Degree.

Table 5.31 Results of binary logistic regressions on the frame element of Degree (gender predictor of confusion markers)

							95% CI for Odds Ratio	
Outcome	Predictor	*B*	*SE*	*Wald*	*p*	Odds Ratio	Lower	Upper
Neutral	Male vs Female	0.032	0.076	0.948	0.242	2.095	0.879	6.433
	Constant	−1.242	0.543	2.324	0.046	0.463		
	$R^2=0.056$ (Cox & Snell); $R^2=0.089$ (Nagelkerke)							
	Model $\chi^2(1)=6.433$, $p=0.553$							
Mitigated	Male vs Female	0.043	0.453	2.524	0.746	0.242	1.543	6.984
	Constant	1.643	0.335	7.542	0.054	1.343		
	$R^2=0.012$ (Cox & Snell); $R^2=0.482$ (Nagelkerke)							
	Model $\chi^2(1)=3.424$, $p=0.053$							
Boosted	Male vs Female	−1.758	0.525	1.531	0.000	0.524	0.955	2.544
	Constant	−2.535	0.143	7.125	0.043	0.046		
	$R^2=0.019$ (Cox & Snell); $R^2=0.114$ (Nagelkerke)							
	Model $\chi^2(1)=16.432$, $p<0.001$							

Peripheral frame element: Experiencer

As summarized in Table 5.32, the binary logistical regressions run on the frame element of Experiencer located a significant gender-based difference for the subcategory of Author as Experiencer ($B=-1.674$, $p<0.001$, Nagelkerke $R^2=0.195$, OR=0.564). The female authors were 1.78 times more likely to describe themselves as Experiencers of confusion than the male authors. No such differences were found for the other subcategories.

Table 5.32 Results of binary logistic regressions on the frame element of Experiencer (gender as predictor of confusion markers)

Outcome	Predictor	*B*	*SE*	*Wald*	*p*	Odds Ratio	95% CI for Odds Ratio Lower	Upper
Implied	Male vs Female	0.035	0.645	0.983	0.445	1.434	1.373	3.435
	Constant	−1.432	0.304	1.432	0.093	0.443		
	R^2=0.012 (Cox & Snell); R^2=0.034 (Nagelkerke)							
	Model $\chi^2(1)=6.534, p=0.053$							
Author	Male vs Female	−1.674	0.224	2.546	0.000	0.564	0.954	5.321
	Constant	1.382	0.553	3.112	0.034	1.636		
	R^2=0.121 (Cox & Snell); R^2=0.195 (Nagelkerke)							
	Model $\chi^2(1)=13.443, p<0.001$							
Author/reader/ other researchers	Male vs Female	0.334	0.394	2.434	0.033	1.334	0.893	3.134
	Constant	−2.434	0.435	1.653	0.012	0.434		
	R^2=0.023 (Cox & Snell); R^2=0.034 (Nagelkerke)							
	Model $\chi^2(1)=7.352, p=0.064$							
Participant	Male vs Female	−1.545	0.434	3.432	0.744	0.432	0.435	4.533
	Constant	−1.532	0.323	12.534	0.035	0.332		
	R^2=0.005 (Cox & Snell); R^2=0.021 (Nagelkerke)							
	Model $\chi^2(1)=4.383, p=0.213$							
Other people	Male vs Female	−2.423	0.444	2.543	0.532	0.424	0.983	6.323
	Constant	−2.242	0.234	4.422	0.021	0.874		
	R^2=0.005 (Cox & Snell); R^2=0.022 (Nagelkerke)							
	Model $\chi^2(1)=3.743, p=0.018$							

5.3 Location-based differences in the use of knowledge emotion markers

In response to RQ4 about possible location-based differences in the use of knowledge emotion markers, binary logistical regressions were run to identify whether there were differences between academics based in the Core and Periphery regions.

5.3.1 Use of surprise markers by authors' geo-academic location

5.3.1.1 Overall distributions of surprise markers by authors' location

As summarized in Table 5.33, the binary logistic regression on the general use of surprise markers between the Core-based academics and Periphery-based academics did not return a statistically significant difference (Nagelkerke R^2=0.036, p=0.062). This indicated that the variable of authors' geo-academic location did not reliably predict their use of surprise markers in RAs. However, significant differences were found for some subcategories of the Surprise frame, as reported below.

Table 5.33 Results of binary logistic regression on the of surprise markers (authors' location as predictor)

Outcome	Predictor	*B*	*SE*	*Wald*	*p*	Odds Ratio (OR)	95% CI for OR	
							Lower	Upper
Surprise markers	Core vs Periphery	2.003	0.229	0.687	0.841	2.112	1.567	5.854
	Constant	0.657	0.674	0.535	0.045	1.212		
	R^2=0.088 (Cox & Snell); R^2=0.036 (Nagelkerke)							
	Model $\chi^2(1)$=3.532, p=0.062							

5.3.1.2 Distributions of the frame elements of surprise markers by authors' geo-academic location

Core frame element: Trigger

As can be seen from Table 5.34, the logistic regressions run on the frame element of Trigger found no significant difference for the subcategories of Attribute, Behavior, and Phenomenon. However, a statistically significant difference was found for the subcateogory of Relationship (B=−1.332, p<0.001, Nagelkerke R^2=0.56, OR= 0.214). Nagelkerke R^2 indicated that 5.6% of the variance in the outcome variable was explained by the full model. The odds ratio showed that academics from the Periphery regions were 4.67 times more likely to express surprise towards findings yielded by the study or from different studies than their counterparts from the Core regions.

Table 5.34 Results of binary logistic regressions on the frame element of Trigger (authors' geo-academic location as predictor of surprise makers)

Outcome	Predictor	*B*	*SE*	*Wald*	*p*	Odds Ratio	95% CI for Odds Ratio	
							Lower	Upper
Relationship	Core vs Periphery	−1.332	0.324	4.441	0.000	0.214	1.643	4.757
	Constant	1.113	0.743	2.842	0.456	1.086		
	R^2=0.021 (Cox & Snell); R^2=0.056 (Nagelkerke)							
	Model $\chi^2(1)=9.525, p<0.001$							
Attribute	Core vs Periphery	1.223	0.231	3.514	0.214	1.141	1.455	4.313
	Constant	−1.313	0.443	5.324	0.046	0.243		
	R^2=0.054 (Cox & Snell); R^2=0.081 (Nagelkerke)							
	Model $\chi^2(1)=5.242, p=0.021$							
Behavior	Core vs Periphery	1.344	0.345	7.535	0.021	1.335	0.896	5.635
	Constant	−1.424	0.546	10.645	0.654	0.452		
	R^2=0.033 (Cox & Snell); R^2=0.058 (Nagelkerke)							
	Model $\chi^2(1)=17.524, p=0.042$							
Phenomenon	Core vs Periphery	−1.424	0.524	7.513	0.056	0.432	0.896	2.635
	Constant	−2.241	0.675	11.324	0.242	0.533		
	R^2=0.022 (Cox & Snell); R^2=0.044 (Nagelkerke)							
	Model $\chi^2(1)=8.214, p=0.562$							

Core frame element: Explanation

As shown in Table 5.35, no significant differences were observed for the identified sources of incongruence, suggesting that geo-academic location was not significantly associated with the subcategories. Nevertheless, the variable significantly predicted the incidence of unidentified sources of expectation (B=1.589, $p<0.001$, Nagelkerke R^2=0.138, OR=3.212). The odds ratio indicated that authors from the Core regions were 3.21 times more likely to leave expressed surprises unexplained than those from the Periphery regions.

Table 5.35 Results of binary logistic regressions on the frame element of Explanation (authors' geo-academic location as predictor of surprise markers)

Outcome	Predictor	*B*	*SE*	*Wald*	*p*	Odds Ratio	95% CI for Odds Ratio Lower	Upper
Unidentified	Core vs Periphery	1.589	0.542	4.125	0.000	3.212	1.234	6.321
	Constant	−1.533	0.456	2.343	0.231	0.789		
	R^2=0.064 (Cox & Snell); R^2=0.138 (Nagelkerke)							
	Model $\chi^2(1)=12.635, p<0.001$							
Internal factor	Core vs Periphery	0.778	0.456	2.438	0.815	1.312	0.666	4.853
	Constant	1.434	0.785	8.663	0.082	2.154		
	R^2=0.022 (Cox & Snell); R^2=0.657 (Nagelkerke)							
	Model $\chi^2(1)=8.567, p=0.066$							
External factor	Core vs Periphery	−2.435	0.153	7.534	0.778	0.345	0.789	6.111
	Constant	−1.355	0.556	13.343	0.564	0.113		
	R^2=0.044 (Cox & Snell); R^2=0.0356 (Nagelkerke)							
	Model $\chi^2(1=16.334, p=0.324$							

Core frame element: Resolution

Authors' geo-academic location did not significantly predict the subcategories of Resolution, indicating that RAs written by authors from the Core and Periphery regions did not differ in the resolution of expressed surprises (see Table 5.36).

Table 5.36 Results of binary logistic regressions on the frame element of Resolution (authors' geo-academic location as predictor of surprise markers)

Outcome	Predictor	*B*	*SE*	*Wald*	*p*	Odds Ratio	95% CI for Odds Ratio Lower	Upper
Unresolved	Core vs Periphery	1.445	0.324	4.235	0.463	1.065	0.964	5.432
	Constant	2.525	0.568	1.457	0.213	1.457		
	R^2=0.033 (Cox & Snell); R^2=0.041 (Nagelkerke)							
	Model $\chi^2(1)=16.346, p=0.346$							

(*to be continued*)

Outcome	Predictor	*B*	*SE*	*Wald*	*p*	Odds Ratio	95% CI for Odds Ratio Lower	Upper
Resolution by context	Core vs Periphery	0.244	0.435	5.235	0.022	2.533	1.432	5.356
	Constant	−2.113	0.547	6.121	0.077	0.235		
	R^2=0.021 (Cox & Snell); R^2=0.046 (Nagelkerke)							
	Model $\chi^2(1)$=5.223, p=0.034							
Resolution by method	Core vs Periphery	−1.353	0.235	3.255	0.075	0.646	0.879	5.466
	Constant	1.434	0.767	8.134	0.563	1.464		
	R^2=0.033 (Cox & Snell); R^2=0.058 (Nagelkerke)							
	Model $\chi^2(1)$=4.324, p=0.033							
Resolution by speculation	Core vs Periphery	1.454	0.354	5.645	0.345	2.087	0.656	6.245
	Constant	1.535	0.443	7.535	0.324	1.544		
	R^2=0.041 (Cox & Snell); R^2=0.431(Nagelkerke)							
	Model $\chi^2(1)$=9.324, p=0.088							
Resolution by multiple factors	Core vs Periphery	−2.433	0.235	6.545	0.076	0.546	1.766	3.332
	Constant	−1.112	0.789	13.436	0.464	0.778		
	R^2=0.022 (Cox & Snell); R^2=0.056 (Nagelkerke)							
	Model $\chi^2(1)$=11.343, p=0.665							

Peripheral frame element: Degree

As for the frame element of Degree (see Table 5.37), the statistical analyses located statistically significant differences for the subcategories of Mitigated and Boosted surprise between authors from different geo-academic locations. Specifically, the variable reliably predicted the mitigation (B=−1.543, p<0.001, Nagelkerke R^2=0.078, OR=0.413) and boosting (B=1.687, p< 0.001, Nagelkerke R^2=0.242, OR=3.112) of expressed surprises, accounting for about 3.4% (mitigated surprise) and 24.2% (boosted surprise) of the variance in the outcome variable, respectively. In other words, academics from the Periphery regions were 2.42 times more likely than their counterparts from the Core regions to tone down their expressed surprises. In contrast, the latter group were 3.11 times more likely to boost their expressed surprises than the former group.

Table 5.37 Results of binary logistic regressions on the frame element of Degree (authors' geo-academic location as predictor of surprise markers)

Outcome	Predictor	*B*	*SE*	*Wald*	*p*	Odds Ratio	95% CI for Odds Ratio Lower	Upper
Neutral	Core vs Periphery	0.224	0.086	1.343	0.332	3.435	1.432	6.332
	Constant	1.325	0.456	3.324	0.446	1.324		
	R^2=0.055 (Cox & Snell); R^2=0.078 (Nagelkerke)							
	Model $\chi^2(1)$=12.324, p=0.241							
Mitigated	Core vs Periphery	−1.543	0.334	5.542	0.000	0.413	0.897	5.346
	Constant	1.321	0.234	11.242	0.055	1.488		
	R^2=0.012 (Cox & Snell); R^2=0.034 (Nagelkerke)							
	Model $\chi^2(1)$=6.435, p=<0.001							
Boosted	Core vs Periphery	1.687	0.436	4.457	0.000	3.112	1.243	8.642
	Constant	1.003	0.324	12.214	0.003	1.435		
	R^2=0.042 (Cox & Snell); R^2=0.242 (Nagelkerke)							
	Model $\chi^2(1)$=14.234, p<0.001							

Peripheral frame element: Experiencer

Geo-academic location significantly predicted the subcategory of Author (B=2.534, p<0.001, Nagelkerke R^2=0.032, OR=3.243), with Core-based scholars being 3.24 times more likely to describe themselves as Experiencers than their Periphery-based counterparts (see Table 5.38).

Table 5.38 Results of binary logistic regressions on the frame element of Experiencer (authors' geo-academic location as predictor of surprise markers)

Outcome	Predictor	*B*	*SE*	*Wald*	*p*	Odds Ratio	95% CI for Odds Ratio Lower	Upper
Implied	Core vs Periphery	−1.324	0.234	2.868	0.011	0.232	1.546	7.656
	Constant	−2.123	0.756	6.435	0.032	0.457		

(*to be continued*)

Outcome	Predictor	*B*	*SE*	*Wald*	*p*	Odds Ratio	95% CI for Odds Ratio Lower	Upper
	R^2=0.022 (Cox & Snell); R^2=0.042 (Nagelkerke)							
	Model $\chi^2(1)$=9.424, p==0.052							
Author	Core vs Periphery	2.534	0.445	6.868	0.000	3.243	0.978	5.757
	Constant	1.076	0.345	9.562	0.043	1.047		
	R^2=0.014 (Cox & Snell); R^2=0.032 (Nagelkerke)							
	Model $\chi^2(1)$=16.853, p<0.001							
Participant	Core vs Periphery	−2.075	0.231	4.864	0.085	0.325	1.978	6.954
	Constant	−1.075	0.533	11.434	0.655	0.543		
	R^2=0.002 (Cox & Snell); R^2=0.012 (Nagelkerke)							
	Model $\chi^2(1)$=5.424, p=0.045							
Another researcher	Core vs Periphery	−1.533	0.545	0.423	0.065	0.424	0.567	4.464
	Constant	−2.443	0.446	2.654	0.036	0.077		
	R^2=0.021 (Cox & Snell); R^2=0.045 (Nagelkerke)							
	Model $\chi^2(1)$=10.126, p=0.056							
Other people	Core vs Periphery	0.133	0.345	2.543	0.543	2.064	0.988	1.343
	Constant	−1.544	0.543	8.544	0.644	0.124		
	R^2=0.034 (Cox & Snell); R^2=0.544 (Nagelkerke)							
	Model $\chi^2(1)$=6.332, p=0.077							

5.3.2 Use of interest markers by authors' geo-academic location

5.3.2.1 Overall distribution of interest markers by authors' location

As shown in Table 5.39, the binary logistic regression on the overall distribution of interest markers did not return a statistically significant difference (Nagelkerke R^2=0.025, p=0.036). This indicated that authors from the Core and the Periphery regions did not differ in their overall use of interest markers. However, just as in the case of surprise markers, location-related differences were detected when binary logistic regressions were run on the subcategories of the Interest frame. The detailed statistical results are presented in the following subsections.

Table 5.39 Results of binary logistic regression on the use of interest markers (authors' geo-academic location as predictor)

Outcome	Predictor	*B*	*SE*	*Wald*	*p*	Odds Ratio (OR)	95% CI for OR	
							Lower	Upper
Interest markers	Core vs Periphery	−1.631	0.445	0.775	0.032	0.843	0.345	4.244
	Constant	0.113	0.754	0.435	0.346	1.324		
	R^2=0.021(Cox & Snell); R^2=0.025 (Nagelkerke)							
	Model $\chi^2(1)=5.245$, $p=0.036$							

5.3.2.2 Distributions of the frame elements of interest markers by authors' location

Core frame element: Trigger

As shown in Table 5.40, the binary logistic regressions run on the frame element of Trigger located statistically significant differences in the subcategories of Appraisal and Proposal as Triggers. No such significant difference was found for expressed interest triggered by Relationship, Attribute, or Phenomenon. Specifically, geo-academic location was a significant predictor for the occurrence of Appraisal ($B=-1.443$, $p<0.001$, Nagelkerke $R^2=0.078$, OR=0.554) and Proposal ($B=0.757$, $p<0.001$, Nagelkerke $R^2=0.122$, OR=2.141). The odds ratios showed that authors from the Periphery regions were 1.81 times more likely to evaluate the value, significance or implications of the results of the current study or previous studies than those based in the Core regions. On the other hand, authors from the Core regions were 2.14 times more likely to express interest triggered by newly proposed hypotheses or potential research trends.

Table 5.40 Results of binary logistic regressions on the frame element of Trigger (authors' geo-academic location as predictor of interest markers)

Outcome	Predictor	*B*	*SE*	*Wald*	*p*	Odds Ratio	95% CI for Odds Ratio	
							Lower	Upper
Appraisal	Core vs Periphery	−1.443	0.333	2.544	0.000	0.554	0.989	4.355
	Constant	−0.554	0.755	5.244	0.065	0.863		

(*to be continued*)

Outcome	Predictor	B	SE	$Wald$	p	Odds Ratio	95% CI for Odds Ratio Lower	Upper
	$R^2=0.045$ (Cox & Snell); $R^2=0.078$ (Nagelkerke)							
	Model $\chi^2(1)=12.433, p<0.001$							
Relationship	Core vs Periphery	1.238	0.334	4.233	0.034	1.345	1.896	6.088
	Constant	−1.754	0.556	11.323	0.233	0.655		
	$R^2=0.221$ (Cox & Snell); $R^2=0.443$ (Nagelkerke)							
	Model $\chi^2(1)=12.076, p=0.055$							
Proposal	Core vs Periphery	0.757	0.865	6.087	0.000	2.141	0.987	4.657
	Constant	−1.544	0.654	9.654	0.066	0.644		
	$R^2=0.221$ (Cox & Snell); $R^2=0.122$ (Nagelkerke)							
	Model $\chi^2(1)=11.807, p<0.001$							
Attribute	Core vs Periphery	1.433	0.544	5.976	0.455	1.885	0.877	3.475
	Constant	−2.444	0.232	12.324	0.644	0.445		
	$R^2=0.321$ (Cox & Snell); $R^2=0.545$ (Nagelkerke)							
	Model $\chi^2(1)=16.534, p=0.076$							
Phenomenon	Core vs Periphery	1.344	0.765	4.654	0.087	2.544	1.654	7.655
	Constant	−1.544	0.444	8.544	0.655	0.444		
	$R^2=0.351$ (Cox & Snell); $R^2=0.443$ (Nagelkerke)							
	Model $\chi^2(1)=18.433, p=0.022$							

Core frame element: Explanation

As presented in Table 5.41, the binary logistic regressions run on the frame element of Explanation only found a significant association between geo-academic location and the incidence of unidentified sources of interest ($B=1.433, p<0.001$, Nagelkerke $R^2=0.143$, OR=2.853). The odds ratio revealed that authors from the Core regions were 2.85 times more likely to leave the source of expressed interest unidentified than their counterparts from the Periphery regions.

Table 5.41 Results of binary logistic regressions on the frame element of Explanation (authors' geo-academic location as predictor of interest markers)

Outcome	Predictor	*B*	*SE*	*Wald*	*p*	Odds Ratio	95% CI for Odds Ratio	
							Lower	Upper
Unidentified	Core vs Periphery	1.433	0.334	3.544	0.000	2.853	1.964	8.446
	Constant	−1.532	0.864	1.532	0.032	0.432		
	R^2=0.021 (Cox & Snell); R^2=0.143 (Nagelkerke)							
	Model $\chi^2(1)=12.071$, p=<0.001							
Internal factor	Core vs Periphery	1.334	0.334	4.654	0.086	2.966	0.987	4.376
	Constant	2.408	0.765	7.345	0.065	1.487		
	R^2=0.015 (Cox & Snell); R^2=0.032 (Nagelkerke)							
	Model $\chi^2(1)=6.233$, $p=0.009$							
External factor	Core vs Periphery	−2.644	0.544	5.035	0.074	0.543	1.544	7.333
	Constant	−1.433	0.543	7.443	0.694	0.766		
	R^2=0.021 (Cox & Snell); R^2=0.036 (Nagelkerke)							
	Model $\chi^2(1)=8.433$, $p=0.076$							

Peripheral frame element: Degree

Table 5.42 shows that geo-academic location significantly predicted the mitigation ($B=-1.893$, $p<0.001$, Nagelkerke $R^2=0.132$, OR=0.301) and boosting of expressed interest ($B=2.123$, $p<0.001$, Nagelkerke $R^2=0.221$, OR=1.974). Specifically, researchers from the Periphery regions were 3.32 times more likely than those from the Core regions to soften the expressed interest. By contrast, researchers from the Core regions were 1.97 times more likely than their counterparts from the Periphery regions to intensify their feeling of interest. The Nagelkerke R^2 statistics indicated that the variable explained about 13% of the variance (for mitigated interest) and 22.1% of the variance (for boosted interest).

Table 5.42 Results of binary logistic regressions on the frame element of Degree (authors' geo-academic location as predictor of interest markers)

						Odds	95% CI for Odds Ratio	
Outcome	Predictor	*B*	*SE*	*Wald*	*p*	Ratio	Lower	Upper
Neutral	Core vs Periphery	1.234	0.643	1.743	0.323	1.123	0.964	6.242
	Constant	−1.423	0.324	3.543	0.034	0.231		
	R^2=0.132 (Cox & Snell); R^2=0.332 (Nagelkerke)							
	Model $\chi^2(1)$=16.234, p=0.743							
Mitigated	Core vs Periphery	−1.893	0.533	4.654	0.000	0.301	0.977	8.335
	Constant	1.133	0.644	10.543	0.075	1.454		
	R^2=0.012 (Cox & Snell); R^2=0.132 (Nagelkerke)							
	Model $\chi^2(1)$=15.324, p<0.001							
Boosted	Core vs Periphery	2.123	0.433	2.485	0.000	1.974	1.543	6.544
	Constant	−1.544	0.254	6.444	0.043	0.654		
	R^2=0.146 (Cox & Snell); R^2=0.221 (Nagelkerke)							
	Model $\chi^2(1)$=18.332, p<0.001							

Peripheral frame element: Experiencer

The statistical analyses (see Table 5.43) revealed a significant location-based difference for the subcategory of Author (B=2.432, p<0.001, Nagelkerke R^2=0.094, OR=1.544), with scholars from the Core regions being 1.54 times more likely to describe themselves as Experiencers of the expressed interest than their counterparts from the Periphery regions were.

Table 5.43 Results of binary logistic regressions on the frame element of Experiencer (authors' geo-academic location as predictor of interest markers)

						Odds	95% CI for Odds Ratio	
Outcome	Predictor	*B*	*SE*	*Wald*	*p*	Ratio	Lower	Upper
Implied	Core vs Periphery	1.654	0.644	3.443	0.064	2.087	0.994	7.533
	Constant	−1.533	0.533	1.654	0.033	0.754		

(*to be continued*)

Outcome	Predictor	*B*	*SE*	*Wald*	*p*	Odds Ratio	95% CI for Odds Ratio Lower	Upper
	R^2=0.143 (Cox & Snell); R^2=0.245 (Nagelkerke)							
	Model $\chi^2(1)$ = 8.332, p=0.063							
Author	Core vs Periphery	2.432	0.644	2.976	0.000	1.544	1.765	4.654
	Constant	1.987	1.144	5.962	0.044	1.764		
	R^2=0.075 (Cox & Snell); R^2=0.094 (Nagelkerke)							
	Model $\chi^2(1)$=11.333, p<0.001							
Author/reader/	Core vs Periphery	−1.233	0.765	1.654	0.075	0.764	0.987	4.544
other researchers	Constant	−1.544	0.654	3.513	0.061	0.543		
	R^2=0.021 (Cox & Snell); R^2=0.024 (Nagelkerke)							
	Model $\chi^2(1)$=8.131, p=0.443							
Another	Core vs Periphery	−2.443	0.644	4.444	0.533	0.643	0.944	6.643
researcher	Constant	−1.443	0.344	8.737	0.785	0.076		
	R^2=0.002 (Cox & Snell); R^2=0.015 (Nagelkerke)							
	Model $\chi^2(1)$=4.126, p=0.336							
Other people	Core vs Periphery	2.533	0.543	2.443	0.353	1.215	0.433	7.441
	Constant	−1.433	0.433	4.433	0.037	0.434		
	R^2=0.005 (Cox & Snell); R^2=0.08 (Nagelkerke)							
	Model $\chi^2(1)$=4.735, p=0.017							

5.3.3 Use of confusion markers by authors' geo-academic location

5.3.3.1 Overall distribution of confusion markers by authors' location

As seen from Table 5.44, the binary logistic regression on the overall distribution of confusion markers did not yield a significant difference (Nagelkerke R^2=0.078, p=0.008), indicating that authors from the different regions did not differ in the overall use of confusion markers in their RAs. Nevertheless, when binary logistic regressions were run on the subcategories of the Confusion frame, some significant location-based differences were observed, similar to the distributional patterns of surprise and interest markers. In what follows, detailed statistical results are presented.

Table 5.44 Results of binary logistic regression on the overall use of confusion markers (authors' geo-academic location as predictor)

Outcome	Predictor	*B*	*SE*	*Wald*	*p*	Odds Ratio (OR)	95% CI for OR Lower	Upper
Confusion markers	Core vs Periphery	−1.213	0.232	0.765	0.632	0.425	0.335	3.134
	Constant	−1.435	0.664	1.532	0.009	0.556		
	R^2=0.055 (Cox & Snell); R^2=0.078 (Nagelkerke)							
	Model $\chi^2(1)=3.453, p=0.008$							

5.3.3.2 Distributions of the frame elements of confusion markers by authors' geo-academic location

Core frame element: Trigger

As summarized in Table 5.45, the logistic regressions run on the frame element of Trigger did not find a significant association between geo-academic location and the subcategories of Conceptualization, Relationship, Attribute, and Phenomenon. However, a statistically significant association was found for the subcategory of Knowledge Gap ($B=2.431$, $p<0.001$, Nagelkerke $R^2=0.182$, OR=2.534). As indicated by Nagelkerke R^2, geo-academic location explained 18% of the variance in the outcome variable. The odds ratio indicated that academics from the Core regions were 2.53 times more likely to express confusion triggered by a Knowledge Gap than their counterparts from the Periphery regions.

Table 5.45 Results of binary logistic regressions on the frame element of Trigger (authors' geo-academic location as predictor of confusion markers)

Outcome	Predictor	*B*	*SE*	*Wald*	*p*	Odds Ratio	95% CI for Odds Ratio Lower	Upper
Conceptualization	Core vs Periphery	1.455	0.233	4.493	0.063	1.765	0.643	4.544
	Constant	−1.442	0.473	2.544	0.654	0.476		

(to be continued)

Outcome	Predictor	*B*	*SE*	*Wald*	*p*	Odds Ratio	95% CI for Odds Ratio Lower	Upper
	R^2=0.012 (Cox & Snell); R^2=0.027 (Nagelkerke)							
	Model $\chi^2(1)=8.121, p=0.009$							
Knowledge gap	Core vs Periphery	2.431	0.754	7.353	0.000	2.534	0.976	7.642
	Constant	−1.334	0.234	11.432	0.075	0.644		
	R^2=0.213 (Cox & Snell); R^2=0.182 (Nagelkerke)							
	Model $\chi^2(1)=17.382, p<0.001$							
Attribute	Core vs Periphery	1.331	0.455	3.953	0.043	1.643	1.454	5.483
	Constant	−1.433	0.655	6.445	0.544	0.345		
	R^2=0.041 (Cox & Snell); R^2=0.064 (Nagelkerke)							
	Model $\chi^2(1)=12.812, p=0.043$							
Relationship	Core vs Periphery	1.432	0.544	4.343	0.865	1.444	0.855	7.843
	Constant	−2.544	0.643	5.048	0.064	0.435		
	R^2=0.014 (Cox & Snell); R^2=0.027 (Nagelkerke)							
	Model $\chi^2(1)=8.132, p=0.433$							
Phenomenon	Core vs Periphery	2.833	0.565	6.875	0.654	3.354	1.556	4.544
	Constant	1.521	0.337	11.433	0.065	1.553		
	R^2=0.032 (Cox & Snell); R^2=0.051 (Nagelkerke)							
	Model $\chi^2(1)=11.433, p=0.045$							

Core frame element: Explanation

A significant difference was found for unidentified sources of confusion ($B=1.013$, $p<0.001$, Nagelkerke $R^2=0.226$, OR=1.675), with Core-based authors being 1.68 times more likely to leave the sources of confusion unidentified than their Periphery-based counterparts (see Table 5.46).

Table 5.46 Results of binary logistic regressions on the frame element of Explanation (authors' geo-academic location as predictor of confusion markers)

Outcome	Predictor	*B*	*SE*	*Wald*	*p*	Odds Ratio	95% CI for Odds Ratio Lower	Upper
Unidentified	Core vs Periphery	1.013	0.346	2.056	0.000	1.675	1.788	5.667
	Constant	0.583	0.654	4.544	0.064	2.144		
	R^2=0.125 (Cox & Snell); R^2=0.226 (Nagelkerke)							
	Model $\chi^2(1)$=16.112, p=<0.001							
Internal factor	Core vs Periphery	1.443	0.755	1.931	0.236	1.824	0.655	7.224
	Constant	0.654	0.344	2.765	0.086	2.655		
	R^2=0.052 (Cox & Snell); R^2=0.073 (Nagelkerke)							
	Model $\chi^2(1)$=8.124, p=0.033							
External factor	Core vs Periphery	−1.435	0.445	4.534	0.076	0.352	1.553	4.744
	Constant	1.434	0.593	6.324	0.344	1.545		
	R^2=0.021 (Cox & Snell); R^2=0.049 (Nagelkerke)							
	Model $\chi^2(1)$=10.223, p=0.075							

Peripheral frame element: Degree

As can be seen in Table 5.47, geo-academic location significantly predicted the mitigation (B=−1.561, p<0.001, Nagelkerke R^2=0.252, OR=0.642) and boosting (B=1.078, p<0.001, Nagelkerke R^2=0.118, OR=1.314) of expressed confusion. The results indicated that scholars from the Periphery regions were 1.56 times more likely than their counterparts from the Core regions to tone down their expressed confusion in RAs. In contrast, scholars from the Core regions were 1.3 times more likely to tone up their expressed confusion than those from the Periphery regions.

Table 5.47 Results of binary logistic regressions on the frame element of Degree (authors' geo-academic location as predictor of confusion markers)

Outcome	Predictor	*B*	*SE*	*Wald*	*p*	Odds Ratio	95% CI for Odds Ratio Lower	Upper
Neutral	Core vs Periphery	1.212	0.231	1.548	0.022	1.041	1.079	3.413

(*to be continued*)

Outcome	Predictor	B	SE	$Wald$	p	Odds Ratio	95% CI for Odds Ratio Lower	Upper
	Constant	−1.345	0.756	2.456	0.546	0.363		
	R^2=0.026 (Cox & Snell); R^2=0.039 (Nagelkerke)							
	Model $\chi^2(1)$=5.133, p=0.053							
Mitigated	Core vs Periphery	−1.561	0.756	3.545	0.000	0.642	0.899	6.455
	Constant	1.013	0.245	6.182	0.074	1.043		
	R^2=0.211 (Cox & Snell); R^2=0.252 (Nagelkerke)							
	Model $\chi^2(1)$=13.124, p<0.001							
Boosted	Core vs Periphery	1.078	0.245	2.041	0.000	1.314	1.078	5.123
	Constant	−2.351	0.564	5.344	0.014	0.226		
	R^2=0.019 (Cox & Snell); R^2=0.118 (Nagelkerke)							
	Model $\chi^2(1)$=6.132, p<0.001							

Peripheral frame element: Experiencer

As summarized in Table 5.48, the binary logistical regressions found a significant location-based difference only for the subcategory of Authors as Experiencers of expressed confusion (B=1.232, p<0.001, Nagelkerke R^2=0.125, OR=1.657). Authors from the Core regions were 1.66 times more likely to describe themselves as Experiencers of expressed confusion than those from the Periphery regions.

Table 5.48 Results of binary logistic regressions on the frame element of Experiencer (authors' geo-academic location as predictor of confusion markers)

Outcome	Predictor	B	SE	$Wald$	p	Odds Ratio	95% CI for Odds Ratio Lower	Upper
Implied	Core vs Periphery	0.863	0.645	1.087	0.033	2.062	0.966	4.864
	Constant	−1.633	0.233	4.481	0.093	0.644		
	R^2=0.112 (Cox & Snell); R^2=0.254 (Nagelkerke)							
	Model $\chi^2(1)$=12.534, p=0.021							
Author	Core vs Periphery	1.232	0.545	2.644	0.000	1.657	1.954	6.321

(*to be continued*)

Outcome	Predictor	*B*	*SE*	*Wald*	*p*	Odds Ratio	95% CI for Odds Ratio	
							Lower	Upper
	Constant	0.382	0.345	3.345	0.067	2.645		
	R^2=0.061 (Cox & Snell); R^2=0.125 (Nagelkerke)							
	Model $\chi^2(1)=6.443, p<0.001$							
Author/reader/ other researchers	Core vs Periphery	0.664	0.744	4.964	0.644	2.341	0.866	4.125
	Constant	−1.444	0.456	2.755	0.066	0.366		
	R^2=0.013 (Cox & Snell); R^2=0.024 (Nagelkerke)							
	Model $\chi^2(1)=4.152, p=0.264$							
Participant	Core vs Periphery	−2.645	0.544	2.057	0.056	0.654	0.835	5.133
	Constant	−1.456	0.656	8.543	0.077	0.342		
	R^2=0.035 (Cox & Snell); R^2=0.071 (Nagelkerke)							
	Model $\chi^2(1)=9.163, p=0.069$							
Other people	Core vs Periphery	−1.432	0.645	2.088	0.456	0.768	1.667	4.245
	Constant	−2.443	0.245	1.032	0.057	0.643		
	R^2=0.105 (Cox & Snell); R^2=0.122 (Nagelkerke)							
	Model $\chi^2(1)=13.543, p=0.048$							

5.4 Diachronic differences in the use of knowledge emotion markers

To address RQ5 about possible time-related differences in the use of knowledge emotion markers, the proposed frame was used to code all instances of knowledge emotion markers in the corpus. Binary logistical regressions were run to determine if there were time-related differences in the use of surprise, interest, and confusion markers. The findings are presented as follows.

5.4.1 Use of surprise markers by time

5.4.1.1 Overall distribution of surprise markers by time

As presented in Table 5.49, a statistically significant difference was found for the overall use of surprise markers between the two time periods (B=1.321, Nagelkerke R^2=0.077, p<0.001, OR=1.964), with authors in the more recent period (2015-2019) being 1.96 times more likely to express surprises in their RAs than those in the earlier period (1985-1989).

Table 5.49 Results of binary logistic regression on the overall use of surprise markers (time as predictor)

Outcome	Predictor	*B*	*SE*	*Wald*	*p*	Odds Ratio (OR)	95% CI for OR Lower	95% CI for OR Upper
Surprise markers	Time 1 vs Time 2	1.321	0.432	0.864	0.000	1.964	1.086	7.968
	Constant	0.425	0.242	0.535	0.026	1.435		
	R^2=0.068 (Cox & Snell); R^2=0.077 (Nagelkerke)							
	Model $\chi^2(1)$=5.612, p<0.001							

5.4.1.2 Distributions of the frame elements of surprise by time

Significant time-related differences were also found when binary logistic regressions were run on the subcategories of the Surprise frame.

Core frame element: Trigger

As shown in Table 5.50, time was not a significant predictor for the different types of Trigger, indicating that RAs published in the two periods of time did not differ in expressing surprise evoked by different factors.

Table 5.50 Results of binary logistic regressions on the frame element of Trigger (time as predictor of surprise markers)

Outcome	Predictor	*B*	*SE*	*Wald*	*p*	Odds Ratio	95% CI for Odds Ratio Lower	95% CI for Odds Ratio Upper
Relationship	Time 1 vs Time 2	2.011	0.345	9.144	0.077	1.514	1.324	7.034
	Constant	0.125	0.224	3.546	0.055	1.054		
	R^2<0.001 (Cox & Snell); R^2=0 .001(Nagelkerke)							
	Model $\chi^2(1)$=0.225, p=0.821							
Attribute	Time 1 vs Time 2	−1.124	0.268	3.514	0.714	0.641	0.455	1.313

(*to be continued*)

Outcome	Predictor	*B*	*SE*	*Wald*	*p*	Odds Ratio	95% CI for Odds Ratio Lower	Upper
	Constant	−1.356	0.246	1.556	0.545	0.678		
	R^2=0.004 (Cox & Snell); R^2=0.011 (Nagelkerke)							
	Model $\chi^2(1)=8.242, p=0.023$							
Behavior	Time 1 vs Time 2	2.444	0.648	8.135	0.088	1.878	0.657	8.697
	Constant	−2.164	0.456	15.356	0.355	0.645		
	R^2=0.013 (Cox & Snell); R^2=0.028 (Nagelkerke)							
	Model $\chi^2(1)=11.324, p=0.642$							
Phenomenon	Time 1 vs Time 2	−1.565	0.324	5.656	0.635	0.234	1.345	6.235
	Constant	−1.035	0.234	19.224	0.057	0.346		
	R^2=0.032 (Cox & Snell); R^2=0.064 (Nagelkerke)							
	Model $\chi^2(1)=18.114, p=0.568$							

Core frame element: Explanation

As shown in Table 5.51, the binary logistic regressions did not find any significant diachronic difference for the identified sources of incongruence (i.e. Internal and External Factors) but yielded a significant difference for Unidentified sources of surprise ($B=-1.628$, $p<0.001$, Nagelkerke $R^2=0.078$, OR=2.538). The RAs written between 1985 and 1989 were 2.54 times more likely to leave the sources of expressed surprises unidentified than those published more recently.

Table 5.51 Results of binary logistic regressions on the frame element of Explanation (time as predictor of surprise markers)

Outcome	Predictor	*B*	*SE*	*Wald*	*p*	Odds Ratio	95% CI for Odds Ratio Lower	Upper
Unidentified	Time 1 vs Time 2	−1.628	0.245	3.464	0.000	0.394	0.796	8.245
	Constant	−2.575	0.323	5.034	0.422	0.534		
	R^2=0.034 (Cox & Snell); R^2=0.078 (Nagelkerke)							
	Model $\chi^2(1)=7.365, p<0.001$							

(*to be continued*)

Outcome	Predictor	*B*	*SE*	*Wald*	*p*	Odds Ratio	95% CI for Odds Ratio Lower	Upper
Internal factor	Time 1 vs Time 2	0.158	0.356	1.738	0.055	2.881	1.674	5.456
	Constant	1.345	0.235	6.234	0.023	1.445		
	R^2=0.011 (Cox & Snell); R^2=0.034 (Nagelkerke)							
	Model $\chi^2(1)=5.511, p=0.645$							
External factor	Time 1 vs Time 2	−1.446	0.355	6.255	0.056	0.656	0.985	4.234
	Constant	−1.234	0.344	12.645	0.754	0.245		
	R^2=0.034 (Cox & Snell); R^2=0.056 (Nagelkerke)							
	Model $\chi^2(1)=5.244, p=0.065$							

Core frame element: Resolution

No statistically significant difference was found for any subcategory of Resolution, indicating that time was not a reliable predictor (see Table 5.52).

Table 5.52 Results of binary logistic regressions on the frame element of Resolution (time as predictor of surprise markers)

Outcome	Predictor	*B*	*SE*	*Wald*	*p*	Odds Ratio	95% CI for Odds Ratio Lower	Upper
Unresolved	Time 1 vs Time 2	2.093	0.345	3.154	0.834	1.983	0.483	7.355
	Constant	1.384	0.763	7.334	0.035	2.045		
	R^2=0.023 (Cox & Snell); R^2=0.055 (Nagelkerke)							
	Model $\chi^2(1)=12.246, p=0.065$							
Resolution by context	Time 1 vs Time 2	0.721	0.233	2.845	0.033	1.305	0.245	3.224
	Constant	−1.938	0.535	5.894	0.341	0.674		
	R^2=0.001 (Cox & Snell); R^2=0.026 (Nagelkerke)							
	Model $\chi^2(1)=3.864, p=0.006$							
Resolution by method	Time 1 vs Time 2	−1.586	0.435	1.935	0.082	0.432	0.735	2.284
	Constant	2.834	0.234	6.434	0.063	1.665		

(*to be continued*)

Outcome	Predictor	*B*	*SE*	*Wald*	*p*	Odds Ratio	95% CI for Odds Ratio Lower	Upper
	R^2=0.013 (Cox & Snell); R^2=0.028 (Nagelkerke)							
	Model $\chi^2(1)$=11.224, p=0.077							
Resolution by speculation	Time 1 vs Time 2	1.454	0.354	5.645	0.345	2.087	0.656	6.245
	Constant	1.535	0.443	7.535	0.324	1.544		
	R^2=0.033 (Cox & Snell); R^2=0.071 (Nagelkerke)							
	Model $\chi^2(1)$=8.194, p=0.232							
Resolution by multiple factors	Time 1 vs Time 2	−1.983	0.372	8.275	0.241	0.457	0.289	4.646
	Constant	−1.214	0.342	11.342	0.465	0.345		
	R^2=0.062 (Cox & Snell); R^2=0.076 (Nagelkerke)							
	Model $\chi^2(1)$=8.146, p=0.053							

Peripheral frame element: Degree

As seen from Table 5.53, time did not predict neutral or mitigated surprises but was a significant predictor of boosted surprises (B=1243, $p<0.001$, Nagelkerke R^2=0.152, OR=2.121), explaining about 15% of the variance in the outcome variable. The RAs published more recently were 2.12 times more likely to tone up expressed surprises than those published in the earlier period.

Table 5.53 Results of binary logistic regressions on the frame element of Degree (time as predictor of surprise markers)

Outcome	Predictor	*B*	*SE*	*Wald*	*p*	Odds Ratio	95% CI for Odds Ratio Lower	Upper
Neutral	Time 1 vs Time 2	1.455	0.323	2.866	0.356	2.255	1.789	5.068
	Constant	2.654	0.456	6.335	0.057	1.976		
	R^2=0.221 (Cox & Snell); R^2=0.354 (Nagelkerke)							
	Model $\chi^2(1)$=4.244, p=0.065							
Mitigated	Time 1 vs Time 2	−1.756	0.646	7.346	0.635	0.756	0.234	7.454
	Constant	1.255	0.545	10.342	0.045	1.768		

(*to be continued*)

Outcome	Predictor	*B*	*SE*	*Wald*	*p*	Odds Ratio	95% CI for Odds Ratio Lower	Upper
	R^2=0.022 (Cox & Snell); R^2=0.046 (Nagelkerke)							
	Model $\chi^2(1)=9.134$, $p=0.038$							
Boosted	Time 1 vs Time 2	1.243	0.345	5.245	0.000	2.121	1.566	4.642
	Constant	1.054	0.655	16.242	0.044	1.242		
	R^2=0.032 (Cox & Snell); R^2=0.152 (Nagelkerke)							
	Model $\chi^2(1)=8.134$, $p<0.001$							

Peripheral frame element: Experiencer

The binary logistical regressions run on the frame element of Experiencer (see Table 5.54) indicated that time reliably predicted the subcategories of Implied Experiencer ($B=-1.435$, $p<0.001$, Nagelkerke $R^2=0.252$, OR=0.314) and Author as Experiencer ($B=1.366$, $p<0.001$, Nagelkerke $R^2=0.041$, OR=2.789). Specifically, the RAs in the earlier period were 3.19 times more likely not to identify the Experiencers of expressed surprises, and those in the more recent period were 2.79 times more likely to present authors themselves as the Experiencers of the emotive responses than those published earlier.

Table 5.54 Results of binary logistic regressions on the frame element of Experiencer (time as predictor of surprise markers)

Outcome	Predictor	*B*	*SE*	*Wald*	*p*	Odds Ratio	95% CI for Odds Ratio Lower	Upper
Implied	Time 1 vs Time 2	−1.435	0.544	3.035	0.000	0.314	0.657	6.244
	Constant	−2.343	0.234	4.543	0.044	0.645		
	R^2=0.112 (Cox & Snell); R^2=0.252 (Nagelkerke)							
	Model $\chi^2(1)=10.313$, $p<0.001$							
Author	Time 1 vs Time 2	1.366	0.234	5.214	0.000	2.789	0.664	4.143
	Constant	1.645	0.343	8.345	0.055	1.777		

(*to be continued*)

Outcome	Predictor	B	SE	$Wald$	p	Odds Ratio	95% CI for Odds Ratio Lower	Upper
	$R^2=0.024$ (Cox & Snell); $R^2=0.041$ (Nagelkerke)							
	Model $\chi^2(1)=6.334, p<0.001$							
Participant	Time 1 vs Time 2	−1.034	0.344	2.534	0.035	0.545	0.243	7.353
	Constant	−1.242	0.335	6.244	0.074	0.244		
	$R^2=0.002$ (Cox & Snell); $R^2=0.012$ (Nagelkerke)							
	Model $\chi^2(1)=4.413, p=0.232$							
Another researcher	Time 1 vs Time 2	1.243	0.544	0.343	0.242	1.646	1.545	6.363
	Constant	−1.545	0.244	2.545	0.033	0.345		
	$R^2=0.011$ (Cox & Snell); $R^2=0.025$ (Nagelkerke)							
	Model $\chi^2(1)=4.436, p=0.022$							
Other people	Time 1 vs Time 2	0.433	0.434	1.333	0.345	1.656	1.646	4.253
	Constant	−1.541	0.645	5.284	0.088	0.657		
	$R^2=0.004$ (Cox & Snell); $R^2=0.044$ (Nagelkerke)							
	Model $\chi^2(1)=4.732, p=0.019$							

5.4.2 Use of interest markers by time

5.4.2.1 Overall distribution of interest markers by time

As shown in Table 5.55, A time-based difference was found for the overall distribution of interest markers ($B=0.822$, Nagelkerke $R^2=0.031$, $p<0.001$, OR=2.311), indicating that authors in the more recent period were 2.31 times more likely to employ interest markers than their counterparts in the 1980s.

Table 5.55 Results of binary logistic regression on the overall use of interest markers (time as predictor)

Outcome	Predictor	B	SE	$Wald$	p	Odds Ratio (OR)	95% CI for OR Lower	Upper
Interest markers	Time 1 vs Time 2	0.822	0.353	0.653	0.000	2.311	0.567	4.235
	Constant	0.342	0.464	0.776	0.321	1.116		

(*to be continued*)

Outcome	Predictor	*B*	*SE*	*Wald*	*p*	Odds Ratio (OR)	95% CI for OR Lower	Upper
	R^2=0.016 (Cox & Snell); R^2=0.031 (Nagelkerke)							
	Model $\chi^2(1)$=3.114, p<0.001							

Likewise, significant time-related differences were also observed when binary logistic regression analyses were run on the subcategories of the Interest frame. The detailed statistical results are presented in the following subsections.

5.4.2.2 Distributions of the frame elements of interest markers by time

Core frame element: Trigger

As seen from Table 5.56, a statistically significant association was found between the time of publication and expressed interest triggered by Appraisal (B=1.443, p<0.001, Nagelkerke R^2=0.078, OR=1.805). As indicated by the odds ratio, the RAs published in the more recent period were 1.81 times more likely to express interest triggered by Appraisal than those published earlier. However, no such relationship was found for interest triggered by other subcategories.

Table 5.56 Results of binary logistic regressions on the frame element of Trigger (time as predictor of interest markers)

Outcome	Predictor	*B*	*SE*	*Wald*	*p*	Odds Ratio	95% CI for Odds Ratio Lower	Upper
Appraisal	Time 1 vs Time 2	1.443	0.423	4.086	0.000	1.805	0.989	4.355
	Constant	−0.254	0.755	5.244	0.065	0.863		
	R^2=0.025 (Cox & Snell); R^2=0.048 (Nagelkerke)							
	Model $\chi^2(1)$=12.433, p<0.001							
Relationship	Time 1 vs Time 2	2.035	0.645	6.329	0.084	2.034	1.134	7.024
	Constant	1.924	0.343	8.025	0.075	1.948		
	R^2=0.003 (Cox & Snell); R^2=0.011 (Nagelkerke)							
	Model $\chi^2(1)$=2.216, p=0.221							
Proposal	Time 1 vs Time 2	0.157	0.461	3.001	0.036	1.161	1.245	6.601
	Constant	−1.938	0.234	7.624	0.072	0.375		

(*to be continued*)

Outcome	Predictor	*B*	*SE*	*Wald*	*p*	Odds Ratio	95% CI for Odds Ratio Lower	Upper
	R^2=0.121 (Cox & Snell); R^2=0.223 (Nagelkerke)							
	Model $\chi^2(1)=8.107, p= 0.051$							
Attribute	Time 1 vs Time 2	2.092	0.274	4.029	0.024	2.035	0.924	5.265
	Constant	−1.385	0.534	12.024	0.131	0.656		
	R^2=0.421 (Cox & Snell); R^2=0.745 (Nagelkerke)							
	Model $\chi^2(1)=6.136, p=0.256$							
Phenomenon	Time 1 vs Time 2	2.835	0.545	2.602	0.141	3.503	1.624	6.025
	Constant	−1.385	0.383	10.513	0.098	0.745		
	R^2=0.051 (Cox & Snell); R^2=0.063 (Nagelkerke)							
	Model $\chi^2(1)=11.353, p=0.073$							

Core frame element: Explanation

As summarized in Table 5.57, a significant diachronic difference was found for unidentified sources of interest ($B=-1.443$ $p<0.001$, Nagelkerke $R^2=0.273$, OR=0.341), with the authors in the earlier period being 2.93 times more likely to leave expressed interest unexplained than those in the more recent period. In addition, a statistically significant association was found between time of publication and External Factor as explanations for the expressed interest ($B=1.743$, $p=0.007$, Nagelkerke $R^2=0.016$, OR=2.232). This suggested that the authors in the recent period were 2.23 times more likely to describe the expressed interest caused by external factors related to results or findings of previous research or characteristics of the research context than their counterparts from the earlier period.

Table 5.57 Results of binary logistic regressions on the frame element of Explanation (time as predictor of interest markers)

Outcome	Predictor	*B*	*SE*	*Wald*	*p*	Odds Ratio	95% CI for Odds Ratio Lower	Upper
Unidentified	Time 1 vs Time 2	−1.433	0.334	3.544	0.000	0.341	1.964	8.446

(*to be continued*)

Outcome	Predictor	*B*	*SE*	*Wald*	*p*	Odds Ratio	95% CI for Odds Ratio Lower	Upper
	Constant	−1.132	0.464	1.911	0.032	0.432		
	R^2=0.121 (Cox & Snell); R^2=0.273 (Nagelkerke)							
	Model $\chi^2(1)$=12.071, p=<0.001							
Internal factor	Time 1 vs Time 2	2.645	0.574	5.374	0.214	1.962	0.039	4.245
	Constant	2.345	0.645	8.635	0.021	1.645		
	R^2=0.022 (Cox & Snell); R^2=0.041 (Nagelkerke)							
	Model $\chi^2(1)$=3.213, p=0.024							
External factor	Time 1 vs Time 2	1.743	0.244	4.054	0.009	2.231	1.094	6.029
	Constant	−2.039	0.574	6.485	0.045	0.325		
	R^2=0.001 (Cox & Snell); R^2=0.016 (Nagelkerke)							
	Model $\chi^2(1)$=5.237, p=0.007							

Peripheral frame element: Degree

Table 5.58 indicated that time significantly predicted boosted interest (B=1.473, p<0.001, Nagelkerke R^2=0.274, OR=1.914). The result suggested that RAs published in 2015-2019 were 1.91 times more likely to intensify the expressed interest than those published earlier. Nagelkerke R^2 indicated that the variable explained about 27% of the variance in the outcome variable. No such relations were found for the other two subcategories of the Degree frame element.

Table 5.58 Results of binary logistic regressions on the frame element of Degree (time as predictor of interest markers)

Outcome	Predictor	*B*	*SE*	*Wald*	*p*	Odds Ratio	95% CI for Odds Ratio Lower	Upper
Neutral	Time 1 vs Time 2	1.843	0.644	5.934	0.054	2.354	0.755	5.034
	Constant	−1.703	0.545	2.743	0.053	0.475		
	R^2=0.032 (Cox & Snell); R^2=0.042 (Nagelkerke)							
	Model $\chi^2(1)$=11.654, p=0.456							

(*to be continued*)

Outcome	Predictor	*B*	*SE*	*Wald*	*p*	Odds Ratio	95% CI for Odds Ratio Lower	Upper
Mitigated	Time 1 vs Time 2	1.313	0.356	3.849	0.021	1.849	0.859	7.824
	Constant	2.903	0.475	10.385	0.214	1.046		
	R^2=0.112 (Cox & Snell); R^2=0.232 (Nagelkerke)							
	Model $\chi^2(1) = 5.345, p=0.071$							
Boosted	Time 1 vs Time 2	1.473	0.435	2.372	0.000	1.914	0.837	7.263
	Constant	−1.242	0.343	8.353	0.034	0.693		
	R^2=0.116 (Cox & Snell); R^2=0.275 (Nagelkerke)							
	Model $\chi^2(1)=6.137, p<0.001$							

Peripheral frame element: Experiencer

Significant diachronic differences were found for the subcategories of Implied Experiencer ($B=-1.271$, $p<0.001$, Nagelkerke $R^2=0.075$, OR=0.423) and Author ($B=1.035$, $p<0.001$, Nagelkerke $R^2=0.076$, OR=1.655). The authors in the earlier period were 2.36 times more likely to leave Experiencers implied than those in the more recent period, whereas the latter were 1.66 times more likely to describe themselves as Experiencers of expressed interest than the former (see Table 5.59).

Table 5.59 Results of binary logistic regressions on the frame element of Experiencer (time as predictor of interest markers)

Outcome	Predictor	*B*	*SE*	*Wald*	*p*	Odds Ratio	95% CI for Odds Ratio Lower	Upper
Implied	Time 1 vs Time 2	−1.271	0.376	2.023	0.000	0.423	0.994	7.533
	Constant	−1.032	0.435	1.382	0.023	0.754		
	R^2=0.043(Cox & Snell); R^2=0.075 (Nagelkerke)							
	Model $\chi^2(1)=9.112, p<0.001$							
Author	Time 1 vs Time 2	1.035	0.428	3.385	0.000	1.655	1.015	6.602
	Constant	1.234	1.242	2.024	0.064	1.231		

(*to be continued*)

Outcome	Predictor	*B*	*SE*	*Wald*	*p*	Odds Ratio	95% CI for Odds Ratio Lower	Upper
	R^2=0.031 (Cox & Snell); R^2=0.064 (Nagelkerke)							
	Model $\chi^2(1)=8.136, p<0.001$							
Author/reader/ other researchers	Time 1 vs Time 2	−1.573	0.545	1.295	0.215	0.734	0.354	4.502
	Constant	−1.247	0.463	4.894	0.024	0.746		
	R^2=0.011 (Cox & Snell); R^2=0.021(Nagelkerke)							
	Model $\chi^2(1)=15.036, p=0.123$							
Another researcher	Time 1 vs Time 2	−1.414	0.744	3.242	0.091	0.453	0.574	5.038
	Constant	−1.756	0.645	6.645	0.033	0.353		
	R^2=0.012 (Cox & Snell); R^2=0.025 (Nagelkerke)							
	Model $\chi^2(1)=7.116, p=0.034$							
Other people	Time 1 vs Time 2	2.598	0.243	6.066	0.082	1.867	0.833	6.453
	Constant	−1.573	0.563	4.401	0.137	0.731		
	R^2=0.001 (Cox & Snell); R^2=0.012 (Nagelkerke)							
	Model $\chi^2(1)=2.136, p=0.021$							

5.4.3 Use of confusion markers by time

5.4.3.1 Overall distribution of confusion markers by time

As shown in Table 5.60, a statistically significant diachronic difference was found for the overall use of confusion markers (B=2.207, Nagelkerke R^2=0.028, $p<0.001$, OR=1.382), with the RAs published more recently being 1.38 times more likely to describe confusion than those published earlier. As reported below, significant diachronic differences were also found for the frame elements.

Table 5.60 Results of binary logistic regression on the overall use of confusion markers (time as predictor)

Outcome	Predictor	*B*	*SE*	*Wald*	*p*	Odds Ratio (OR)	95% CI for OR Lower	Upper
Confusion markers	Time 1 vs Time 2	2.207	0.645	2.343	0.000	1.382	0.915	4.322
	Constant	1.635	0.434	4.644	0.013	2.544		

(*to be continued*)

Outcome	Predictor	*B*	*SE*	*Wald*	*p*	Odds Ratio (OR)	95% CI for OR Lower	Upper
	R^2=0.015 (Cox & Snell); R^2=0.028 (Nagelkerke)							
	Model $\chi^2(1)=10.151, p<0.001$							

5.4.3.2 Distributions of the frame elements of confusion markers by time

Core frame element: Trigger

As summarized in Table 5.61, a statistically significant difference was found in the subcategory of Knowledge Gap as Trigger ($B=1.465$, Nagelkerke $R^2=0.261$, $p<0.001$, OR$=1.541$), with the RAs published more recently being 1.64 times more likely to express confusion triggered by a Knowledge Gap than those published earlier. No significant differences were located for the other subcategories.

Table 5.61 Results of binary logistic regressions on the frame element of Trigger time as predictor of confusion markers)

Outcome	Predictor	*B*	*SE*	*Wald*	*p*	Odds Ratio	95% CI for Odds Ratio Lower	Upper
Conceptualization	Time 1 vs Time 2	2.152	0.436	1.064	0.124	2.143	0.975	6.645
	Constant	1.664	0.243	2.654	0.034	1.545		
	R^2=0.002 (Cox & Snell); R^2=0.017 (Nagelkerke)							
	Model $\chi^2(1)=6.124, p=0.024$							
Knowledge gap	Time 1 vs Time 2	1.465	0.353	4.654	0.000	1.541	0.756	5.655
	Constant	−1.532	0.542	8.573	0.024	0.544		
	R^2=0.116 (Cox & Snell); R^2=0.261 (Nagelkerke)							
	Model $\chi^2(1)=11.186, p<0.001$							
Attribute	Time 1 vs Time 2	1.865	0.341	6.243	0.013	1.866	1.131	8.431
	Constant	−1.475	0.343	4.524	0.142	0.644		
	R^2=0.002 (Cox & Snell); R^2=0.011 (Nagelkerke)							
	Model $\chi^2(1)=6.117, p=0.213$							
Relationship	Time 1 vs Time 2	2.419	0.345	2.318	0.053	1.473	0.976	8.462

(*to be continued*)

Outcome	Predictor	*B*	*SE*	*Wald*	*p*	Odds Ratio	95% CI for Odds Ratio	
							Lower	Upper
	Constant	−1.564	0.435	6.052	0.215	0.656		
	R^2=0.004 (Cox & Snell); R^2=0.007 (Nagelkerke)							
	Model $\chi^2(1)$=9.034, p=0.321							
Phenomenon	Time 1 vs Time 2	1.643	0.324	4.825	0.092	2.313	1.013	2.013
	Constant	2.591	0.532	8.644	0.213	1.945		
	R^2=0.038 (Cox & Snell); R^2=0.055 (Nagelkerke)							
	Model $\chi^2(1)$=7.136, p=0.022							

Core frame element: Explanation

Time significantly predicted Unidentified sources of confusion ($B=-2.064$, $p<0.001$, Nagelkerke $R^2=0.217$, OR=1.742). As in the case of surprise and interest markers, researchers in the recent period were 1.74 times more likely to explain why they felt confused than those in the earlier period (see Table 5.62). No diachronic differences were found for the other subcategories of Explanation.

Table 5.62 Results of binary logistic regressions on the frame element of Explanation (time as predictor of confusion markers)

Outcome	Predictor	*B*	*SE*	*Wald*	*p*	Odds Ratio	95% CI for Odds Ratio	
							Lower	Upper
Unidentified	Time 1 vs Time 2	−2.064	0.245	3.363	0.000	0.574	1.242	6.603
	Constant	1.634	0.343	5.645	0.022	1.645		
	R^2=0.113 (Cox & Snell); R^2=0.217 (Nagelkerke)							
	Model $\chi^2(1)$=10.164, p=<0.001							
Internal factor	Time 1 vs Time 2	2.045	0.533	1.524	0.064	2.801	0.878	4.635
	Constant	0.654	0.344	2.765	0.086	2.655		
	R^2=0.012 (Cox & Snell); R^2=0.023 (Nagelkerke)							
	Model $\chi^2(1)$=6.127, p=0.214							
External factor	Time 1 vs Time 2	1.352	0.345	5.645	0.224	1.785	1.796	7.736

(*to be continued*)

Outcome	Predictor	*B*	*SE*	*Wald*	*p*	Odds Ratio	95% CI for Odds Ratio Lower	Upper
	Constant	2.455	0.514	8.535	0.144	2.636		
	R^2=0.006 (Cox & Snell); R^2=0.017 (Nagelkerke)							
	Model $\chi^2(1)=7.282, p=0.022$							

Peripheral frame element: Degree

As shown in Table 5.63, a significant diachronic difference was located for the subcategory of Boosted confusion ($B=2.074$, $p<0.001$, Nagelkerke $R^2=0.029$, OR=1.772), with the RAs in the more recent time being 1.77 times more likely than those published earlier to scale up expressed confusion.

Table 5.63 Results of binary logistic regressions on the frame element of Degree (time as predictor of confusion markers)

Outcome	Predictor	*B*	*SE*	*Wald*	*p*	Odds Ratio	95% CI for Odds Ratio Lower	Upper
Neutral	Time 1 vs Time 2	2.088	0.544	1.622	0.088	2.353	0.975	4.465
	Constant	−1.766	0.435	2.877	0.064	0.455		
	R^2=0.016 (Cox & Snell); R^2=0.029 (Nagelkerke)							
	Model $\chi^2(1)=8.155, p=0.211$							
Mitigated	Time 1 vs Time 2	1.554	0.343	3.655	0.065	1.644	1.644	6.635
	Constant	1.535	0.534	6.111	0.032	1.956		
	R^2=0.231 (Cox & Snell); R^2=0.452 (Nagelkerke)							
	Model $\chi^2(1)=12.465, p=0.118$							
Boosted	Time 1 vs Time 2	2.074	0.343	2.756	0.000	1.772	1.464	5.635
	Constant	−2.351	0.564	5.344	0.014	0.226		
	R^2=0.019 (Cox & Snell); R^2=0.044 (Nagelkerke)							
	Model $\chi^2(1)=7.155, p<0.001$							

Peripheral frame element: Experiencer

As summarized in Table 5.64, significant diachronic differences were detected for the subcategories of Implied Experiencer ($B=-1.891$, $p<0.001$, Nagelkerke R^2=

0.561, OR=0.464) and Author as Experiencer (B=2.116, p<0.001, Nagelkerke R^2= 0.115, OR=1.251). The RAs published earlier were 2.16 times more likely to leave the Experiencers of expressed confusion implied than those published more recently. In contrast, the latter were 1.25 times more likely than the former to describe authors as Experiencers of expressed confusion.

Table 5.64 Results of binary logistic regressions on the frame element of Experiencer (time as predictor of confusion markers)

Outcome	Predictor	B	SE	$Wald$	p	Odds Ratio	95% CI for Odds Ratio Lower	Upper
Implied	Time 1 vs Time 2	−1.891	0.533	2.542	0.551	0.464	0.966	4.864
	Constant	−1.545	0.431	5.649	0.021	0.544		
	R^2=0.032 (Cox & Snell); R^2=0.561 (Nagelkerke)							
	Model $\chi^2(1)$=9.137, p=0.023							
Author	Time 1 vs Time 2	2.116	0.352	2.614	0.000	1.251	1.064	7.315
	Constant	1.364	0.463	2.214	0.044	1.641		
	R^2=0.041 (Cox & Snell); R^2=0.115 (Nagelkerke)							
	Model $\chi^2(1)$=12.103, p<0.001							
Participant	Time 1 vs Time 2	0.235	0.242	2.534	0.431	1.388	1.864	5.164
	Constant	−1.341	0.437	4.753	0.022	0.645		
	R^2=0.023 (Cox & Snell); R^2=0.034 (Nagelkerke)							
	Model $\chi^2(1)$=6.177, p=0.091							
Another researcher	Time 1 vs Time 2	−1.645	0.544	1.053	0.027	0.433	0.544	4.125
	Constant	−1.767	0.635	4.555	0.212	0.644		
	R^2=0.005 (Cox & Snell); R^2=0.011 (Nagelkerke)							
	Model $\chi^2(1)$=6.183, p=0.012							
Other people	Time 1 vs Time 2	−1.545	0.455	2.524	0.092	0.544	1.977	6.223
	Constant	−2.442	0.365	1.875	0.054	0.643		
	R^2=0.125 (Cox & Snell); R^2=0.222 (Nagelkerke)							
	Model $\chi^2(1)$=6.145, p=0.077							

Chapter Six

Use of Knowledge Emotion Markers in Research Articles: Qualitative Findings

6.1 Cross-disciplinary differences in the use of knowledge emotion markers

6.1.1 Disciplinary knowledge-making conventions: shared vs distinct

The interviews began with questions about the nature of different disciplines and the expected writing format in the disciplines concerned.

All informants from Applied Linguistics unanimously stated that their discipline is interdisciplinary and practice-driven, aiming to address language-based problems in real life. The discipline covers a wide range of topics, such as language teaching, language acquisition, language testing, discourse analysis, literacy studies, and language policy. Regarding the research methodology, Informant 4 stated that "the methods adopted are determined by what you want to research." Informants 2 and 3 commented that "there is no universally agreed-upon research method for a specific topic."

When informants were asked about the expected article structure in Applied Linguistics, they commented that "there is some freedom or variation" in structuring the article, depending on the specific issues examined or the journal-preferred format. However, the IMRD (introduction, methods, the results, and discussions) pattern is generally expected.

We usually follow the IMRD pattern, but there could be some variations. Researchers are expected to follow a stricter IMRD format in more experiment-oriented fields such as psycholinguistics. (I-4)

As regards the discipline of History, the informants perceived the nature of this discipline as being "conceptual rather than empirical" (I-5). In addition, all the informants emphasized the skillful use of argumentation, interpretation, and explanation in writing.

History concerns using written evidence and information available to interpret the human past. Historians should take a deliberative stance and synthesize, interpret or even question materials or sources from the past. (I-2)

There are different methods to show that our inferences of the past are factual. We generally draw on many resources available to argue with potential readers. Historians often have different opinions, so the evidence we draw on becomes critical. (I-4)

When asked about the expected article structure in history studies, the interviewees commented that "there is greater freedom in writing" and "the genre structure is variable." In other words, there is no obligatory pattern or genre-structural guidance historians should follow strictly.

The article structure is negotiable, depending on topics, target audiences, publication language, or writers' personal preferences. However, there is a rough structure: introduction, a body part, and a concluding section in history papers. (I-8)

For the discipline of Biology, the informants agreed that it is "multidisciplinary and complex by nature," dealing with various subtopics involving living creatures' molecular interactions, evolution, chemical processes, and the natural environment. Hypothesis testing and explanation are essential in this discipline.

We are looking for explanations of how a biological phenomenon works. I have been researching molecular biology for quite a long time. This field combines biochemistry, genetics, physics, and chemistry. (I-10)

In biology studies, we usually test many hypotheses and try to explain what we have found in our labs. (I-12)

Regarding the genre structure of research articles in biology, all the biologists interviewed said that the basic IMRD structure is expected to be followed strictly with very little variation. The only variations lie in the journal-specific style, such as the use of footnotes or the resolution of diagrams/figures/pictures.

As far as the discipline of Mechanical Engineering is concerned, all the informants commented on the practical nature of this discipline because an engineer's job is to "bring a product from an idea to its use in the marketplace."

We have many measurements and mathematical computations in the lab. We generate concepts, design experiments, use analytical tools, and determine the manufacturing approach...We pay much attention to the use of technology. This discipline has strong links to the industrial field. (I-14)

For the preferred article structure in mechanical engineering studies, three interviewees (I-13, I-14, I-16) stated that the basic IMRD structure dominates the field. Notably, Informant 15 added that the main part allows for some freedom, depending on the nature of the study (experimental vs theoretical or applied).

These responses indicated that each discipline has its distinct characteristics and knowledge-making conventions. In the interview, all the informants highlighted the importance of adhering to these norms and conventions. Otherwise, they put themselves at the risk of appearing to be outsiders. They stated that,

You will be accepted by the community only when you follow what has been accepted. (I-2, Applied Linguistics)

We work in the field, and we have to know and respect the rules of the game. (I-10, Biology)

Due to a more experimental orientation, we are not expected to write creatively and differently. (I-15, Mechanical Engineering)

Since the responses given by the informants revealed the discipline-distinct knowledge-making practices valued by them, they were asked to explain if their use of knowledge emotion markers was discipline-specific and their purpose intended to achieve by employing these markers. They responded that the deployment of these markers helped draw readers' attention to what was stated. It was an "eye-catching" strategy, as illustrated by Informant 3 and Informant 13,

It was a reader-oriented strategy. It aimed to draw readers' attention and

engage the readers or ask them to pursue the argument with the authors. (I-3, Applied Linguistics)

In my opinion, this was a strategy to generate readers' interest. Many people said their research was interesting because they needed money for the project. It was a way of drawing people's attention so that we could get the money... (I-13, Mechanical Engineering)

Moreover, when the informants were asked to comment on possible differences between their and fellow academics' use of knowledge emotion markers and that of academics in other disciplines, they stated that these markers were used similarly across disciplines.

I couldn't tell the difference. This is not an area I work for, but I feel we used these markers in quite similar ways. As these extracts showed, we all expressed surprises towards the unexpected findings... (I-15, Mechanical Engineering)

Well, I have worked with some engineers before. I saw the use of these markers in their papers, too. I think it is just a kind of language choice to express our attitudes. For example, we would use surprise markers to describe something we did not expect... (I-4, Applied Linguistics)

Notably, when Informant 7 was asked to explain why he resolved the expressed surprise by way of speculations (Example 56) in his RA, this soft-discipline specialist's comments shed some light on the interpretative nature of his discipline.

Compared to natural sciences, my discipline doesn't need to report lots of statistics or data. We primarily deal with texts, readings or historical materials. We provide accounts of historical events instead of discovering some general patterns. When we interpret our results, we are more likely to speculate because we can't be 100 percent sure about that. Interpretations sometimes can be quite subjective. That is why using hedges is important... (I-7, History)

Conversely, the hard scientists put much emphasis on the "reliable data" obtained from experiments in the labs, as illustrated by the responses given by informant 15 from Mechanical Engineering for her use of interest markers to explain the interesting results (Example 111). She stated that,

When the methods are reliable, the data and the results are reliable. Only trustworthy data can help improve the models or the actual system. In our research, we had interesting findings because the results were obtained from

a different computational approach to the old combustion model...(I-15, Mechanical Engineering)

Unlike soft-discipline academics who tended to offer explanations for the expressed surprise or confusion, their hard-discipline counterparts were prone to leave the induced emotive responses unexplained. When Informant 8 from History and Informant 11 from Biology were asked about their respective linguistic choices (Example 110 and Example 3), their responses also revealed the discipline-specific knowledge-making conventions valued by disciplinary communities.

It was essential to tell why I felt this was interesting (evidence). In history, we have to explain what we have found. My claim here was based on the discussions with my readers. I believe there might be some scholars who would disagree with my interpretations... Well, that happens a lot in this field. So if we explain our point clearly and show how we draw that conclusion, people are more willing to follow and accept... (I-8, History)

I chose not to explain why this was surprising because the results were obviously unexpected. If people read my paper, they would have the same reaction. This is not a large community, and different labs actually are building on each other's work. We all have the necessary expertise to understand this. We read our rivals' paper and they read ours... (I-11, Biology)

When Informant 10, a researcher in Biology, was asked to comment on her use of confusion markers (Example 162), she highlighted the necessity of creating a research gap and offering new/alternative evidence in Biology.

I used ***equivocal*** *to tell the readers the evidence provided by some research was not clear enough or well explained. Their claims need to be backed up with more lab experiments. My team conducted an experiment related to the metabolic rate, and we found some new evidence. That was why we published this paper to share the enthusiasm for the result. In my discipline, the gap should be pointed out explicitly because this helps people understand why you do this experiment. This is the general rule. We have to emphasize the significance of the evidence or the new explanations; otherwise, you can't get your paper published. (I-10, Biology)*

In contrast, when Informant 7, a historian was asked if his use of confusion markers (Example 179) was aimed to identify a niche as the hard scientist did, his comments again revealed the interpretative nature of history as a soft/pure science.

Of course, we need to bridge the research gap. But in history, we mostly hold discussions or reexamine some old topics from a different perspective... It doesn't need to be a completely new thing. You don't have to identify a gap every time in your paper. In this extract, I used ***muddled*** *here because previous explanations, I think, were a bit misleading. I mean I just wanted to add another round of discussion to make it more clear... (I-7, History)*

Finally, when the interviewees were asked if these markers caught their attention, they commented that they would pause, think, or evaluate if the information was surprising, interesting, or confusing when encountering such expressions in their peers' work.

When I read the sentences, my attention would be drawn to the information. The authors said something was fascinating, but I would think about that to see if it was true. I sometimes would go back to read that information several times. (I-6, History)

Yes, I would stop for a while to read that sentence carefully because this was probably something the authors wanted us to pay attention to... (I-10, Mechanical Engineering)

Overall, the responses elicited from the interviewees suggested that academics were conscious of the importance of conforming to the dominant norms and expected conventions in disciplinary communities to become recognized members. Regarding the disciplinary use of knowledge emotion markers, a majority of informants considered their use of these markers as an attention grabber shared by different disciplines. Nevertheless, there were discipline-specific ways of knowledge-making conventions associated with the use of knowledge emotion makers for academic communication. Notably, the informants' attention could be drawn to the extracts containing the knowledge emotion markers to evaluate the information together with the authors.

6.1.2 Legitimating knowledge claims: knowledge-oriented vs knower-oriented

In the interviews, all the informants emphasized the importance of demonstrating legitimacy in knowledge claiming to enhance the persuasiveness of their argumentation. Extending Bernstein's characterization of horizontal/hierarchical knowledge structures in the academic fields, Maton (2000, 2014) proposed knowledge-knower structures and legitimation codes in disciplinary knowledge-making. He maintained that epistemological orientations prevailing in disciplines prioritized different legitimation codes in knowledge-making practices. The hard disciplines operated on a knowledge code basis, in contrast to the soft disciplines, which were dominated by a knower code. As such, the hard disciplines relied more on methodological rigor and adequacy of accepted procedures to legitimate knowledge. Conversely, the soft fields depended on the researchers' authority, voice, and expertise to verify knowledge.

The informants' responses concerning cross-disciplinary differences in the use of knowledge emotion markers indicated that epistemological orientations of different disciplines were at work in knowledge-making practices. Knowledge in the soft disciplines was validated based on researchers' reputation, their interpretations or speculations of the results, as commented by the informants from the soft disciplines.

The use of these markers, I think, probably had something to do with researchers' seniority. These well-established scholars knew what was interesting and what was unclear. Ideas proposed by them carried more weight, right?...They evaluated the information as surprising or interesting...and I think they had the expertise to do that... (I-1, Applied Linguistics)

We resort to interpretations and speculations in history because it is the way to write in the field... Many history texts do not have a Method section due to the nature of historical data. Sometimes, references to previous research in history are scarce because we usually do not have a theoretical consensus. In this case, who writes the article actually becomes important...The markers showed our personal attitude to what we wrote, and I think they might help project our image as a professional. For example, if I said some historical records were puzzling, I highlighted my own viewpoints and personal voice... (I-5, History)

In contrast, knowledge in the hard sciences was verified based on the acknowledged methodologies and objectivity, as illustrated by the hard scientists,

Our paper should emphasize that the findings are obtained from a rigorous and credible method. We must clearly describe the method so that other people can

follow. There is a general procedure to report what we did...Well, I think we can use these linguistic resources to highlight our methodology. When I read a paper, I will pay special attention to the methods adopted in the experimental design. (I-14, Mechanical Engineering)

*We need to offer explanations for the biological phenomenon, but we are not expected to speculate what has happened. That speculation would devalue the study and make it less reliable...For your question, I proposed a new hypothesis in the conclusions and use **interesting** here because this was something I planed to work on in another project. So somehow, I wanted to draw the editor's attention to this new idea... (I-12, Biology)*

Notably, when one biologist was asked why he described his expressed surprise toward characteristics of research variables (Example 32), he responded that the manipulation of variables in doing biological experiments could possibly lead to new findings. Therefore, the surprise markers helped highlight his methodological approach.

*It is quite important for us to highlight what methods are used, particularly, how the new findings were obtained if a variable was modified in the experiment. The expressed surprise in this extract intended to show we had noticed the moderator effects didn't work, so we used another method. Then, we had different findings. The word **unexpected** might help our readers to notice the innovative methods used in my lab. You know, we should let our data talk... (I-9, Biology)*

Different from highlighting the methodological procedures in communicating science in the hard disciplines, soft-discipline academics seemed to lay emphasis on their authority and expertise in the field. When one historian was asked about his use of interest markers (Example 88) to evaluate another researcher's work, he responded that this could add perceived importance to his own research, particularly if his work was based on an important scholar's study.

I intended to highlight the relevance of my study to other people's work. I wanted to give credit to people who did similar research. They probably would read my work. If I rèlated my study to theirs, I could show where I was and where I stood. This made my work important, too. People would read it with more interest if their paper was cited... Yes, if my work was important, it would be more likely to be recognized. (I-6, History)

While acknowledging or citing other researchers' work could add potential value to the current study, projecting an authorial presence with linguistically boosted emotions in the argument would, according to the academics, emphasize the authors' active role in claiming and legitimating knowledge. Informants from the soft disciplines elaborated on their linguistic choices in the texts (Example 165 and Example 119) as follows:

Making our argument convincing was central in the field. ***We*** *and* ***rather*** *used here with our expressed confusion helped emphasize our unique perspectives and win the "battle". This gave the readers the impression that you were giving interpretations or explanations, not somebody else. (I-4, Applied Linguistics)*

You know, some scholars believe that in our field, what we have found may not provide a factual record of the past. When setting out my views in the area, I preferred to express my points with force. I think the emphatics ***particularly*** *could add strength to the argument, and this was related to the spirit of arguing and questioning in history. (I-5, History)*

As shown by these excerpts, the ways to verify disciplinary knowledge were influenced by epistemological assumptions underpinning the hard and soft disciplines. Specifically, researchers from the hard sciences legitimated disciplinary knowledge by highlighting the widely accepted methods and experimental procedures. Conversely, academic authors from soft disciplines validated knowledge claims by stressing the authors' attributes and authoritativeness as privileged knowers.

6.2 Gender-based differences in the use of knowledge emotion markers

6.2.1 Perceptions of successful academic communication: clarity vs conciseness

When the interviewees were asked to comment on their perceived differences in knowledge emotion markers employed by male and female academics, 12 informants responded that they could not tell the authors' gender when reading the extracts given to them.

When I read those texts, I didn't know whether the authors were males or females. We wrote pretty much the same way for academic purposes... In academic writing, females also need to project a so-called poker face, you know... (I-1, Male)

When I write, I think I write like a man. What matters is the strength of the argument, not who you are. We are all researchers and writers, not men and women. However, I am not so sure if my feminine writing style would sometimes engage them in the conversation. (I-10, Female)

The other four informants, however, were not certain since they held the belief that gender may play a role in the linguistic choice, as one of them stated,

Maybe there were some differences..., because I knew that women tended to be more dramatic and emotional. However, I am not sure if this is true for academic writing... (I-12, Male)

Although most of them stated that males and females did not differ much in academic writing, when the informants were asked about what contributed most to effective academic communication, their answers pointed to some potential gender-linked differences.

Female researchers emphasized the importance of clarity of ideas. For example, Informants 3 and 10, two female scholars, talked about why they chose to provide explanations for the expressed surprise (Examples 45 and 48).

You know, you couldn't expect the audience to truly understand this... it was a complex issue. When the audience got the idea, they probably went along with your point. Oh, yes, this was surprising! (I-3, Female)

It was essential to make everything clear and easy for my readers by telling them why this was surprising... My colleagues and those outside the field may read my article, and I couldn't assume readers had the same knowledge or background. (I-10, Female)

In contrast, male researchers highlighted the importance of being concise in scholarly communication when they chose not to explicitly identify the sources of the elicited emotive responses (Example 44).

I knew who was going to be my readers when I was writing. You didn't need to put everything there... be concise..., so I didn't see the need to explain too much.

They knew what I was talking about. Anyway, this was not the kind of novel for everybody... They could understand because we have been working in the field for many years... (I-6, Male)

When I asked the male informants to comment on their female counterparts' preference for explaining the elicited confusion (Example 174), they stated that female researchers intended to make their points more straightforward, as Informant 16 elaborated,

I noticed females preferred to explain something. They were more concerned with if they could be understood... (I-16)

In general, the male and female scholars had different perceptions of what language choices contributed to effective academic communication. The female scholars tended to explain their expressed emotions because they thought the explanation would help recover the readers' background knowledge to facilitate their understanding of the propositions under discussion.

6.2.2 Status in academia: visible vs invisible

In the interviews, the female academics were asked to explain their use of boosting expression with self-mentions instantiated in expressions such as to *our greatest surprise*. A majority of them (6 out 8) commented that the more linguistically emphatic and assertive style helped project a more confident image and construct a more visible "self" in the publication market, while two female researchers associated the choice with their personal writing style.

Notably, some female informants offered their views of the gender imbalance in male-dominated academia,

In our field, many researchers are male... You needed to present your writing in a very confident manner. That affected how you would be perceived. (I-15, female)

If we want to get promoted, we have to be "in the market"...publish, publish and publish..., otherwise we are not visible. So in order to be as visible as those well-known male researchers, we had to stress that this study was ***very intriguing****... (I-15, female)*

We publish less than men. Male scholars are more influential... However, we have the same or even more pressure for career promotion than male scholars...

We have lots of stuff to deal with, like kids, family, teaching... Well, back to our topic, I simply wanted to show I was arguing for this, and the readers would see why I offered this information, I explained that in my discussion... It was a good way to invite the readers' responses of that information... (I-8, female)

Overall, the female researchers expressed that they were under-represented and less visible in top-ranked journals than their male counterparts. Their disadvantaged position in academia motivated them to highlight their agency in aligning their authorial stance with the prevalent perceptions of significant research problems and claim their authority as disciplinary experts. Moreover, the female researchers were willing to assume a more intrusive and personal manner to facilitate the co-construction of knowledge in a text. According to the female informants, these endeavors could make their work more easily accepted.

6.3 Location-based differences in the use of knowledge emotion markers

6.3.1 English as a linguistic choice: advantageous vs disadvantageous

When the informants were asked about their attitudes toward using English for international publication, all the interviewees stated that scholars based in the Periphery had linguistic disadvantages compared to those from the Core. However, they also added that this linguistic handicap was not a decisive influence on the rejection of a paper. Two Core-based scholars (I-6, I-16) commented that academic writing was also challenging to native speakers, so they did not believe that this linguistic superiority would make it easier for them to publish. Although a majority of the Periphery-based scholars expressed their linguistic concerns about using English to write up manuscripts by commenting that "English norms somehow are different," they acknowledged that English publications allowed them to reach a wider audience and become more visible in the globalized research community.

Using English is something we can't change... I feel it is sometimes difficult to achieve persuasiveness when writing in English, like striking the right "tone" or modulating the strength of claims. You know, academic writing in English and Chinese is very different. You basically have to restructure everything when you write in another language. It takes you more time and energy. However, English publications allow me to reach a wider audience and get more recognition. (I-2, scholar from the Periphery regions)

Yes, it will take more time to produce a high-quality English paper. I don't write as quickly as I do in Portuguese. In Portuguese, I can always find the words I like. I know if these words are accurate or not. However, when writing in English, I sometimes don't say what I know, only what I can. (I-4, scholar from the Periphery regions)

In addition to the general linguistic constraints reported by the Periphery-based academics, most of them expressed their concerns about the proper use of knowledge emotion markers in writing in particular, as illustrated by two informants' responses,

When I wrote the paper, I felt it was not easy for me to decide if I should express surprises here... I didn't want to make it dramatic by using these markers. But the findings were truly not expected and I wanted my readers to pay attention to this. So I used this expression. When polishing my manuscript the last time before the submission, I hesitated again because I was not sure if this use was proper. Should I add a hedging device before that? What if the editors thought this was not surprising? Anyway, I kept this expression...and the decisions about linguistic styles bothered me...(I-7, scholar from the Periphery regions)

I got my Ph. D. in America and I learned how to write academically in English. It is not difficult for me to write about subject-related materials. But for the accurate use of these linguistic markers, I have to say, it is challenging. I have tried to imitate authors who use these expressions because my attention will be drawn to the information if the author states what confuses them or surprises them in the paper. I think they are useful in expressing our stance. However, probably I overused them or underused them in my previous papers, I am not quite sure...(I-4, scholar from the Periphery regions)

When the interviewees were asked to comment on possible differences in the use of knowledge emotion markers by scholars from the Core and Periphery regions, they responded that they could not tell any differences. However, seven of them (3 from the Core, 4 from the Periphery) speculated that there might be some differences in language choice across regions by stating that "how your teammates write would influence how you write," particularly when collaborative writing is quite common in a globalized research community. In the interviews, 6 informants from the Periphery regions expressed their willingness to collaborate with scholars based in the Core because these "high-level" scholars would "take care of the language issues."

Moreover, the efforts made by the scholars from the Periphery regions to provide explanations for expressed knowledge emotions also signaled their concerns with language clarity. They held the belief that explanations for the expressed emotions would be conducive to getting the message across and achieving consensus building with readers. Informant 4 explained as follows:

I provided the reasons here so the readers could better understand what I was trying to say here. This explanation gave readers more information about why I thought it was a very surprising result. I think the explanation could make the message clearer and better understood...The explanation was essential to invite the readers into the dialogue, so they would be with me on that... (I-4, scholar from the Periphery regions)

Overall, the informant's attitude toward using English as an academic lingua franca was positive, although scholars from the Periphery regions commented that they had linguistic disadvantages when writing in another foreign language. Particularly, they reported their concerns with the accurate or proper use of linguistically expressed emotions in English academic writing.

6.3.2 Accessibility to the knowledge production market: dominant vs marginalized

Regarding accessibility to academic resources such as labs or research equipment, scholars from the Periphery regions reported a lack of resources such as funding. Compared with their counterparts, researchers from the Core regions admitted their easier access to the research grant. As one of them commented,

Doing research needs money. We have different types of funding each year. However, your grant would be approved if you can convince the reviewers you are in a key lab, you have a strong team, and you have everything that could guarantee the successful completion of this project. Yes, we have more access to facilities and experimental equipment than researchers from the developing countries. However, these countries are catching up, right? I wouldn't say they have been marginalized, but we would look at which research labs they come from when recommending their papers to publish... It is more difficult for them to get into the prestigious journals. (I-12, scholar from the Core regions)

While academics from the Core regions are endowed with the resources needed to conduct good-quality research and more possibilities of getting their paper published in top-tier journals, scholars from the Periphery regions have to make more strenuous efforts to promote their research using knowledge emotion markers. As an illustration, Informant 11 emphasized his intention to employ confusion markers in his paper,

I think the expressed confusion may help the paper get accepted because it highlighted the contribution of this paper. Something like, you know, to create a gap... If you didn't address the gap, your research would not be published. (I-13, scholar from the Periphery regions)

Then he continued to express his preference for co-authorship with academics from the Core regions because that could help improve the research quality as a whole. Apparently, this kind of collaboration accentuates the privileged and dominant position of the Core-based scholars in the knowledge production market.

In addition, the Periphery-based scholars' responses regarding their use of knowledge emotion markers to describe their surprising findings or evaluate other academics' work highlighted the hierarchical structure of the field. These practices seemed to be "strategies" to increase the likelihood of making their research visible in the international sphere. They elaborated,

The number of good journals has been growing a lot! However, it seems that it is even more difficult to publish in a good journal these days, perhaps because we are not considered important scholars... In this case, if you don't emphasize how your findings are different from the previous research or interesting enough, the editors will put it away... Why your paper? There are many original research papers out there... (I-10, scholar from the Periphery regions)

If you give credit to the existing studies, especially an important researcher's work, somehow, you add significance to your own research. It is not easy for us to get published in a top journal when scholars from the United States dominate the field. We have to persuade editors that our study is good enough because we have extended a famous researcher's work. (I-7, scholar from the Periphery regions)

I used ***interesting*** *because I thought it was an interesting study... That study really inspired me. More importantly, I mentioned this scholar's work because he was quite influential. His words carried great force, I think. To tell you the truth, I tended to cite the scholars from the West because they might be the reviewers. (I-4, scholar from the Periphery regions)*

Moreover, the Periphery-based scholars' propensity to mitigate their expressed emotions indicated their tentativeness and cautious commitment because they thought it was safer not to be "overconfident in the claims." As Informant 15 commented on her choice (Example 170),

I thought this was confusing, but I didn't know if readers would take my point, so I used ***somewhat****... well, it was safer to hedge here, I mean, to leave some space for possible disagreement (I-15, scholar from the Periphery regions).*

Unlike the Periphery-based scholars' tactics of opening up a dialogic space for knowledge negotiation with readers, scholars from the Core regions emphasized that constructing a confident, authoritative persona to convince potential readers was critical to successful publication. According to them, the employment of boosted knowledge emotion markers with self-mentions could help achieve the persuasiveness of the argument. Informant 3 and Informant 16, two scholars from the Core regions, explained their choices in their articles (Examples 181 and 118).

I suppose we should stand behind our work. However, we needed to let the readers know this was our perspective... It was important to construct a credible image to persuade. If you didn't give that image, nobody would like to read your work and accept your work. (I-3, scholar from the Core regions)

I tried to show my role as an arguer and, more importantly, a researcher responsible for the findings. This was the time for showing credibility rather than modesty. This was the time to argue and convince. I was not sure if I could gain credit for this finding, but I wanted to engage my readers and let them see "me" in the argument. (I-16, scholar from the Core regions)

In general, in the knowledge production market primarily dominated by scholars from the Core regions, the academics from the Peripheral regions had to invest more effort to "sell" the research by strategically deploying knowledge emotion markers to highlight the significance of their work. Moreover, the Periphery-based academics' preference for mitigating their expressed emotions indicated that they were more willing to negotiate readers' expectations in knowledge claims. Furthermore, the Core-based scholars, being at the top of the hierarchy of academia, seemed to be assigned the role of "knowledge keepers," which gave them more confidence and willingness to display a professional and authoritative discoursal self in the disciplinary conversation. This probably explained why they tended to employ boosted knowledge emotion markers accompanied by self-mentions in the argumentation.

6.4 Diachronic differences in the use of knowledge emotion markers

6.4.1 Gaining acceptance and recognition: publish vs perish

When the informants were asked if they would use knowledge emotion markers in their recent publications, they all gave a positive answer because they regarded these markers as important linguistic resources that helped gain acceptance of their research in an increasingly competitive publication market.

> *The competition in our field is intense, and the publication pace is very fast. We sometimes have to give up a top journal like Science to reduce the turnaround time of a paper... If you fail to attract the editors' attention or convince editors that your paper has great value, your paper will be rejected. (I-16)*
>
> *My university has given more and more credit to international publications these years. You will get the monetary rewards, or bonus schemes for a SCI-indexed, Q1 paper. However, we feel it is more difficult to publish in top journals than five years ago... The competition, the pressure, you know, have penetrated into every aspect of our academic life. (I-10)*
>
> *Research institutions have placed increasing emphasis on scientific performance. The publication market has indeed become more competitive. I would say my paper published in the 1980s probably would be rejected now... People are producing very high-quality papers these days... (I-5)*
>
> *Publish or perish, this is what I have currently experienced. Obtaining tenure track and getting career promotion drive me to publish more papers of good*

quality. However, we are competing with lots of teams in the world. It isn't that easy. You know it is so funny that each staff member in my department has to publish at least one refereed paper each year. This is how we are assessed... (I-7)

Currently, universities and research institutes give more weight to international publishing than to domestic publications, as illustrated by the comments above. Given the fierce competition for limited international publication slots, academics had to resort to these linguistic markers to claim the novelty, highlight the significant results, or the contributions of the study to "avoid the danger of perishing from the field."

You wanted to tell other people what you had discovered. I used ***surprise*** *because I wanted to show that this finding contradicted what I had expected. It was essential to let people notice what you had done. (I-10)*

The gap in history was implicit. You needed to state what had not been investigated or discussed. The journals were strict in their selection process. So if you wanted to sell your paper, you needed to point out your contribution. (I-7)

I wanted to identify something that still puzzled researchers in the field. This was why you wanted to test a new hypothesis. It showed that you had done much work. It was important to let the audience, especially the editor, know this was your contribution. (I-12)

6.4.2 Evolving scholarly ethos: impersonal vs interpersonal

When scholars were asked to comment on their use of knowledge emotion markers with self-mentions in recent publications, they responded that the authorial presence could contribute to the build-up of a tie with potential readers. Informant 10 talked about her choice of intruding into the text (Example 181):

I think it could increase the visibility of "me" in the research. It helped invite the readers to join me in that opinion. It was like a conversation between the readers and me. I wanted to make the readers feel included in the conversation. (I-10)

When scholars were asked to explain their use of boosted knowledge emotion markers in their recent publications, they stated that the "scaled-up emotional vigor" demonstrated their assurance of conviction in knowledge claiming and contributed to constructing an authoritative persona for more effective negotiation with readers.

Notably, two disciplinary informants who published in the earlier period perceived some changes in terms of more assurance of conviction in knowledge claiming than three decades ago.

I felt people these days are more and more confident about their claims. This seems to contradict what I have learned about scientific writing. We were told not to be 100 percent sure about what we had found because people would accept something more easily if you showed your cautiousness in your argument. (I-13)

Overall, it seemed that scholars were more willing to engage readers with interpersonal elements by creating a sense of proximity, dialogic exchange with readers, and a level of authoritative reliability to enhance persuasiveness.

6.4.3 Changing academic context: specialized field vs expanded readership

In the interview, when the informants were asked if they perceived any changes regarding knowledge practices in their fields, many informants talked about the emergence of subfields and the increasing specialization of their fields.

Applied linguistics has been fragmented into different subfields. Language policy, language testing, language acquisition, you know, this area has expanded quite a lot. The research paradigms have witnessed many changes as well. In the past, quantitative methods were preferred. Later, the qualitative research was favored. Currently, a mix-methods approach seems to be more popular... (I-4)

Since 2000, there have been more subfields emerging in biology studies, like Evolutionary Biology, Computational Biology, Marine Biology... The topics have become more and more specialized and focused... (I-10)

The expanding disciplines would probably involve a disciplinary readership consisting of researchers who are more divided. Thus, it could lead to possible comprehension difficulties among disciplinary community members. When the informants publishing in the more recent period were asked to explain the reasons for providing explanations for the emotions expressed in their publications, they responded that the explanation helped a non-specialist audience better understand why they evaluated what they had found to be unexpected or interesting.

These days, I am not sure if I can appeal to the readers' background knowledge to understand something I have discussed in the paper. As I said earlier, maybe the technology company manager would be interested in my research because what I have been doing is quite practical. The readers are less predictable than before. You can't expect they are all the specialists and experts in the field and understand everything you have said. (I-15)

In the more globalized research community, the readership has expanded enormously. Thirty years ago, your readers were mainly the people you knew in your small or regional communities. Now, your readers could be anybody from the field, the neighboring field, or even outside the field. They may come from any place in the world. (I-12)

Notably, when Informant 7 was asked why he explained the expressed interest by referring to the findings of the previous research (Example 110), he commented,

The study conducted by Woods and his colleagues was very important. My work was based on their research. However, I found something new, I mean, the new evidence that was different from what they had used to back up their claims. If the readers were willing to know the origin of this argument, they could read the previous research. The literature cited here showed how this line of research was extended, and it helped provide more background information about how my work was situated. The citation, in my opinion, could provide useful references to those who wanted to enter this area. (I-7)

To conclude, the responses given by the informants revealed how societal changes might affect academics' knowledge-making practices in their fields. Due to the huge pressure imposed on them to publish in prestigious journals, scholars have endeavored to underline the novelty, significance, and contributions of their research in the competitive publication market. Moreover, researchers held the belief that taking an involved, credible affective stance was conducive to evoking personal responses in their intended readers to align with their viewpoints. In addition, the increasingly specialized disciplines and expanding readership with various backgrounds made them be more explicit in their arguments and take non-specialist readers into consideration.

Chapter Seven
Discussion

7.1 Disciplinary influences on the use of knowledge emotion markers

7.1.1 Overall use of knowledge emotion markers across disciplines

The quantitative results reported previously indicated that researchers from different disciplines did not prefer a specific type of knowledge emotion markers for scientific communication. This result was perhaps related to the general metadiscursive function of knowledge emotion markers for writer-reader communication (Hyland, 2005b) and their distinctive function for knowledge production (Hu & Chen, 2019; Chen & Hu, 2020a, 2020b). In the interviews, the informants associated the function of these markers with an eye-catching rhetorical strategy to align with readers and promote their study. In a highly competitive academic arena where scholars have to rapidly publish their research in prestigious journals (Lillis & Curry, 2013; Millar et al., 2019), highlighting surprising results, interesting data, or ambiguous methods employed by previous research through linguistically expressed emotions helps enliven the text and draw readers' attention to the worthiness of the research (Millar et al., 2019). As such, knowledge emotion markers are viewed as "emotional framing of persuasive appeals" (DeSteno et al., 2004, p.43) or "persuasive promotional rhetoric" (Martín & Pérez, 2014, p.1), which could have a positive influence on the audience's assessment of one's study. In addition, the informants' responses suggested that the linguistically expressed emotions were triggered by their cognitive evaluation of the propositional content in relation to their scientific activities. In other words, the affective emotions helped foster new knowledge when academics resolved encountered surprises, pursued what was of interest, and addressed what confused them. Given the association of knowledge construction with knowledge emotion markers and RAs as a key genre for scientific communication (Hu & Cao, 2015), expressed emotions in academic writing essentially signal academics' epistemic attitudes regardless of their disciplinary background.

Notably, the finding that discipline did not have an impact on the overall use of knowledge emotion markers corroborated what Chen and Hu (2020b) found about the general use of surprise markers in Applied Linguistics and Clinical Psychology. However, it seemed to be inconsistent with the findings regarding disciplinary influence on the use of attitude markers in scholarly communication reported by Abdi (2002) and Qiu and Jiang (2021). The former study found that the soft disciplines preferred to deploy more attitude markers than the hard disciplines did, whereas the latter study revealed that the hard sciences employed more attitude markers than the soft disciplines. The discrepancy may be ascribed to two factors. First, the two aforementioned studies treated attitude markers as one broad category and did not distinguish subtypes of attitude markers. Second, the data in Abdi's (2002) study were limited to the discussion part of RAs, and Qiu and Jiang's (2021) research examined stance and engagement in academic spoken discourse, i.e. doctoral students' three Minute Theses presentations. In fact, the inconsistent findings from various studies accentuated the necessity of conducting more fine-grained analyses of the use of attitude markers in academic discourse.

7.1.2 Disciplinary influences on the occurrence of the knowledge emotion frame elements

Although differences in the overall use of knowledge emotion markers were not observed across disciplines, the quantitative results pointed to some cross-disciplinary differences in the frame elements of the knowledge emotion frame. These differences could be attributed to the epistemological assumptions and legitimation codes (Maton, 2014) prevailing in disciplinary knowledge-making practices. In the interviews, the informants' responses shed light on the underlying epistemological orientations across the disciplines by highlighting discipline-specific ways of constructing and disseminating scientific knowledge.

Broadly speaking, research in soft disciplines involves human subjects, actions, events, or participants, and thus has a greater likelihood of expressing surprises toward Behavior (Chen & Hu, 2020a) and describing research participants as Experiencers of expressed surprises. Moreover, soft disciplines are open to different interpretations, subject to contextual dynamics, and contingent on contestation (Becher & Trowler, 2001). Consequently, it was understandable for academic authors in the soft disciplines to rely more on speculations to resolve the expressed surprises in scholarly communication. In contrast, the hard sciences are oriented to establish empirical uniformity with precisely controlled variables and measurements typically involving recognized lab experiments and instrumentation (Becher & Trowler, 2001; Fløttum et al., 2006; Hu, 2018). It is very likely that the manipulation of a variable in experimental methods could lead to different discoveries, making the methodology "a unique selling-point" in the hard sciences (Omidian et al., 2018, p.12). Therefore, it could be expected that the hard scientists described their expressed surprises toward characteristics related to methodological issues to highlight the experimental basis for the study. As confirmed by the interview data, the informants from the soft disciplines depended on interpretations and explanations in knowledge claims, in contrast to their counterparts from the hard disciplines, who believed that speculations and interpretations would devalue the study and that the methodological rigor should be underlined.

Furthermore, pure disciplines were primarily concerned with interpreting, explicating, and developing new theories and perspectives, whereas applied ones were more functional and pragmatic, focusing on how knowledge could be used (Becher & Trowler, 2001; Nesi & Gardner, 2006). The epistemological beliefs underpinning the pure disciplines could explain why researchers were more motivated to express surprises triggered by Relationship highlighting innovative results or findings obtained than their applied-discipline counterparts were. Additionally, since the pure disciplines placed much emphasis on "validating knowledge through examining conflicting evidence and exploring alternative explanations" (Neumann et al., 2002, p.408), it was reasonable for the authors in these disciplines to describe their expressed interest toward a newly proposed hypothesis or alternative evidence. Apparently, expressed interest associated with a new research hypothesis would enhance the conceptual or theoretical contributions of a study.

According to Legitimation Code Theory (Maton, 2000, 2014), knowledge claims in the soft disciplines are dominated by a knower code, relying on displaying researchers' "aptitudes, attitudes and dispositions" (Maton, 2014, p.92). In other words, such a knower-oriented code prioritizes researchers' voices, authority, and expertise to legitimate disciplinary knowledge. Thus, it was plausible for the authors from the soft disciplines in my corpus to evaluate the interesting aspects of the extant literature to assert their authority and expertise in the field. Different from the soft disciplines, which value the "unique insight of the knower" (Maton, 2000, p.157), knowledge in the hard sciences is developed linearly and generated cumulatively (Zou & Hyland, 2020) and is expected to fill in knowledge gaps in the field. Consequently, it was not surprising that the hard-science authors of the articles in my corpus were prone to express their surprises triggered by what remained ambiguous and obscure, whereby the need for new hypothesis testing could be justified, and the contribution of the current study could be claimed.

For the frame element of Explanation associated with surprise and confusion markers, the hard-discipline researchers were more inclined not to explain what elicited these emotive responses. This could be ascribed to the epistemological codes prevailing in the hard sciences. As argued by Maton (2014), hard sciences operate with a knowledge code. In such an epistemological context, the individual characteristics of scientists are downplayed, and scientists depend more on methodological rigor and adequacy of accepted procedures to verify disciplinary knowledge. Therefore, hard sciences are more likely to reach a consensus on theoretical perspectives, procedures, and methods due to their relatively homogeneous and objective knowledge base (Fløttum et al., 2006). Specific research problems always emerge from an established knowledge context where audiences are assumed to be familiar with prior research (Zou & Hyland, 2020). As such, a convergent view of logical and causal relationships obtained from experimental observations is easier to establish with more homogeneous readers in a specialized field (Nesi & Holmes, 2010). This could probably explain why the hard scientists in my study had no need to explain the sources of expressed surprise and confusion when communicating scientific ideas with other disciplinary members.

However, interestingly, if the hard scientists chose to explain what aroused their interest, they were more likely to associate the source with internal factors pertaining to the characteristics of the methods, objects, or variables of the study. It could be speculated that this perhaps had much to do with the unique property of interest as a knowledge emotion involving the ability to cope with discrepant information encountered (Silvia, 2019). As explained earlier, hard disciplines operate on a knowledge code, and epistemic persuasiveness could be enhanced by justifying methodological innovations/rigor and explaining how a study is conducted by following scientific procedures. Consequently, it would not be difficult to understand why the authors in my study tended to show their comprehension of and anticipated satisfaction with methodological breakthroughs to highlight methodological contributions.

Finally, the finding that boosted surprise, interest, and confusion were more likely to be found in RAs from the soft disciplines corroborated previous research on the cross-disciplinary use of boosters in scientific communication (Hu & Cao, 2015; Hyland, 2005a; Liu, 2019; Peacock, 2006; Yoon & Römer, 2020). As soft disciplines foreground researchers' agency in knowledge verification (Maton, 2014) and are more subjective, interpretative, and discursive (Hyland 2005a; Qiu & Jiang, 2021), researchers need to accentuate their epistemic conviction to "restrict alternative voices" (Hyland, 2011, p.205). As such, intensified affective expressions that assist academic writers in highlighting their distinct voice and negotiating readers' expectations can be expected to be deployed more frequently in soft disciplines.

7.2 Gender influences on the use of knowledge emotion markers

7.2.1 Overall use of knowledge emotion markers across gender

The quantitative results yielded suggested that gender was not a determining factor in deploying knowledge emotion markers for scholarly communication. This finding appeared to run counter to some research arguing that females were more emotionally expressive than males in writing communication (Chaplin & Aldao, 2013; Hess et al., 2000). However, given that academic writing is a highly formal and conventionalized genre, the expected argument style might override gendered traits in writing (e.g. Francis et al., 2001; Rubin & Greene, 1992). In other words, male and female scientists probably share more similarities than differences because the dominant norms in disciplinary communities shape the socially defined ways of constructing and disseminating scientific knowledge. Understandably, scholars are expected to communicate science in a way that is recognizable and acceptable by disciplinary insiders (Hyland, 2009). As demonstrated by the interview data, the informants emphasized the necessity of adhering to a set of discoursal practices in scientific writing. In addition, some researchers argued that academic writing style essentially reflects masculinity manifested in values such as detachment from emotion, competition and aggression (Madera et al., 2009; Tse & Hyland, 2008). It could be possible that female academics have been socialized into such a style. This possibly accounted for why they could not tell any gender-linked differences in the use of knowledge emotion markers by reading the extracts written by their male/female counterparts.

7.2.2 Influences of gender on the occurrence of knowledge emotion frame elements

As reported previously, gender could reliably predict the presence of unidentified sources of expressed surprise, interest, and confusion, boosted emotive responses, and the frame element of author-related Experiencer. These gender-based differences concurred with some scholarly inquiries that revealed gender-specific writing styles (Newman et al., 2008; Stenström, 1999).

First, female researchers were more likely to explain why the triggered emotions were surprising, interesting, and confusing (2.8 times for surprise makers, 1.86 times for interest markers, and 1.87 times for confusion markers) than their male counterparts. This was probably attributable to different assumptions held by men and women about what constituted successful and friendly writer-reader communication, as illustrated by the interview responses presented in the preceding chapter. It was found that the females were inclined to adopt a more facilitative and cooperative style (Coates, 1993) by taking the reader's comprehension into account. Moreover, they tended to favor a more rhetorically elaborated exposition for the sake of eliminating ambiguities (Tse & Hyland, 2008). Consequently, the female researchers in the present study were more willing to explicitly state the reasons for the expressed surprise, interest, and confusion to facilitate readers' understanding of the propositional content.

Second, female academics' greater use of boosted knowledge emotion markers indicated that these scholars, compared to their male counterparts, generally showed a linguistically emphatic and assertive style in scientific communication. This finding concurred with what was found by Newman et al. (2008), who reported that female writers were more inclined to express a high degree of assurance in their interpretation of prepositional information and stronger commitment to arguments in writing.

However, the results obtained in the present study diverged from what was reported by Tse and Hyland (2008) and Liu (2019). The former study found that male researchers tended to show a more assertive writing style to scale up their confidence in evaluations through boosters. The latter one also suggested that male academics preferred to use more intensifiers than females in scholarly communication. The inconsistencies with Tse and Hyland (2008) and Liu (2019) could be plausibly ascribed to genre differences and the stance features under investigation. While the present study examined the interaction of a specific type of attitude markers with hedges or boosters in RAs, Tse and Hyland (2008) and Liu (2019) were concerned with the use of hedges or boosters by male and female academics in book reviews and spoken lectures, respectively. As remarked by Tse and Hyland (2008), the genre of book reviews was "a direct, public, and often critical encounter with a particular text and its author" (p.1235). In such a confrontational communication context, it was expected that female writers tended to be less assertive and take a more compromising line to avoid conflicts. This was essentially related to the male authors' seniority in a male-dominated academy, which allowed them to display their masculine aggressivity (Tse & Hyland, 2008). In addition, according to Liu (2019), the nature of university academic lectures was characterized by more consensus building with students. In such a setting, the male lecturers' preference for using hyperboles through intensifers was associated with their intention to signpost key points, create a dramatic effect, add politeness and, above all, achieve effective and efficient delivery of knowledge. In fact, it was argued that the use of intensifiers is associated with a kind of "positively polite style" (Fuchs, 2017, p.350) and is a typical feature of female language. Thus, Liu (2019) speculated that the special features of the lecture genre probably inclined males to use more intensifiers than their female counterparts. This suggested that genre could possibly influence male and female discoursal behavior and practice.

With respect to academic writing, as discussed earlier, the female and male informants had different perceptions of polite and effective academic communication. Since female academics prioritized politeness in scholarly practice, it was understandable for them to "scale up" linguistically expressed surprises, interest, and confusion in their RAs.

It was noteworthy that the female academics' boosted emotive responses tended to co-occur with self-mentions. In the interviews, the female academics' comments on this linguistic choice revealed their preferred authorial intrusion into the text to convey a more personal, authoritative persona. The female researchers stated that they were "less visible" in the publication market than their male counterparts, so they preferred boosting emotions accompanied by self-mentions to project an image of authoritative discipline insider in their arguments.

As a matter of fact, female scholars' disadvantaged positions in the male-dominated academic discourse or community are well documented (Belcher, 1997; Jackson, 2002; Lillis & Curry, 2018). Although they are more recognized for their contributions academically (Thieme & Saunders, 2018), the gender gap in terms of research productivity persists in the male-dominated STEM disciplines (Monroe et al., 2014) and even in social sciences where female scholars probably outnumber male researchers (Lillis & Curry, 2018; Nygaard & Bahgat, 2018). As reported by the female informants in the interviews, they were under more pressure for rapid publication in competitive and high-profile journals for career advancement. Given the female researchers' enormous career pressure in the hierarchical academia (Maxwell et al., 2019), they were motivated to make their presence and arguments strongly felt to construct a more engaged, enthusiastic, and confident persona in order to be recognized.

7.3 Regional influences on the use of knowledge emotion markers

7.3.1 Overall use of knowledge emotion markers across regions

In line with the quantitative results presented earlier, academic authors based in the Core and Periphery research sites did not differ in their preference for a particular type of knowledge emotion makers in RAs. While academic writing is deemed a locally situated practice in specific regional or national contexts, in the current international scientific community, academic discourse practices are shaped by the complex interplay of national network building and the processes of globalization (Lillis & Curry, 2010). Notably, when institutional policies give more credit to Center-affiliated journals, Periphery-based scholars have to accommodate to the norms of Anglo-influenced discursive practices although they suffer from the geolinguistic imbalance (Canagarajah, 2001; Hanauer et al., 2019; Pérez-Llantada, 2018). As such, their academic writing might exhibit "interdiscursive hybridity" (Mauranen et al., 2020), that is, the mix of locally established rhetorical practices with prevalent Anglophone rhetorical models.

Despite the Periphery-based scholars' linguistic concerns with the proper discursive style in English publication, they agreed that collaborations with scholars based in the Core regions provided great opportunities for them to learn how to make their manuscripts grammatically correct, stylistically acceptable, and rhetorically persuasive. As cross-border research cooperation between the Core- and Periphery-based scholars has been on the increase, the discursive practices valued locally might change. This could possibly explain why scholars based in the Core and the Periphery did not differ in the frequencies with which they used different types of knowledge emotion markers in their scholarly communication.

7.3.2 Regional influences on the occurrence of knowledge emotion frame elements

As indicated by the quantitative results, the researchers from the Periphery regions were more likely to express surprise toward Relationship pertaining to the novel findings obtained from their study than their Core-based counterparts. The informants' responses indicated that the knowledge production market is dominated by the Core-based scholars, who are at the top of the academic hierarchy (Moletsane, 2015). Conversely, the Periphery-based scholars are likely to be deprived of access to scholarly centers or material resources and suffer from disproportionate representation (Curry & Lillis, 2004; Salager-Meyer, 2008). Consequently, they have to invest considerably more effort to persuade the "gatekeepers" of high-ranking journals to accept their research by claiming the novelty of their study. As shown in the interviews, the Periphery-based informants accentuated the importance of highlighting the findings to add to the perceived importance of their study's contribution.

Regarding the frame element of Trigger for interest markers, scholars from the Peripheral regions were more likely than their Core-based counterparts to associate what caused interest with Appraisal. This might plausibly be related to what the Periphery-based scholars deemed a legitimate way to claim knowledge. As noted by Samraj (2008), an author's contribution to knowledge is "not usually presented in a disciplinary vacuum but as relevant to the research questions pursued by other researchers in that disciplinary field" (p.56). This indicates that researchers need to establish suitable grounds for convincing readers of the significance of their new knowledge claims by relating them to previous research or demonstrating how the literature is built upon. The Periphery-based informants' responses suggested that due to their marginalization in academia, the evaluation of previous studies as interesting was essential because it helped establish the centrality of their research. More importantly, the contribution of their research could be more easily recognized if previous lines of interesting research were extended.

In contrast, the scholars from the Core regions were more likely to express their interest elicited by proposed new hypotheses or a potential research direction than those from the Periphery regions. Moreover, they were more likely to express their confusion triggered by a Knowledge Gap pertinent to the under-explored issues in the field. In the academic field, where English-speaking voices dominate (Curry & Lillis, 2017), academics based in the Core regions dictate potential research trends and what count as valuable research topics, similar to what Hyland (2015b, p.72) stated "scholars based in the leading Anglophone countries play a key role in setting research agendas and deciding what gets published". As gatekeepers of prestigious journals or insiders of the disciplinary community (Hyland, 2007), they are likely to construct an authoritative image to highlight their expert status by proposing what research topics merit further explorations. In this sense, academic knowledge production, bound with knowing and knowers (Maton & Moore, 2010), involves epistemological forms of power and diverse ecological resources (Canagarajah, 2013; Maton, 2010).

Notably, the researchers from the Core regions preferred not to provide the sources for the expressed surprise, interest, and confusion compared to their counterparts from the Periphery regions. These patterns suggested that they tended to bring readers into the same discursive space for the negotiation of knowledge claims by foregrounding readers' shared epistemological beliefs within the disciplinary community. In contrast, the Periphery-based authors, who used English as an additional language (Hanauer et al., 2019; Pérez-Llantada, 2018), were inclined to explain the emotive responses induced to solicit solidarity with potential readers. In the interviews, the Periphery-based informants indicated their concerns with language clarity. As a result, they provided explanations to ensure that the propositional content could be fully understood. Apparently, their language-related problems and concerns, to some extent, revealed the linguistic imperialism in the publishing arena (Canagarajah, 2002; Phillipson, 2013; Pennycook, 2017).

Notably, the Core-based scholars were more likely to tone up expressed feelings of surprise, interest, and confusion. These results indicated that they preferred to construct a confident persona by investing a higher degree of authorial certainty in evaluating propositions. As illustrated by the interview data, the scholars from the Core regions underlined the contributory role of solid convictions in securing the alignment of potential readers with their viewpoints. In contrast, the scholars from the Periphery regions tended to tone down the elicited emotive responses by claiming knowledge with tentativeness and cautious commitment. This was perhaps related to their epistemic belief that opening up a dialogic space was critical to establishing the validity of propositional content. As noted by Yakhontova (2002), Periphery-based researchers such as Ukrainian and Russian scholars resorted to a defensive position and anticipated criticism and disputes. Less arguably, such discoursal practices also signal the Periphery-based scholars' disadvantaged position in the knowledge production market.

In addition, the Core-based scholars' preference for identifying themselves as Experiencers of the elicited emotions could be ascribed to their intention to construct a more prominent authorial stance by emphasizing their interpretations of the proposition. On the one hand, the authorial presence could be explained by the Anglophone writing practice characterized by a writer-responsible culture (Hinds, 2001). On the other hand, it could help project the authors as recognizable, representative, and privileged disciplinary knowers (Hu & Cao, 2015; Hyland & Jiang, 2017), and enabled them to seek agreement, highlight their contributions to the field, and promote their research (Hyland & Jiang, 2017; Walkova, 2019).

In contrast to their Core-based counterparts, the Periphery-based scholars tended to convey a more impersonal stance with authorial detachment toward the knowledge claims. One plausible explanation could be that they positioned themselves as aligned with the scholarly ethos of the academic community, such as neutrality and objectivity, and thus were trying to avoid impositions on target readers via depersonalization (Yakhontova, 2006). Another possible explanation could be that the culture of the non-Core regions valued humility rather than self-promotion. For example, Sabaj et al.'s (2013) study revealed that the trait of modesty contributed to academic persuasion in Spanish academic discourse. Although this did not conform to the "self-promotional" feature of scholarly writing in English (Hyland, 2001), the locally valued discursive style of relying on findings rather than authorial visibility was probably deemed appropriate to validate knowledge claims by the Periphery-based scholars.

7.4 Influences of time on the use of knowledge emotion markers

7.4.1 Overall use of knowledge emotion markers across time

The quantitative results regarding the diachronic changes in the overall use of knowledge emotion markers showed that academic scholars preferred a greater use of these markers in their scholarly communication than 30 years ago. This indicated that academic communication today relies more on interpersonal elements manifested by affective stance-taking than on empirical and factual data, compared to 30 years ago. However, the researchers' increasing use of knowledge emotion markers for authorial standpoints in the present study ran counter to the overall decline of attitude markers in academic prose reported in Hyland and Jiang's (2018) diachronic study. In particular, this observation also contradicted the results reported by Chen and Hu (2020a), who found that the time of publication did not influence the use or non-use of surprise markers in applied linguistics RAs published over a time span of 30 years. It could be speculated that the differences from Hyland and Jiang's (2018) findings may be attributable to their investigation into attitude markers as a broad category, and the inconsistencies with Chen and Hu's (2020a) research may be due to the different disciplines examined. Chen and Hu (2020a) probed into diachronic changes in the use of surprise markers in a single discipline (i.e. Applied Linguistics), whereas the present study explored the use of surprise markers in both hard and soft disciplines over a period of 30 years. It is possible that specific types of attitude markers might exhibit different patterns of diachronic changes when examined in one discipline and multiple disciplines.

The more prominent authorial evaluations manifested in the use of surprise and interest markers in RAs published more recently corroborated what was reported in Wen and Lei (2022). Drawing on a large corpus of articles in 12 disciplines in the life sciences, the study found that researchers tended to employ more positive words, such as *surprisingly, remarkably*, or *interestingly*, over 50 years. They attributed this upward trend of linguistic positivity in the sciences to publication pressure, the need to promote research, and the pursuit of political correctness.

At first blush, the finding that academic writers expressed their confusion more frequently than 30 years ago was puzzling. When disciplines have matured and solidified with a massive growth of literature, researchers undoubtedly have understood the field better than before and could be expected to feel confused less frequently. A close examination of expressed confusion in the articles in my corpus revealed that the linguistically expressed confusion was inherently strategic, helping underscore the significance of the study. As the informants explained in the interviews, they used confusion markers to identify a research niche so that the necessity of their study was justified.

In summary, the upward trend of linguistically expressed surprise, interest, and confusion in RAs examined indicated that scholarly ethos evolved as a response to societal changes. In the academic world, where scientific output has grown exponentially and the publication market has become more commercially oriented (Lillis & Curry, 2013; Wen & Lei, 2022), how knowledge is claimed, disseminated, and accepted has also changed. Academic writing, traditionally expected to refrain from emotions, has witnessed the increasing use of emotionally evaluative expressions as promotional tactics to sell research.

7.4.2 Influences of time on the occurrence of knowledge emotion frame elements

The findings that time of publication was not associated with the occurrence of frame elements of Trigger and Unresolved surprise were inconsistent with those of Chen and Hu (2020a). In the study, RAs published more recently were found to be more likely to describe surprise triggered by information already known to a scientist and leave expressed surprise unresolved than those published 30 years before. As noted earlier, the discrepancy was perhaps related to the specific disciplines under investigation. The inconclusive findings about diachronic changes in the use of knowledge emotion markers reported by different studies have confirmed the need to undertake more fine-grained scholarly work in this line of research.

For interest markers, the longitudinal data indicated that RAs published in the more recent period were 1.81 times more likely to express interest triggered by evaluating the research findings of one's study or previous studies than those published earlier were. The informants' responses regarding this linguistic choice revealed their purpose of establishing the significance of their study and garnering recognition. As noted by some previous research, academic writers tend to positively evaluate others' work (Catalini et al., 2015) to demonstrate their membership in a disciplinary community.

As regards the use of confusion markers, the quantitative findings indicated that the authors of more recently published articles were more likely to express their confusion triggered by a Knowledge Gap than those of articles published 30 years ago. It seemed that researchers were increasingly prone to pinpoint inadequately addressed issues by articulating their unresolved confusion. As discussed earlier, linguistically expressed confusion functioned as "persuasive promotional rhetoric" (Martín & León Pérez, 2014, p.1) to accentuate and justify current scholarly endeavors. When a current study carves out a niche, bridges the gap, and increases our understanding of a particular issue in the field, its significance is highlighted.

For the frame element of Explanation, the findings showed that publications in the more recent period were more likely to explain the reason for the expressed emotive responses than those published 30 years ago. This suggests that academic writers publishing in the earlier period interacted with community readers by appealing to their shared epistemological beliefs, in contrast to the more recent period, when writers tended to claim knowledge more transparently and explicitly. In addition, they were more likely to express interest caused by external factors concerning previous research findings than their counterparts publishing 30 years ago. These changing knowledge-making practices, according to the informants, were related to the continuous growth of new fields, sub-disciplines and interdisciplinary sciences (see also Vanderstraeten, 2010). Because of the expansion of academic disciplines, the readership is no longer comprised of only informed insiders but has become less homogeneous and predictable (Hyland & Jiang, 2018). Those readers might include, but are not limited to, expert specialists of the field, external funders, tenure and promotion committees, nonspecialists outside the immediate discipline, policymakers from the government, or even the general public (Berkenkotter & Huckin, 2016; Hyland & Jiang, 2017; Rakedzon et al., 2017). In the interviews, many informants talked about the increasing specialization of their disciplinary field with more expanded or broader audiences. In order to align readers with their viewpoints, they needed to consider the readers' background knowledge or lack thereof and guide those readers who were probably unfamiliar with the related theories, methodologies, and practices of a field through explicit explanations. This could explain why the sources of expressed surprise, interest, and confusion were more explicitly identified in the more recent period of publication examined in this study.

Regarding the diachronic variation concerning the frame element of Degree, an increase in the incidence of boosted knowledge emotions in RAs was noted, suggesting academic writers' higher level of confidence in making arguments and formulating propositions than before. This result diverged from Chen and Hu's (2020a) finding that no significant difference was observed in the use of boosted surprise over a 30-year period. As noted earlier, this discrepancy was perhaps related to the different disciplines examined in Chen and Hu (2020a) and the present study. However, the upward trend in the use of boosted emotions aligned with what was reported by Poole et al. (2019). Poole et al. examined the stance features of biochemical RAs published between 1972 and 2017 and found increasing use of boosters over time.

With respect to the academics' preference for boosted emotions in the more recent time, the informants' responses also shed some light on that linguistic choice. Currently, academic authors have a greater need to construct an authoritative image and shut down the dialogical space for readers to challenge their interpretations due to the escalating pressure in the publication market. Moreover, in the more recent decade, the development and maturation of a field has made it increasingly acceptable to claim knowledge with assurance in a particular domain of study. As argued by Poole et al. (2019), epistemic devices signaling greater certainty about an issue would increase along with the solidification of knowledge in a field.

Finally, concerning the frame element of Experiencer, RAs published more recently were more likely to describe "authors" as the people who experienced expressed surprise, interest, and confusion. In other words, the authors were more willing to increase their authorial visibility than 30 years ago. In the interviews, the informants' responses revealed that such an intrusion into text helped reinforce their role as an arguer responsible for the propositional content. More importantly, it helped highlight their authoritativeness and contribution to their disciplinary community. In addition, the informants believed that co-construction of meaning in a disciplinary dialogue through building up a close tie with potential readers would enhance the persuasiveness of their knowledge claims. When a deeper level of bonding with potential readers is achieved, readers are likely to be more involved in the knowledge claims and more willing to accept them (Li, 2021). In support of this interpretation, changes in academic writing from a more detached way to a more personal way have been evidenced in the more frequent use of "self-mentions" in academic prose over the years (e.g. Hyland & Jiang, 2018a, 2018b; Li, 2021). These changes indicate a shift in scholarly ethos characterized by an author-evacuated and data-oriented style toward more personal, engaging, intimate, and egalitarian relationship-building with readers. Arguably, the diachronic variations manifested in the more frequent association between "self" and linguistically expressed emotions over time were also related to the increasingly competitive academic world, where researchers feel an ever growing need to construct a discoursal persona of visible agents for professional recognition and promotion.

7.5 Knowledge emotion markers and knowledge-making practices

As made clear in the above discussions, it is safe to conclude that knowledge emotion markers have at least two major functions in academic writing: a metadiscursive function in writer-reader communication (Hyland, 2005b) and an epistemic function in knowledge production (Hu & Chen, 2019; Chen & Hu, 2020). Notably, their unique properties for cognitive operations, i.e. information processing, logical argumentation, and new knowledge construction in scholarly communication, cannot be overlooked (Chevrier et al., 2019; Silvia, 2019; Vogl et al.,2021). Linguistically expressed surprise, interest, and confusion index academic writers' engagement with and processing of cognitive dissonance and unfamiliarity brought about by new knowledge. This new knowledge can be fostered and generated when researchers propose explanations, resolutions, and potentially worthwhile explorations or argue for a lack of sufficient understanding of a topic.

The comments provided by the disciplinary informants confirmed the epistemic features of knowledge emotion markers in academic communication. On the one hand, the informants were conscious of exploiting knowledge emotion markers to indicate their epistemic attitude toward propositions in knowledge making. They employed surprise markers to alert themselves and readers to cognitive discrepancies and look for resolutions; they deployed interest markers to signal their anticipated satisfaction with the findings obtained; they used confusion markers to suggest how their study bridged a knowledge gap by addressing an unresolved issue. On the other hand, when encountering these markers in their peer's writing, they were motivated to pause and evaluate whether the information concerned was surprising, interesting, or confusing and even to take action to address the triggered incongruity or ignorance of scientific knowledge. Therefore, the emotions elicited by discrepancy, novelty, and complexity were associated with cognitive reappraisal (Muis et al.,

2015; Pekrun & Stephens, 2012; Silva, 2019; Vogl et al., 2019). New knowledge can be gained by directing attention to examining the relationship between one's current knowledge and unexpected/confusing discrepancies in the world. In this sense, the definition of attitude markers given by Hyland (2005a) is debatable since he argued that attitude markers "indicate the writer's affective, rather than epistemic, attitude to propositions" (p.180).

To conclude, given the inherent connection of knowledge-making practices and the epistemic purposes served by knowledge emotion markers, these linguistically expressed emotions in academic writing are epistemically motivated. This is probably why Silva (2009, 2019) has included surprise, interest, and confusion in the family of knowledge emotions.

Chapter Eight Conclusions

8.1 Major Findings

This study, drawing on the frame semantic approach, conducted a fine-grained analysis of the employment of knowledge emotion markers (surprise, interest, and confusion markers) in RAs from an integrated perspective that attend simultaneously to disciplinary, gender-based, geo-academic, and historical influences on academic discourse. The synchronic and diachronic perspectives help increase our understanding of current academic writing as a complex and negotiated task. This section summarizes the primary findings concerning the five research questions that guided this study.

1) The knowledge emotion frame in RAs

Informed by frame semantics, this study generated semantic frames of surprise, interest, and confusion markers in scholarly communication based on the analyses of their distinct frame elements and the interconnections among frames. Specifically, the Surprise frame was found to comprise five frame elements: Trigger, Degree, Explanation, Resolution, and Experiencer with different subcategories. The Interest frame and the Confusion frame encompassed four similar frame elements: Trigger, Degree, Explanation, and Experiencer, with each frame element having its distinctive subcategories.

Given the shared cognitive characteristics of the semantic frames evoked by surprise, interest, and confusion markers, a generic knowledge emotion frame was generated. The proposed knowledge emotion frame enabled a coherent frame-based analysis of knowledge emotion markers deployed in academic discourse and redefined the evoked frame elements' core/peripheral status characterized in FrameNet. It assigned Trigger, Explanation and Resolution as core frame elements, Degree and Experiencer as peripheral frame elements.

In addition, this analytical framework integrated key attributes of the Surprise, Interest and Confusion frames and thus well accounts for the shared and distinctive semantic properties of knowledge emotion markers deployed by academics for scientific communication. For example, the frame element of Resolution was found to be unique for the Surprise frame, while Trigger, Explanation, Degree, and Experiencer were found to be shared by the Surprise, Interest and Confusion frames. Relationship, Phenomenon, and Attribute, the three subcategories of Trigger, were shared by the Surprise, Interest and Confusion frames, whereas the other two subcategories of Trigger (i.e. Appraisal and Knowledge Gap) were distinctive to the Interest frame and Confusion frame, respectively. Furthermore, this framework sheds light on the interaction of knowledge emotion markers with other metadiscursive resources. For instance, linguistically expressed emotions indexing academic authors' epistemic attitudes could be boosted, mitigated, and accompanied by self-mentions in scholarly communication.

2) Use of knowledge emotion markers across disciplines

Quantitative findings based on corpus analyses

Academic writers in the four disciplines (Applied Linguistics, History, Biology, and Mechanical Engineering) did not differ in the frequencies with which they employed knowledge emotion markers in their RAs. However, some discipline-related differences were noted in their employment of some frame elements of these markers for academic communication.

Regarding the use of surprise markers, scholars from the pure disciplines were 3.24 times more likely than those from the applied disciplines to express their surprises triggered by Relationship. Moreover, the hard scientists were 2.34 times more likely to express surprises triggered by Attribute than their counterparts from the soft disciplines were. In addition, linguistic expressions of surprise caused by Behavior were 4.22 times more likely to be found in RAs written by scholars from the soft disciplines than those from the hard disciplines. Furthermore, academic authors from the hard disciplines were 1.66 times more likely than their soft-discipline counterparts to leave the expressed surprises unexplained. Additionally, RAs written by scholars from the soft disciplines were 2.72 times more likely than those from the hard fields to provide speculative resolutions to the expressed surprise. The former group of RAs were 2.9 times more likely than the latter group to tone up expressed surprises. Finally, they were 4.65 times more likely to describe the expressed surprises toward Participants than the latter group.

Regarding the use of interest markers, RAs in the soft disciplines were 3.92 times more likely to evaluate the value, significance, or implications of the findings obtained from the current study or previous studies than those in the hard sciences were. Moreover, expressed interest triggered by newly proposed hypotheses or potential research trends was 2.8 times more likely to be found in RAs in the pure disciplines than the applied ones. In addition, researchers from the hard disciplines were 1.72 times more likely to express interest caused by internal factors related to the characteristics of research objects, procedures, and variables than the soft ones. Finally, the latter group of researchers were 3.42 times more likely than the former group to intensify their expressed interest in scientific communication.

Concerning the use of confusion markers, RAs in the hard disciplines were 3.74 times more likely than those in the soft ones to describe confusion evoked by a Knowledge Gap. Moreover, linguistic expressions of confusion triggered by Attribute were 2.98 times more likely to be found in RAs written by scholars from the soft disciplines than those written by the hard scientists. Furthermore, the latter group were twice more likely not to explain the source of expressed confusion than the former group were. Finally, soft-discipline scholars were 1.53 times more likely than their hard-discipline counterparts to tone up their expressed confusion in RAs .

Qualitative findings based on semi-structured interviews

The disciplinary experts' responses in the interviews indicated that the epistemological assumptions underpinning their disciplines shaped disciplinary norms and conventions. The academics' deployment of knowledge emotion markers to draw readers' attention, validate their knowledge claims, and, above all, promote their research was a shared knowledge-making practice across the four disciplines. Nevertheless, disciplinary knowledge-making conventions and knowledge/knower structure prevailing in different disciplines accounted for academics' use of knowledge emotion markers for scientific communication. Notably, knowledge emotion markers deployed in RAs motivated academic authors to process cognitive discrepancies and thus signal their epistemic attitudes.

3) Use of knowledge emotion markers by male and female academics

Quantitative findings based on corpus analyses

The male and female authors of the articles in my corpus did not show different preferences for the use or non-use of knowledge emotion markers in general. Nevertheless, some gender-linked discoursal characteristics related to the use of these markers were detected.

Regarding the use of surprise markers, the male scientists were 2.75 times more likely than their female counterparts to leave sources of the expressed surprises unidentified. Furthermore, the female scholars were 3.1 times more likely than their male counterparts to scale up expressed surprise. In addition, they were more likely (i.e. 4.1 times) to associate themselves with the expressed surprise than the male researchers were.

Regarding the use of interest markers, the female authors were 1.85 times more likely to explain the reason for the expressed interest than the male researchers were. Moreover, they were 2.92 times more likely to tone up the expressed interest than their male counterparts were. Furthermore, they were 2.43 times more likely to describe themselves as the experiencers of the expressed interest.

Regarding confusion markers, the female researchers were 1.87 times more likely to explain the source of confusion than their male counterparts were. In addition, they were 1.9 times more likely than the male academics to tone up their expressed confusion. Finally, they were 1.78 times more likely to describe themselves as the people who experienced the expressed confusion.

Qualitative findings based on semi-structured interviews

The male and female informants' comments on their deployment of knowledge emotion markers in gender-specific ways demonstrated that they had different perceptions of what was deemed essential in effective academic communication. The male scholars attached much importance to conciseness in academic writing, while their female counterparts valued clarity. Moreover, the female researchers' under-representation and disadvantaged position in academia motivated them to seek writer-reader solidarity-building and co-construction of knowledge through their authorial presence as disciplinary experts.

4) Use of knowledge emotion markers by Core- and Periphery-based academics

Quantitative findings based on corpus analyses

It was found that scholars from the Core and Periphery research communities did not show many differences in the overall use of knowledge emotion markers in their RAs. However, these two groups of scholars exhibited some location-based differences in their deployment of some frame elements of knowledge emotion markers.

Regarding the use of surprise markers, academics based in the Periphery regions were 4.67 times more likely to express their surprise toward findings yielded by the current study than their counterparts from the Core regions were. Moreover, the latter group was 3.21 times more likely to leave the expressed surprises unexplained than the former group were. Furthermore, the Periphery-based scholars were 2.42 times more likely than their Core-based counterparts to tone down their expressed surprise, while the latter group was 3.11 times more likely to boost their expressed surprise than the former group. In addition, RAs written by the Core-based scholars were more likely (i.e. 3.24 times) to describe themselves as experiencers of expressed surprise than their Periphery-based counterparts were.

Regarding the use of interest markers, the Periphery-based academics were 1.81 times more likely to evaluate the significance or implications of the findings from the current study or previous studies than their Core-based counterparts were. Moreover, expressions of interest triggered by newly proposed hypotheses or potential research trends were 2.14 times more likely to be found in RAs written by the Core-based scholars. Furthermore, the Core-based academics were 2.85 times more likely not to identify the source of the expressed interest than their Periphery-based counterparts were. In addition, the Periphery-based academics were 3.32 times more likely than their Core-based counterparts to soften their expressed interest, whereas the latter group were 1.97 times more likely than the former group to intensify the expressed interest. Finally, the Core-based scholars were 1.54 times more likely to describe themselves as experiencers of expressed interest than those from the Periphery were.

Concerning the use of confusion markers, scholars from the Core regions were 2.53 times more likely to express confusion triggered by a Knowledge Gap than their counterparts from the Periphery regions were. Additionally, the Periphery-based academics were 1.56 times more likely than their Core-based counterparts to tone down their expressed confusion. In contrast, the latter group was 1.3 times more likely to tone up their expressed confusion than the former group was. Finally, academics from the Core were 1.66 times more likely to describe themselves as the people who experienced confusion than those from the Periphery were.

Qualitative findings based on semi-structured interviews

The informant's attitudes toward English publications were positive, although scholars from the Periphery regions expressed their concerns related to the accuracy and appropriateness of linguistically expressed emotions to achieve persuasiveness of their arguments in English academic writing. Furthermore, their responses showed that their choice of knowledge emotion markers was associated with where they were in the pyramid of academia. In the publication market dominated by scholars from the Core, the Periphery-based academics were motivated to invest more effort to claim the centrality and novelty of their research by deploying knowledge emotion markers in order to increase their chances of publication. In addition, they were more willing to open up a dialogic space by softening the expressed emotions for the sake of soliciting solidarity with potential readers. In contrast, the Core-based scholars' role of "knowledge keepers" gave them a privileged position in the knowledge production market. This advantage inclined them to boost their expressed emotions with self-mentions to construct an authoritative, credible and confident discoursal persona in scholarly communication.

5) Use of knowledge emotion markers over time

Quantitative findings based on corpus analyses

Many diachronic differences in the use of knowledge emotion markers were found in RAs published in the two periods of time. Overall, academic writers publishing in the more recent period tended to use knowledge emotion markers more frequently than did their counterparts publishing 30 years ago. Specifically, scholars in the more recent period (2015-2019) were 1.96 times more likely to express surprise, 2.31 times more likely to express interest, and 1.38 times more likely to express confusion than their counterparts in the earlier period (1985-1989).

Regarding the use of surprise markers, academics publishing during the two time periods were not found to differ in the frequencies with which they described what triggered expressed surprises. However, the RAs published more recently were 1.81 times more likely to express interest triggered by Appraisal than those published earlier were. Regarding what caused confusion, the former group of RAs were more likely to describe confusion triggered by a Knowledge Gap than the latter group were.

Notably, for the frame elements of Explanation, Degree, and Experiencer, the knowledge emotions expressed in the corpus of RAs exhibited shared patterns. Specifically, academics in the more recent period were 2.54 times more likely to explain the expressed surprise, 2.93 times more likely to explain the expressed interest, and 1.74 times more likely to explain the expressed confusion than those from the earlier period were. In particular, the former group was 2.23 times more likely than the latter group to describe the expressed interest caused by external factors related to the findings of previous research. Furthermore, academics publishing in the more recent period were 2.12 times more likely to tone up the expressed surprise, 1.91 times more likely to intensify the expressed interest, and 1.77 times more likely to scale up the expressed confusion than those publishing in the earlier period. Moreover, academics in the recent period were more likely to identify who experienced these emotive responses: 3.19 times more likely for surprise markers, 2.36 times more likely for interest markers, and 2.16 times more likely for confusion markers. Furthermore, the articles published in the more recent period were more likely to describe authors as experiencers of the expressed surprise (2.79 times), expressed interest (1.66 times), and expressed confusion (1.25 times) than those published in the earlier period.

Qualitative findings based on semi-structured interviews

The informants' responses regarding diachronic changes in the use of knowledge emotion markers depicted a picture of an increasingly competitive publication market where the "publish or perish" dictum swept across research institutes and universities (Hyland, 2015). In such an academic context, researchers need to promote the novelty, significance, and contributions of their research through deploying these evaluative resources. Moreover, to enhance the persuasiveness of their knowledge claims, they tend to take a more involved, personal affective stance to persuade readers of the significance of their research than their counterparts did 30 years ago. Furthermore, with the increasing specialization of disciplines, the emergence of subfields and interdisciplinary fields, and a less predictable readership, academics are expected to claim knowledge more explicitly rather than relying on readers' disciplinary knowledge to assess the value of their research.

8.2 Contributions of the present study

The investigation into linguistically expressed surprise, interest, and confusion in RAs through the lens of frame semantics has made several significant contributions to the current body of literature on academic writing.

First, this study represents a new attempt to investigate academic writing from a cognitive perspective and has extended the application of frame semantics to academic discourse studies. Theoretically, the proposed knowledge emotion frame assigns the frame elements found in FrameNet with a new core/peripheral status. It enables us to capture the salient linguistic and semantic properties of expressed emotions for scholarly communication. Moreover, this framework reveals the shared and distinctive cognitive characteristics of surprise, interest, and confusion markers manifested in various linguistic forms, such as verbs, nouns, adjectives, or phrases for knowledge construction in academic writing. Furthermore, the frame-based analyses offer a new perspective for examining metadiscoursal resources in academic prose and, notably, make it possible to analyze the contextualized interplay of different metadiscursive resources deployed by academic writers. The proposed generic frame offers a means for research on academic discourse to draw on current psychological work on cognitive underpinnings, joint antecedents and interrelations of emotions such as surprise, interest, and confusion (Nerantzaki & Efklides, 2019; Nerantzaki et al., 2021; Muis et al., 2015; Vogl et al., 2021). Recent psychological research has revealed that these emotions are dynamic and can change when cognitive processing progresses. For example, surprise may trigger confusion if novelty leads to cognitive impasses (Nerantzaki et al., 2021), and dissolved confusion may prompt interest (Pekerun & Stephens, 2012). The proposed knowledge emotion frame provides a semantic perspective on how such underpinnings and interconnections may be construed and realized linguistically in academic discourse to serve particular rhetorical and communicative purposes. Methodologically, the combination of corpus-based analyses and ethnographic inquiry probing into the situational context of academic writing has yielded evidence of what motivates scholars to employ knowledge emotion markers in scientific communication. Such an attempt could shed new light on the context in which written texts are produced and thus provide us with a fuller understanding of how academic authors' epistemic considerations help shape their academic writing.

Second, this study contributes to the existing research on cross-disciplinary variations in academic writing by revealing discipline-specific use of knowledge emotion markers for knowledge construction and writer-reader interaction in RAs. These observed differences help us better understand the epistemological beliefs and discursive knowledge-making practices espoused by academics across disciplines and in particular, the impact of disciplinarity on stance-taking manifested in the choice of linguistically expressed emotions.

Third, the study provides new empirical evidence of gender-specific discourse in science communities and adds new empirical support to the current debate on the question of to what extent academic discourse is gendered. The observed gender-based differences in the use of knowledge emotion markers point to the mediating role of gender in shaping the way scientific knowledge is constructed and communicated. It furthers our understanding of how gender is enacted in the practices of academia.

Fourth, this study offers some insights into how authors' geo-academic location may influence the use of knowledge emotion markers. Academic values, attitudes, and conventions are socially constitutive and inseparable from the physical space where texts are produced. The location-based differences suggest possible connections of different geographically located research communities and their specific ways of valuing, constructing, and transmitting knowledge. These findings add valuable insights into scholarly discursive practices in research communities to which academics geographically belong.

Finally, this study adds a diachronic perspective on academic discourse by investigating the use of specific types of attitude markers over a period of 30 years. These identified changes in the deployment of knowledge emotion markers reveal the evolution of scientific thoughts and academic writing to communicate such ideas. The diachronic changes observed in this study regarding the use of attitude markers differ from those reported in some previous research, underscoring the need to conduct more scholarly inquiries into the interplay of time-related factors and the deployment of metadiscursive resources. Such endeavors would allow us to gain more historically embedded knowledge of academic prose.

8.3 Pedagogical implications of the present study

Apart from the contributions mentioned above, this study has important pedagogical implications. The findings can inform students, L2 writers, and novice researchers of the heuristic role that linguistically expressed knowledge emotions can play in establishing knowledge claims and effectively communicating scientific information. These linguistic resources are helpful and useful for them to learn to anchor their affective and epistemic stance in relation to their readers' expectations, construct a credible image, and build up an interpersonal relation contributing to legitimating their knowledge claims.

First, the discipline-specific way of using knowledge emotion markers found in the present study focused on linguistic realizations at the micro level in academic writing. It helps raise the awareness of students or novice researchers about the nature of disciplinary discourse in general and the importance of discipline-specific language in particular. Such understandings would assist them in acquiring a more disciplinary-sensitive repertoire of discursive resources to convey an appropriate authorial identity for more effective academic communication. Particularly in a research context where cross-disciplinary or interdisciplinary research is encouraged, it is essential to give them language support because a good understanding of disciplinary conventions can facilitate and enhance interdisciplinary collaborations.

Second, the gendered patterns of employing knowledge emotion markers could add to students' understanding of gender-specific penchants for metadiscursive resources, empower them with a wider range of effective stance-taking resources that include other-sex preferred ones, and encourage "successful boundary crossing" (Belcher, 1997, p.15). The location-based differences found in the corpus regarding the use of knowledge emotion markers could help students develop better awareness of the mediating impact of these linguistic markers on preferred knowledge-making practices that are geographically defined. The non-core based academics or novice writers can probably better acculturate themselves into appropriate ways of claiming knowledge consistent with the "promotional" feature of English academic writing.

Third, time-based differences in deploying knowledge emotion makers for communicating science revealed by the present study enable students to develop understandings of the relationship between diachronic changes in knowledge-making practices and discursive practices, notably the impact of broader socio-historical factors on academic prose. More importantly, the evolving academic discourse suggests that students should be instructed with updating text examples using such linguistic resources for academic communication.

Finally, this study sheds some light on the design of academic writing curricula and programs. Informed by the findings, I argue that EAP instructors should teach the use of metadiscourse resources such as linguistic expressions of emotions explicitly. Such instructions will better help students command a repertoire of linguistic resources of knowledge emotion markers. In addition to giving pedagogical attention to generic approaches (e.g. moves and rhetorical structure) to academic writing, course designers should incorporate rhetorical strategies realized by knowledge emotion markers into classroom teaching. Moreover, tailor-made or discipline-specific courses should be offered to meet students' rhetorical needs. The knowledge emotion frame with elaborated frame elements and typical examples of the deployment of knowledge emotion markers found in the corpus have potential pedagogical value and can be incorporated into EAP-related classroom teaching and learning activities. These materials could help enhance students' understanding of the strategic deployment of discursive resources for legitimating knowledge claims. Moreover, the materials would help expand students' knowledge of how metadiscursive linguistic resources contribute to interpersonal meaning beyond sentences.

8.4 Limitations of the study and directions for future research

Despite the contributions of and the implications derived from the study, it has some limitations that future studies can address. First, the proposed knowledge emotion frame was based on RAs sampled from four disciplines. It is unclear whether it applies to the subdisciplines within a discipline since subdisciplines may have their distinct writing conventions. Furthermore, it needs to be validated whether this framework can be extended to other academic genres, such as book reviews, grant proposals, doctoral theses, academic blogs, or spoken discourse such as conference presentations, lectures, and seminars. Thus, studies covering more disciplines and investigating other academic genres are called for. In particular, it is worthwhile to examine whether interdisciplinarity may impact the use of knowledge emotion markers as more trans-disciplinary and interdisciplinary research is emerging.

Second, it is possible that an author's writing style or journal-preferred stylistic features may influence the linguistic expression of knowledge emotions for epistemic purposes. Furthermore, authors' affiliations do not necessarily reflect locally defined knowledge-making practices due to academics' increasing mobility. Moreover, this study did not consider the authors' nationality, L1 background, ethnicity, educational background, or cultural background. The binary categories adopted such as the Core/Periphery may blur some intra-group differences. It would be interesting to examine the interplay of these demographic factors and the deployment of knowledge emotion markers. In addition, it would be potentially revealing to examine the interactive effects of different variables, for example, the interaction of disciplinarity and geo-academic locations or gender and historical context. Such attempts could add to our understanding of the complex nature of scholarly practices in communicating science.

Third, the proposed knowledge emotion frame for academic communication could be used to conduct comparative research across languages, writing groups (e.g. L2 writers and expert writers), research paradigms (quantitative vs qualitative) and different sections (introduction, discussions, or conclusions) of research articles. Moreover, the use of knowledge emotions can be examined together with a move analysis to reveal how they are used in tandem with discoursal moves/steps in the progression of macro logico-semantic structures and in the furtherance of rhetorical purposes. These scholarly inquiries are expected to yield a more in-depth understanding of the role that these markers play in knowledge construction and scientific communication.

Appendix: Interview Schedule

- Introduction: greetings and briefings on the interview
- Warm-up questions

  1) number of international publications

  2) age, academic background (title), first language

  3) the purpose of academic writing
- General questions

  4) How would you describe the nature of your discipline? Is there a particular way to write to claim knowledge in your field?

  5) As an author, why did you express surprise/interest/confusion in your research article? As a reader, why do you think the author(s) choose to use these expressions in research articles?

  6) Do you think male and female academic writers in your discipline have different writing styles? Why or why not?

  7) What do you think about the use of English as the international language for scientific communication?

  8) Do you think that the dominance of English in international publication gives an advantage to native speakers? If yes, in what ways?

  9) Have you perceived any changes in academic writing in your discipline across 30 years?
- Text-based questions

  10) Please look at this extract in which you have used surprise/interest/confusion markers. Why did you use this kind of expression? Is this a rhetorical strategy? Is this use discipline-specific?

  11) Please look at this extract in which you have used surprise/interest/confusion markers. Do you think your male/female colleagues would use it in a

different way?

12) Please look at this extract in which you have used surprise/interest/confusion markers. Do you think academics based in the core/peripheral research institutions would use it in a different way?

13) Please look at this extract of a publication in 1980s. Do you think the use of such expressions has changed over 30 years? Is such use more popular than 30 years ago?

- Wrap-up

14) Thank you for providing me with the information regarding the use of linguistically expressed surprise/interest/confusion in scientific communication. Is there anything you would like to further comment on or to add?

15) Thank you so much for your valuable time for this interview! I highly appreciate your kind help in this study!

References

Abdi, R. Interpersonal metadiscourse: An indicator of interaction and identity [J]. *Discourse Studies*, 2002, *4*(2): 139-145.

Acharya, A. Global international relations (IR) and regional worlds: A new agenda for international studies [J]. *International Studies Quarterly*, 2014, *58*(4): 647-659.

Ädel, A. *Metadiscourse in L1 and L2 English*[M]. Amsterdam: John Benjamins, 2006.

Agnew, J. Know-where: Geographies of knowledge of world politics[J]. *International Political Sociology*, 2007, *1*(2): 138-148.

Agnew, J. A., & Livingstone, D. N. *The Sage handbook of geographical knowledge*[M]. Thousand Oaks: Sage, 2011.

Alejandro, A. *Western dominance in international relations? The internationalisation of IR in Brazil and India*[M]. London: Routledge, 2018.

Baker, C. F., Fillmore, C. J., & Cronin, B. The structure of the FrameNet database[J]. *International Journal of Lexicography*, 2003, *16*(3): 281-296.

Becher, T. *Academic tribes and territories*[M]. Milton Keynes: Open University Press, 1989.

Belcher, D. An argument for nonadversarial argumentation: on the relevance of the feminist critique of academic discourse to L2 writing pedagogy[J]. *Journal of Second Language Writing*, 1997(6): 1-21.

Becher, T., & Trowler, P. *Academic tribes and territories: Intellectual enquiry and the culture of disciplines*[M]. Buckingham: Open University Press, 2001.

Belcher, D. D. How research space is created in a diverse research world[J]. *Journal of Second Language Writing*, 2009, *18*(4): 221-234.

Bennett, K. (Ed.). *The semiperiphery of academic writing: Discourses, communities and practices*[M]. Basingtoke: Palgrave Macmillan, 2014.

Berkenkotter, C., & Huckin, T. N. *Genre knowledge in disciplinary communication: Cognition/culture/power*[M]. New York: Routledge, 2016.

Boyatzis, R. E. *Transforming qualitative information: Thematic analysis and code development*[M]. London: Sage, 1998.

Braun V., & Clarke V. *Thematic analysis: A practical guide*[M]. London: Sage, 2021.

Cameron, D. Sex/Gender, language and the new biologism[J]. *Applied Linguistics,* 2010, *31*(2): 173-192.

Canagarajah, A. S. *A geopolitics of academic writing*[M]. Pittsburgh: University of Pittsburgh Press, 2002.

Canagarajah, S. *Translingual practice: Global Englishes and cosmopolitan relations*[M]. New York: Routledge, 2013.

Canagarajah, S. Agency and power in intercultural communication: Negotiating English in translocal spaces[J]. *Language and Intercultural Communication*, 2013, *13*(2): 202-224.

Candiotto, L. From philosophy of emotion to epistemology: Some questions about the epistemic relevance of emotions[M]// L. Candiotto (Ed.). *The value of emotions for knowledge*. Cham: Palgrave Macmillan, 2019: 3-24.

Cao, F., & Hu, G. Interactive metadiscourse in research articles: A comparative study of paradigmatic and disciplinary influences[J]. *Journal of Pragmatics*, 2014 (66): 15-31.

Catalini, C., Lacetera, N., & Oettl, A. The incidence and role of negative citations in science[J]. *Proceedings of the National Academy of Sciences*, 2015, *112*(45): 13823-13826.

Chaplin, T. M., & Aldao, A. Gender differences in emotion expression in children: a meta-analytic review[J]. *Psychological Bulletin*, 2013, *139*(4):735-765.

Chen, L., & Hu, G. Surprise markers in applied linguistics research articles: A diachronic perspective[J]. *Lingua*, 2020a(248): 102992.

Chen, L., & Hu, G. Mediating knowledge through expressing surprises: A frame-based analysis of surprise markers in research articles across disciplines and research paradigms[J]. *Discourse Processes*, 2020b, *57*(8): 659-681.

Chevrier, M., Muis, K. R., Trevors, G. J., Pekrun, R., & Sinatra, G. M. Exploring the antecedents and consequences of epistemic emotions[J]. *Learning and Instruction*, 2019 (63): 101209.

Coates, J. *Women, men and language*[M]. London: Longman, 1993.

Cohen, L., Manion, L., & Morrison, K. *Research methods in education* [M]. 7th ed. London: Routledge, 2011.

Collyer, F. M. Global patterns in the publishing of academic knowledge: Global North, global South[J]. *Current Sociology*, 2018, *66*(1): 56-73.

Connelly, D. A. Applying Silvia's model of interest to academic text: Is there a third appraisal?[J]. *Learning and Individual Differences*, 2011, *21*(5): 624-628.

Cottone, R. R. Paradigms of counseling and psychotherapy, revisited: Is social constructivism a paradigm? [J]. *Journal of Mental Health Counseling*, 2007 (29): 189-203.

Creswell, J. W., & Creswell, J. D. *Research design: Qualitative, quantitative, and mixed methods approaches*[M]. London: Sage Publications, 2017.

Crismore, A., Markkanen, R., & Steffensen, M. S. Metadiscourse in persuasive writing: A study of texts written by American and Finnish university students[J]. *Written Communication*, 1993, *10*(1): 39-71.

Curry, M. J., & Lillis, T. Problematizing English as the Privileged Language of Global Academic Publishing[M]// M. J. Curry & T. Lillis (Eds.). *Global academic publishing: Policies, perspectives and pedagogies*. Clevedon: Multilingual Matters, 2017: 1-20.

Dahl, T. Textual metadiscourse in research articles: A marker of national culture or of academic discipline?[J]. *Journal of Pragmatics*, 2004, *36*(10): 1807-1825.

Del Olmo, S. O. Hedging and attitude markers in Spanish and English scientific medical writing[M]// A. Zuczkowski, R. Bongelli, I. Riccioni & C. Canestrari (Eds.). *Communicating certainty and uncertainty in medical, supportive and scientific contexts*. Amsterdam: John Benjamins, 2014: 273-290.

DeSteno, D., Petty, R. E., Rucker, D. D., Wegener, D. T., & Braverman, J. Discrete emotions and persuasion: the role of emotion-induced expectancies[J]. *Journal of Personality and Social Psychology*, 2004, *86*(1): 43-56.

D'Mello, S., & Graesser, A. Dynamics of affective states during complex learning[J]. *Learning and Instruction*, 2012, *22*(2): 145-157.

D'Mello, S., Lehman, B., Pekrun, R., & Graesser, A. Confusion can be beneficial for learning[J]. *Learning and Instruction*, 2014 (29): 153-170.

Dontcheva-Navratilova, O. Cross-cultural variation in the use of hedges and boosters in academic discourse[J]. *Prague Journal of English Studies*, 2016, *5*(1):163-184.

Dörnyei, Z. *Research methods in applied linguistics*[M]. Oxford: Oxford University Press, 2007.

Faber, P. *A Cognitive linguistics view of terminology and specialized language*[M]. Berlin: De Gruyter Mouton, 2012.

Faber, P., Araúz, P. L., Prieto Velasco, J. A., & Reimerink, A. Linking images and words: The description of specialized concepts[J]. *International Journal of Lexicography*, 2007, *20*(1): 39-65.

Faber, P., León, P., & Prieto, J. A. Semantic relations, dynamicity, and terminological knowledge bases[J]. *Current Issues in Language Studies*, 2009, *1*(1): 1-23.

Fewer, G. Beyond the language barrier[J]. *Nature*, 1997, *385*(6619): 764-764.

Fillmore, C. J. Frames and the semantics of understanding[J]. *Quaderni Di Semantica*, 1985, *6*(2): 222-254.

Fillmore, C. J., & Baker, C. Frame approaches to semantic analysis[M]// In B. Heine & H. Narrog (Eds.). *The Oxford handbook of linguistic analysis*. Oxford: Oxford University Press, 2010: 313-340.

Fillmore, C. J., Johnson, C. R., & Petruck, M. R. Background to framenet[J]. *International Journal of Lexicography*, 2003, *16*(3): 235-250.

Fløttum, K., Dahl, T., & Kinn, T. *Academic voices: Across languages and disciplines* (Vol. 148)[M]. London: John Benjamins, 2006.

Francis, B. Gender monoglossia, gender heterglossia: The potential of Bakhtin's work for re-conceptualising gender[J]. *Journal of Gender Studies*, 2012, *21*(1): 1-15.

Francis, B., Robson, J., & Read, B. An analysis of undergraduate writing styles in the context of gender and achievement[J]. *Studies in Higher Education*, 2001, *26*(3): 313-326.

Francis, B., Read, B., Melling, L., & Robson, J. University lecturers' perceptions of gender and undergraduate writing[J]. *British Journal of Sociology of Education*, 2003, *24*(3): 357-373.

Fuchs, R. Do women (still) use more intensifiers than men?: Recent change in the sociolinguistics of intensifiers in British English[J]. *International Journal of Corpus Linguistics*, 2017, *22*(3): 345-374.

Gardner, S. Genres and registers of student report writing: An SFL perspective on texts and practices[J]. *Journal of English for Academic Purposes*, 2012, *11*(1): 52-63.

Garfield, E. The history and meaning of the journal impact factor[J]. *Journal of the American Medical Association*, 2006, *295* (1): 90-93.

Gillaerts, P., & Van de Velde, F. Interactional metadiscourse in research article abstracts[J]. *Journal of English for Academic Purposes*, 2010, *9*(2): 128-139.

Graham, M., Hale, S., & Stephens, M. *Geographies of the world's knowledge*[M]. London: Convoco! Edition, 2011.

Greene, J. C. *Mixed Methods in Social Inquiry*[M]. San Francisco: Jossey-Bass, 2007.

Gregson, N. A., Simonsen, K., & Vaiou, D. Writing (across) Europe: On writing spaces and writing practices[J]. *European Urban and Regional Studies*, 2003, *10*(1): 5-22.

Hallgren, K. A. Computing inter-rater reliability for observational data: An overview and tutorial[J]. *Tutorials in Quantitative Methods for Psychology*, 2012, *8*(1): 23-34.

Halliday, M. A. K., & Matthiessen, C. M. I. M. *Halliday's introduction to Functional Grammar* [M]. 4th ed. London: Routledge, 2013.

Hanauer, D. I., Sheridan, C. L., & Englander, K. Linguistic injustice in the writing of research articles in English as a second language[J]. *Written Communication*, 2019, *36*(1):136-154.

Hess, U., Senécal, S., Kirouac, G., Herrera, P., Philippot, P., & Kleck, R. E. Emotional expressivity in men and women: Stereotypes and self-perceptions[J]. *Cognition & Emotion*, 2000, *14*(5): 609-642.

Hidi, S., & Renninger, K. A. The four-phase model of interest development[J]. *Educational Psychologist*, 2006, *41*(2): 111-127.

Hinds, J. Reader versus writer responsibility: A new typology [M]// T. Silva & P. K. Matsuda (Eds.). *Landmark essays on ESL writing*. New York: Routledge, 2001: 63-72.

Hookway, C. Affective states and epistemic immediacy[J]. *Metaphilosophy*, 2003,

34 (1): 78-96.

Hu, G., & Cao, F. Disciplinary and paradigmatic influences on interactional metadiscourse in research articles[J]. *English for Specific Purposes*, 2015 (39): 12-25.

Hu, G., & Chen, L. "To our great surprise…": A frame-based analysis of surprise markers in research articles[J]. *Journal of Pragmatics*, 2019 (143): 156-168.

Hu, G., & Wang, G. Disciplinary and ethnolinguistic influences on citation in research articles[J]. *Journal of English for Academic Purposes*, 2014 (14): 14-28.

Hyland, K. Humble servants of the discipline? Self-mention in research articles[J]. *English for Specific Purposes*, 2001, *20*(3): 207-226.

Hyland, K. Stance and engagement: A model of interaction in academic discourse[J]. *Discourse Studies*, 2005a, *7*(2): 173-192.

Hyland, K. *Metadiscourse: Exploring interaction in writing*[M]. London: Continuum, 2005b.

Hyland, K. Genre and academic writing in the disciplines[J]. *Language Teaching*, 2008, *41*(4): 543-562.

Hyland, K. Disciplines and discourses: Social interactions in the construction of knowledge[M]// D. Starke-Meyerring, A. Paré, N. Artemeva, M. Horne, & L. Yousoubova (Eds.). *Writing in knowledge societies: Perspectives on writing*. West Lafayette: Parlor Press, 2011: 193-214.

Hyland, K. *Academic publishing: Issues and challenges in the construction of knowledge*[M]. Oxford: Oxford University Press, 2015.

Hyland, K. Metadiscourse: What is it and where is it going?[J]. *Journal of Pragmatics*, 2017 (113): 16-29.

Hyland, K., & Bondi, M. (Eds.). *Academic discourse across disciplines* (Vol. 42)[M]. Bern: Peter Lang, 2006.

Hyland, K., & Jiang, F. K. "We must conclude that…": A diachronic study of academic engagement[J]. *Journal of English for Academic Purposes*, 2016a (24): 29-42.

Hyland, K., & Jiang, F. K. Change of attitude? A diachronic study of stance[J]. *Written Communication*, 2016b, *33*(3): 251-274.

Hyland, K., & Jiang, F. K. Is academic writing becoming more informal?[J]. *English for Specific Purposes*, 2017 (45): 40-51.

Hyland, K., & Jiang, F. K. "We Believe That… ": Changes in an academic stance marker[J]. *Australian Journal of Linguistics*, 2018a, *38*(2): 139-161.

Hyland, K., & Jiang, F. K. "In this paper we suggest": Changing patterns of disciplinary metadiscourse[J]. *English for Specific Purposes*, 2018b (51): 18-30.

Hyland, K., & Jiang, F. K. Points of reference: Changing patterns of academic citation[J]. *Applied Linguistics*, 2019, *40*(1): 64-85.

Jackson, C. Disciplining gender?[J]. *World Development*, 2002, *30*(3): 497-509.

Jiang. F. K., & Hyland, K. Nouns and academic interactions: A neglected feature of metadiscourse[J]. *Applied Linguistics*, 2016, *39*(4): 508-531.

Jiang, F. K., & Hyland, K. Metadiscursive nouns: Interaction and cohesion in abstract moves[J]. *English for Specific Purposes*, 2017 (46): 1-14.

Jiang, F. K., & Hyland, K. "The goal of this analysis…": Changing patterns of metadiscursive nouns in disciplinary writing[J]. *Lingua*, 2021 (252): 103017.

Kachru, B. Standards, codification and sociolinguistic realism: The English language in the outer circle[M]// R. Quirk and H.G. Widdowson (Eds.). *English in the world: Teaching and learning the language and literatures*. Cambridge: Cambridge University Press, 1985: 11-30.

Kang, M. J., Hsu, M., Krajbich, I. M., Loewenstein, G., McClure, S. M., Wang, J. T. Y., & Camerer, C. F. The wick in the candle of learning: Epistemic curiosity activates reward circuitry and enhances memory[J]. *Psychological Science*, 2009, *20*(8): 963-973.

Khedri, M., Heng, C. S., & Ebrahimi, S. F. An exploration of interactive metadiscourse markers in academic research article abstracts in two disciplines[J]. *Discourse Studies*, 2013, *15*(3): 319-331.

Kieńć, W. Authors from the periphery countries choose open access more often[J]. *Learned Publishing*, 2017, *30*(2): 125-131.

Kövecses, Z. Surprise as a conceptual category[J]. *Review of Cognitive Linguistics*, 2015, *13*(2): 270-290.

Kukla, A. *Social constructivism and the philosophy of science*[M]. London: Routledge, 2000.

Landis, J. R., & Koch, G. G. An application of hierarchical kappa-type statistics in the assessment of majority agreement among multiple observers[J]. *Biometrics*,

1977, *33*(2): 363-374.

Larson, J. Other voices: Authors' literary-academic presence and publication in the discursive world system[J]. *Discourse: Studies in the Cultural Politics of Education*, 2018, *39*(4): 521-535.

Lau, K., & Gardner, D. Disciplinary variations in learning styles and preferences: Implications for the provision of academic English[J]. *System*, 2019 (80): 257-268.

Lazarus, R. S. Cognition and motivation in emotion[J]. *American Psychologist*, 1991, *46*(4): 352.

Lehman, B., D'Mello, S., & Graesser, A. Confusion and complex learning during interactions with computer learning environments[J]. *The Internet and Higher Education*, 2012, *15*(3):184-194.

Li, Z. Authorial presence in research article abstracts: A diachronic investigation of the use of first person pronouns[J]. *Journal of English for Academic Purposes*, 2021(51): 100977.

Lillis, T. Ethnography as method, methodology, and "Deep Theorizing" closing the gap between text and context in academic writing research[J]. *Written Communication*, 2008, *25*(3): 353-388.

Lillis, T., & Curry, M. J. *Academic writing in a global context: The politics and practices of publishing in English*[M]. London: Routledge, 2010.

Lillis, T., & Curry, M. J. English, scientific publishing and participation in the global knowledge economy[M]// E. J. Erling, & P. Seargeant (Eds.). *English and development: Policy, pedagogy and globalization*. Bristol: Multilingual Matters, 2013: 220-242.

Lillis, T., & Curry, M. J. Trajectories of knowledge and desire: Multilingual women scholars researching and writing in academia[J]. *Journal of English for Academic Purposes*, 2018 (32): 53-66.

Litman, J. A. Interest and deprivation factors of epistemic curiosity[J]. *Personality and Individual Differences*, 2008 (44): 1585-1595.

Liu, C. Y. Gender and discipline: Intensifier variation in academic lectures[J]. *Corpus Pragmatics*, 2019, *3*(3): 211-224.

L'Homme, M.-C., & Robichaud, B. Frames and terminology: Representing predicative terms in the field of the environment[M]// M. Zock., R. Rapp., &

C.-R. Huang (Eds.). *Proceedings of the 4th Workshop on Cognitive Aspects of the Lexicon*. Dublin: Association for Computational Linguistics and Dublin City University, 2014: 186-197.

Loewenstein, G. The psychology of curiosity: A review and reinterpretation[J]. *Psychological Bulletin*, 1994, *116*(1): 75-98.

Lynch, C. M., & Strauss-Noll, M. Mauve Washers: Sex differences in freshman writing[J]. *The English Journal*, 1987, *76*(1): 90-94.

Mackey, A., & Gass, S. *Second language research: Methodology and design*[M]. New York: Routledge, 2016.

Mansell, R. Power and interests in information and communication and development: Exogenous and endogenous discourses in contention[J]. *Journal of International Development*, 2014, *26*(1): 109-127.

Martin, J. R., & White, P. R. *Language of evaluation: Appraisal in English*[M]. New York: Palgrave Macmillan, 2005.

Martín, P., & Pérez, I. K. L. Convincing peers of the value of one's research: A genre analysis of rhetorical promotion in academic texts[J]. *English for Specific Purposes*, 2014 (34): 1-13.

Martínez, I. A. Native and non-native writers' use of first person pronouns in the different sections of biology research articles in English[J]. *Journal of Second Language Writing*, 2005, *14*(3): 174-190.

Maton, K. Languages of legitimation: The structuring significance for intellectual fields of strategic knowledge claims[J]. *British Journal of Sociology of Education*, 2000, *21*(2): 147-167.

Maton, K. & Moore, R. (Eds.). *Social realism, knowledge and the sociology of education: Coalitions of the mind*[M]. London: Continuum, 2010.

Maton, K. *Knowledge and knowers: Towards a realist sociology of education*[M]. London: Routledge, 2014.

Mauranen, A., Pérez-Llantada, C., & Swales, J. M. Academic Englishes: A standardised knowledge?[M]// A. Kirkpatrick (Ed.). *The Routledge handbook of world Englishes*. New York: Routledge, 2020: 634-652.

Maxwell, N., Connolly, L., & Ní Laoire, C. Informality, emotion and gendered career paths: The hidden toll of maternity leave on female academics and researchers[J]. *Gender, Work & Organization*, 2019, *26*(2): 140-157.

Meyer, W. U., Reisenzein, R., & Schützwohl, A.Toward a process analysis of emotions: The case of surprise[J]. *Motivation and Emotion*,1997, *21*(3): 251-274.

McGrath, L., & Kuteeva, M. Stance and engagement in pure mathematics research articles: Linking discourse features to disciplinary practices[J]. *English for Specific Purposes*, 2012, *31*(3): 161-173.

Mignolo, W. *Local histories/global designs: Coloniality, subaltern knowledges, and border thinking*[M]. Princeton: Princeton University Press, 2012.

Millar, N., Salager-Meyer, F., & Budgell, B. "It is important to reinforce the importance of…": "Hype" in reports of randomized controlled trials[J]. *English for Specific Purposes*, 2019 (54): 139-151.

Moletsane, R. Whose knowledge is it? Towards reordering knowledge production and dissemination in the global South[J]. *Educational Research for Social Change*, 2015, *4*(2): 35-48.

Monroe, K. R., Choi, J., Howell, E., Lampros-Monroe, C., Trejo, C., & Pérez, V. Gender equality in the ivory tower, and how best to achieve it[J]. *PS: Political Science & Politics*, 2014, *47*(2): 418-426.

Mu, C., Zhang, L. J., Ehrich, J., & Hong, H. The use of metadiscourse for knowledge construction in Chinese and English research articles[J]. *Journal of English for Academic Purposes*, 2015 (20): 135-148.

Muis, K. R., Psaradellis, C., Lajoie, S. P., Di Leo, I., & Chevrier, M. The role of epistemic emotions in mathematics problem solving[J]. *Contemporary Educational Psychology*, 2015 (42): 172-185.

Mur-Dueñas, P. Attitude markers in business management research articles: A cross-cultural corpus-driven approach[J]. *International Journal of Applied Linguistics*, 2010, *20*(1): 50-72.

Nerantzaki, K., & Efklides, A. Epistemic emotions: Interrelationships and changes during task processing[J]. *Hellenic Journal of Psychology*, 2019, *16*(2): 177-199.

Nerantzaki, K., Efklides, A., & Metallidou, P. Epistemic emotions: Cognitive underpinnings and relations with metacognitive feelings[J]. *New Ideas in Psychology*, 2021(63): 100904.

Nesi, H., & Gardner, S. Variation in disciplinary culture: University tutors' views on assessed writing tasks[J]. *British Studies in Applied Linguistics*, 2006(21): 99-117.

Nesi, H., & Holmes, J. Verbal and mental processes in academic disciplines[M]// M. Charles, D. Pecorari, & S. Hunston (Eds.). *Academic writing: At the interface of corpus and discourse*. New York: Continuum, 2010: 58-72.

Neumann, R., Parry, S., & Becher, T. Teaching and learning in their disciplinary contexts: A conceptual analysis[J]. *Studies in Higher Education*, 2002, *27*(4): 405-417.

Newman, M. L., Groom, C. J., Handelman, L. D., & Pennebaker, J. W. Gender differences in language use: An analysis of 14,000 text samples[J]. *Discourse Processes*, 2008, *45*(3): 211-236.

Noordewier, M. K., Topolinski, S., & Van Dijk, E. The temporal dynamics of surprise[J]. *Social and Personality Psychology Compass*, 2016, *10*(3): 136-149.

Nygaard, L. P., & Bahgat, K. What's in a number? How (and why) measuring research productivity in different ways changes the gender gap[J]. *Journal of English for Academic Purposes*, 2018 (32): 67-79.

Omidian, T., Shahriari, H., & Siyanova-Chanturia, A. A cross-disciplinary investigation of multi-word expressions in the moves of research article abstracts[J]. *Journal of English for Academic Purposes*, 2018 (36): 1-14.

Paltridge, B. *Genre, frames and writing in research settings*[M]. Amsterdam: John Benjamins, 1997.

Parzuchowski, M., & Szymkow-Sudziarska, A. Well, slap my thigh: Expression of surprise facilitates memory of surprising material[J]. *Emotion*, 2008, *8*(3): 430-434.

Peacock, M. A cross-disciplinary comparison of boosting in research articles[J]. *Corpora*, 2006, *1*(1): 61-84.

Peek, R. P., & Pomerantz, J. P. Electronic scholarly journal publishing[J]. *Annual Review of Information Science and Technology*, 1998 (33): 321-356.

Pennycook, A. *The cultural politics of English as an international language*[M]. London: Routledge, 2017.

Pekrun, R., & Linnenbrink-Garcia, L. Introduction to emotions in education[M]//R. Pekrun & L. Linnenbrink-Garcia (Eds.). *International handbook of emotions in education*. New York: Routledge, 2014: 1-10.

Pekrun, R., & Stephens, E. J. Academic emotions[M]// K. Harris, S. Graham, T. Urdan, S. Graham, J. Royer, & M. Zeidner (Eds.). *APA educational psychology handbook: Individual differences and cultural and contextual factors*. Washington DC: American Psychological Association, 2012: 3-31.

Pekrun, R., Vogl, E., Muis, K. R., & Sinatra, G. M. Measuring emotions during epistemic activities: The epistemically-related emotion Scales[J]. *Cognition and Emotion*, 2017, *31*(6): 1268-1276.

Pérez-Llantada, C. Bringing into focus multilingual realities: Faculty perceptions of academic languages on campus[J]. *Lingua*, 2018 (212): 30-43.

Peterson, S. Gender meanings in grade eight students' talk about classroom writing[J]. *Gender and Education*, 2002, *14*(4): 351-366.

Phillipson, R. *Linguistic imperialism continued*[M]. London: Routledge, 2013.

Polanyi, M. *Personal knowledge*[M]. London: Routledge, 2012.

Poole, R., Gnann, A., & Hahn-Powell, G. Epistemic stance and the construction of knowledge in science writing: A diachronic corpus study[J]. *Journal of English for Academic Purposes*, 2019 (42): 100784.

Qiu, X., & Jiang, F. K. Stance and engagement in 3MT presentations: How students communicate disciplinary knowledge to a wide audience[J]. *Journal of English for Academic Purposes*, 2021 (51): 100976.

Rakedzon, T., Segev, E., Chapnik, N., Yosef, R., & Baram-Tsabari, A. Automatic jargon identifier for scientists engaging with the public and science communication educators[J]. *PloS One*, 2017, *12*(8): e0181742.

Read, B., Robson, J., & Francis, B. Reviewing undergraduate writing: Tutors' perceptions of essay qualities according to gender[J]. *Research in Post-Compulsory Education*, 2004, *9*(2): 217-238.

Reeve, J. *Understanding motivation and emotion*[M]. Hoboken: John Wiley and Sons, 2005.

Reeve, J. How students create motivationally supportive learning environments for themselves: The concept of agentic engagement[J]. *Journal of Educational Psychology*, 2013, *105*(3): 579-595.

Reeve, J., Lee, W., & Won, S. Interest as emotion, as affect, as schema[M]// K. A. Renninger, M. Nieswandt, & S. Hidi (Eds.). *Interest in mathematics and science learning*. Washington, D.C.: American Educational Research Association, 2015:

79-92.

Reisenzein, R. Exploring the strength of association between the components of emotion syndromes: The case of surprise[J]. *Cognition & Emotion*, 2000, *14*(1): 1-38.

Reisenzein, R., Horstmann, G., & Schützwohl, A. The cognitive-evolutionary model of surprise: A review of the evidence[J]. *Topics in Cognitive Science*, 2019, *11*(1): 50-74.

Renninger, K. A., & Hidi, S. *The power of interest for motivation and engagement*[M]. New York: Routledge, 2016.

Renninger, K. A., Hidi, S., Krapp, A., & Renninger, A. *The role of interest in learning and development*[M]. Brandon: Psychology Press, 2014.

Rezaei, S., Kuhi, D., & Saeidi, M. Diachronic corpus analysis of stance markers in research articles: The field of applied linguistics[J]. *Cogent Arts & Humanities*, 2021 (8): 1872165.

Robson, J., Francis, B., & Read, B. Writes of passage: Stylistic features of male and female undergraduate history essays[J]. *Journal of Further and Higher Education*, 2002, *26*(4):351-362.

Rozin, P., & Cohen, A. B. High frequency of facial expressions corresponding to confusion, concentration, and worry in an analysis of naturally occurring facial expressions of Americans[J]. *Emotion*, 2003, *3*(1): 68-75.

Rubin, D. L., & Greene, K. Gender-typical style in written language[J]. *Research in the Teaching of English*, 1992, *26*(1): 7-40.

Ruppenhofer, J., Ellsworth, M., Petruck, M. R. L., Johnson, C. R., & Scheffczyk, J. *FrameNet II: Extended theory and practice*, 2016. Retrieved from: https://framenet2.icsi.berkeley.edu/docs/r1.5/book.pdf.

Sabaj, O., Fuentes, M., & Matsuda, K. Verbal inflection in research article sections[J]. *Estud. Filol*, 2013 (52): 129-142.

Samraj, B. Discourse features of the student-produced academic research paper: variations across disciplinary courses[J]. *Journal of English for Academic Purposes*, 2004, *3*(1): 5-22.

Samraj, B. Introductions in research articles: Variations across disciplines[J]. *English for Specific Purposes*, 2002, *21*(1): 1-17.

Samraj, B. A discourse analysis of master's theses across disciplines with a focus on introductions[J]. *Journal of English for Academic Purposes*, 2008(7): 55-67.

Salager-Meyer, F. Referential behavior in scientific writing: A diachronic study (1810-1995) [J]. *English for Specific Purposes*, 1999, *18*(3): 279-305.

Salager-Meyer, F. Scientific publishing in developing countries: Challenges for the future[J]. *Journal of English for Academic Purposes*, 2008, *7*(2): 121-132.

Salager-Meyer, F., Alcaraz Ariza, M., & Zambrano, N. The scimitar, the dagger and the glove: Intercultural differences in the rhetoric of criticism in Spanish. French and English medical discourse (1930-1995)[J]. *English for Specific Purposes*, 2003 (22): 223-247.

Scherer, K. R. Appraisal considered as a process of multilevel sequential checking[M]// K. R. Scherer, A. Schorr & T. Johnstone (Eds.). *Appraisal processes in emotion: Theory, methods, research*. New York: Oxford University Press, 2001: 92-120.

Schraw, G., Flowerday, T., & Lehman, S. Increasing situational interest in the classroom[J]. *Educational Psychology Review*, 2001, *13*(3): 211-224.

Shaw, P., & Vassileva, I. Co-evolving academic rhetoric across culture; Britain, Bulgaria, Denmark, Germany in the 20th century[J]. *Journal of Pragmatics*, 2009, *41*(2): 290-305.

Shirzad & Jamali. *Gender differences in EFL academic writing*[M]. New York: Lambert Publishing, 2013.

Silvia, P. J. What is interesting? Exploring the appraisal structure of interest[J]. *Emotion*, 2005a, *5*(1): 89-102.

Silvia, P. J. Cognitive appraisals and interest in visual art: Exploring an appraisal theory of aesthetic emotions[J]. *Empirical Studies of the Arts*, 2005b, *23*(2): 119-133.

Silvia, P. J. Interest—the curious emotion[J]. *Current Directions in Psychological Science*, 2008, *17*(1): 57-60.

Silvia, P. J. Looking past pleasure: Anger, confusion, disgust, pride, surprise, and other unusual aesthetic emotions[J]. *Psychology of Aesthetics, Creativity, and the Arts*, 2009, *3*(1): 48-51.

Silvia, P. J. Confusion and interest: The role of knowledge emotions in aesthetic experience[J]. *Psychology of Aesthetics, Creativity, and the Arts*, 2010, *4*(2): 75-80.

Silvia, P. J. Interested experts, confused novices: Art expertise and the knowledge emotions[J]. *Empirical Studies of the Arts*, 2013, *31*(1): 107-115.

Silvia, P. Knowledge emotions: Feelings that foster learning, exploring, and reflecting[M]// R. Biswas-Diener, & E. Diener (Eds.). *Noba textbook series: Psychology*. Champaign: DEF Publishers, 2019: 31-48.

Silvia, P. J., & Berg, C. Finding movies interesting: How appraisals and expertise influence the aesthetic experience of film[J]. *Empirical Studies of the Arts*, 2011, *29*(1): 73-88.

Stenström, A. He was really gormless—She's bloody crap: Girls, boys and intensifers[M]// H. Hasselga'rd, & S. Okesfell (Eds.). *Out of corpora: Studies in honour of Stig Johansson* Amsterdam: Rodopi, 1999: 69-78.

Swales, J. The futures of EAP genre studies: A personal viewpoint[J]. *Journal of English for Academic Purposes*, 2019 (38): 75-82.

Talbot, M. *Language and gender*[M]. Cambridge: Polity, 2010.

Tannen, D. *Gender and discourse*[M]. London: Oxford University Press, 1994.

Teigen, K. H., & Keren, G. Surprises: Low probabilities or high contrasts?[J]. *Cognition*, 2003, *87*(2): 55-71.

Thieme, K., & Saunders, M. A. S. How do you wish to be cited? Citation practices and a scholarly community of care in trans studies research articles[J]. *Journal of English for Academic Purposes*, 2018 (32): 80-90.

Tight, M. Bridging the divide: A comparative analysis of articles in higher education journals published inside and outside North America[J]. *Higher Education*, 2007, *53*(2): 235-253.

Topolinski, S., & Strack, F. Corrugator activity confirms immediate negative affect in surprise[J]. *Frontiers in Psychology*, 2015 (6): 134.

Tsang, N. M. Surprise in social work education[J]. *Social Work Education*, 2013, *32*(1): 55-67.

Tse, P., & Hyland, K. "Robot Kung fu": Gender and professional identity in biology and philosophy reviews[J]. *Journal of Pragmatics*, 2008, *40*(7): 1232-1248.

Tulving, E. *Elements of episodic memory*[M]. New York: Oxford University Press, 1985.

Tutin, A. Surprise routines in scientific writing: A study of French social science articles[J]. *Review of Cognitive Linguistics*, 2015, *13*(2): 415-435.

Vanderstraeten, R. Scientific communication: Sociology journals and publication practices[J]. *Sociology*, 2010, *44*(3): 559-576.

Vogl, E., Pekrun, R., Murayama, K., Loderer, K., & Schubert, S. Surprise, curiosity, and confusion promote knowledge exploration: Evidence for robust effects of epistemic Emotions[J]. *Frontiers in Psychology*, 2019 (10): 1-16.

Vogl, E., Pekrun, R., Murayama, K., & Loderer, K. Surprised-curious-confused: Epistemic emotions and knowledge exploration[J]. *Emotion*, 2020, *20*(4): 625-641.

Vogl, E., Pekrun, R., & Loderer, K. Epistemic emotions and metacognitive feelings[M]// D. Moraitou, & P. Metallidou (Eds.). *Trends and prospects in metacognition research across the life span: A tribute to anastasia Efklides*, 2021: 41-58.

Vold, E. T. Epistemic modality markers in research articles: A cross-linguistic and cross-disciplinary study[J]. *International Journal of Applied Linguistics*, 2006, *16*(1): 61-87.

Walková, M. A three-dimensional model of personal self-mention in research papers[J]. *English for Specific Purposes*, 2019 (53): 60-73.

Wemheuer-Vogelaar, W. B., Nicholas J., Morales, M. N., & Tierney, M. J. The IR of the beholder: Examining global IR using the 2014 TRIP survey[J]. *International Studies Review*, 2016 (18): 16-32.

Wemheuer-Vogelaar, W. B., & Peters, I. Global(izing) international relations: Studying geo-epistemological divides and diversity[M]// I. Peters, & W. Wemheuer-Vogelaar (Eds.). *Globalizing international relations*. London: Palgrave Macmillan, 2016: 1-27.

Wen, J., & Lei, L. Linguistic positivity bias in academic writing: A large-scale diachronic study in life sciences across 50 years[J]. *Applied Linguistics*, 2022, *43*(2): 340-364.

Yakhontova, T. “Selling” or “Telling”? The issue of cultural variation in research genres.[M]// J. Flowerdew (Ed.). *Academic discourse*. Harlow: Pearson Education, 2002: 216-232.

Yakhontova, T. Cultural and disciplinary variation in academic discourse: The issue of influencing factors[J]. *Journal of English for Academic Purposes*, 2006, *5*(2): 153-167.

Yoon, H. J., & Römer, U. Quantifying disciplinary voices: An automated approach to interactional metadiscourse in successful student writing[J]. *Written Communication*, 2020, *37*(2): 208-244.

Zou, H. J., & Hyland, K. "Think about how fascinating this is": Engagement in academic blogs across disciplines[J]. *Journal of English for Academic Purposes*, 2020 (43): 100809.

Notice

本书稿的部分研究成果已经见刊于以下知名国际期刊：

1) Wang, Q., & Hu, G. Disciplinary and gender-based variations: A frame-based analysis of interest markers in research articles[J]. *English for Specific Purposes*, 2023a (70): 177-191. (SSCI)

2) Wang, Q., & Hu, G. Expressions of interest in research articles: Geo-academic location and time as influencing factors[J]. *Lingua*, 2023b (293). (SSCI & AHCI)

3) Wang, Q., & Hu, G. What surprises, interests and confuses researchers? A frame-based analysis of knowledge emotion markers in research articles[J]. *Lingua*, 2022 (279). (SSCI & AHCI)